WRITING
FROM THE
INSIDE _____

WRITING FROM THE INSIDE

Walter Sullivan
VANDERBILT UNIVERSITY

George Core
THE UNIVERSITY OF THE SOUTH

W. W. NORTON & COMPANY • NEW YORK • LONDON

ACKNOWLEDGMENTS

Malcolm Cowley: from *The View from 80* by Malcolm Cowley. Copyright © 1976, 1978, 1980 by Malcolm Cowley. Reprinted by permission of Viking Penguin Inc.

David Dempsey: "Low Moans in the Attic. Oh! A Creak! *Another!*" © 1980 by The New York Times Company. Reprinted by permission.

William Bragg Ewald, Jr.: from the book *Eisenhower the President* by William Bragg Ewald, Jr. © 1981 by William Bragg Ewald, Jr. Published by Prentice-Hall, Inc., Englewood Cliffs, NJ 07632.

C. S. Lewis: from *Mere Christianity* by C. S. Lewis. Copyright 1943, 1945, 1952 by Macmillan Publishing Co., Inc. Copyrights renewed. Reprinted by permission of Macmillan Publishing Co., Inc. Copyright The Estate of C. S. Lewis 1942, 1943, 1944. Used by permission of William Collins Sons & Co., Ltd., Great Britain.

Robert M. Lienert: "Moving Backward" from *Michigan Quarterly Review,* Volume XIX, No. 4/XX, No. 1. University of Michigan, Ann Arbor, MI 48109. Reprinted by permission of the publisher and the author.

Steve Nikitas: "Riding the Rails." © 1981 by The New York Times Company. Reprinted by permission.

Noel Perrin: from *First Person Rural* by Noel Perrin. Copyright © 1978 by Noel Perrin. Reprinted by permission of David R. Godine, Publisher, Inc.

Hugh Thomas: from pp. 590–591 in *A History of the World* by Hugh Thomas. Copyright © 1979 by Hugh Thomas. Reprinted by permission of Harper & Row, Publishers, Inc., and Hamish Hamilton Ltd., the English Canadian publishers.

Barbara W. Tuchman: from *The Guns of August* by Barbara W. Tuchman. © Barbara W. Tuchman 1962. Reprinted with permission of Macmillan Publishing Co., Inc.

John Updike: "Beer Can." Copyright © 1964 by John Updike. Reprinted from *Assorted Prose,* by John Updike, by permission of Alfred A. Knopf, Inc. First appeared in *The New Yorker.*

E. B. White: abridged from "Mrs. Wienckus" (p. 204) in *Poems & Sketches of E. B. White.* Copyright 1951 by E. B. White. Originally appeared in *The New Yorker.* Reprinted by permission of Harper & Row, Publishers, Inc.

Published simultaneously in Canada by George J. McLeod Limited, Toronto.

Printed in the United States of America.

First Edition

Book design by Antonina Krass

ISBN 0-393-95246

W. W. Norton & Company, Inc., 500 Fifth Avenue, New York, N.Y. 10110

W. W. Norton & Company Ltd., 37 Great Russell Street, London WC1B 3NU

1 2 3 4 5 6 7 8 9 0

TO JANE AND SUSAN

Contents

9 / The Research Paper   205

A Writer's Checklist   240

A Glossary of Diction, Grammar, and Usage   246

Index   279

Preface

Writing from the Inside springs from our conviction that composition provides an indispensable element in any college's first-year curriculum. We believe that good writing can best be taught and learned from such a course, a course which explores the idea that the beginning writer most effectively achieves knowledge and gains insight about composition by seeing how professional writers work, by understanding how they, like the rest of us, nervously confront a blank sheet of paper, painfully find a workable subject, and fully develop that subject through successive stages of revision.

In our judgment the finest books about composition, such as Will Strunk's and E. B. White's *The Elements of Style,* are lively succinct anatomies of writing, not rambling tomes in which essential matters are overwhelmed by tangential considerations and by excessive detail. We have tried to present the writing transaction in a way that is as simple and clear and brief and convincing as a sentence by White or John McPhee or Joan Didion.

We believe that good writing results largely from good reading and that one way of showing students the importance of writing well is to present them with a wide variety of well-written prose—not only literary classics but writing that comes from many different disciplines and perspectives.

Our examples—some models of how to do it, some of how not to do it—are drawn from many newspapers, magazines, and books; they constitute a wide range of writing about many subjects—from riding the range to riding the rails, from common labor to scientific research, from the problems of being young to the complications of being old; and they come from writers great and small, famous and obscure, most of whom are alive and working. We agree with E. B. White that "the best writing is often done by persons who are snatching the time from something else—from an occupation, or from a profession, or from a jail term—something that is either burning them up, as religion, or love, or politics, or that is boring them to tears, as prison, or a brokerage house, or an advertising firm."

Writing, whether it be to carry out a classroom assignment or to provide a report for a business meeting or to meet a newspaper deadline or to fulfill a contract for a book, is one of the most difficult things on earth, even for the professional writer. Teaching writing effectively is only a little less demanding and frustrating. We are all students: no writer, no matter how good, should ever stop learning; and none of us is above criticism. *Writing from the Inside* doubtless does not always live up to its authors' best intentions and precepts. But we think we have made the hard task of teaching and learning writing easier and more effective than it would be without this book. We offer you principles to go by, approaches to take, rules to follow; we give you advice that will help you. Read the book, wrestle with it, respond to it.

Nobody ever wrote a book without help. We are especially grateful to Barry Wade, our editor, and to Professor H. L. Weatherby for assistance and advice that are gratifying to note but impossible to express properly here. We also wish to thank Donald Fusting for enabling us to get this book under way with Norton. For editorial assistance and typing we thank Mary Lucia Snyder Cornelius; for typing and photocopying we thank Audrey Johnston Reynolds. We appreciate the detailed and useful readers' reports that have been provided by John Auchard (University of Maryland), Peter Dowell (Emory University), H. Ramsey Fowler (Memphis State University), William Gracie (Miami University), Sandra Kurtinitis (Prince George's Community College), and Charles Schuster (University of Washington). In this connection we are particularly indebted to Richard Marius (Harvard University) and Linda Peterson (Yale University). The dedication records our most profound obligations.

W. S.
G. C.

WRITING FROM THE INSIDE _____

1

Writing from the Inside

The mind travels faster than the pen; consequently, writing becomes a question of learning to make occasional wing shots, bringing down the bird of thought as it flashes by. A writer is a gunner, sometimes waiting in his blind for something to come in, sometimes roaming the countryside hoping to scare something up.

—E. B. White

When we read, probably the most universal and important question that we and all other readers are continually asking is *What does this have to do with me?* We may pose the question subconsciously; we may put it in different words; but it is always before us. We want to be certain that some connection exists between the words on the page that confront us and the common experience of humankind in which we discover and claim our own involvement. That is why good writers always use people and their concerns as the best way of measuring the world around us. The human dimension creates interest.

We bring our whole nature into the act of composition, and both our intellect and our emotions are involved when we choose a subject and an approach to that subject. So remember that knowing the material is not enough: you will

3

do your best work only if you are fully engaged in it, deeply committed to it—and if you respond to it temperamentally as well as intellectually. Write about what you admire or what offends you, about subjects that move you to laughter or pity or outrage. Knowing and feeling deeply about your subject will help you in establishing and maintaining your tone and your point of view.

Finding a Subject

The first step in writing a theme is finding your subject. Sometimes this will be done for you; when this happens, you will have to gather information about whatever subject you are assigned and try to discover something in that subject that interests you and that you hope will interest your reader. We will talk about how to do this later. But if you have a choice of subject, the best course to follow is one that you have probably been advised to follow previously: write about something with which you are familiar, something you know.

Because you know more about yourself than you know about any other fact or idea or person in the world, your instructor will often ask you to write your first theme about something that you have experienced or thought or done. You might be given sample topics such as "My Big Day in High School," or "Memories of a Beachcomber," or "Freaking Out at the Zoo," or "College Registration in One Easy Lesson." These suggestions will be designed to start your mind and your memory working. If you spent last summer at the seashore, and spent a lot of time on the beach looking for rare shells and friendly members of the opposite sex, you can go to work at once, finding your own particular theme in the general topic about beachcombing. But if none of the suggested topics appeals to you or fits your own experience, use the topics as points of departure. You may not have any experience of or interest in the zoo, but perhaps you babysat once for a pet rattlesnake, or picketed a laboratory for its inhumane use of rhesus monkeys for experiments. Perhaps the last time you had a chance to visit the zoo, you decided on a canoe trip instead. Extend the other suggested topics in the same way, and something will come to you.

Some instructors like to assign "free" themes: in such instances you choose the subject without any suggestions to guide you. In such cases make full use of your imagination. Perhaps because writing is a formal endeavor—you are expected to compose well-constructed and grammatically correct sentences and to submit clean copy—some of us think that only formal and well-bred topics can be used as subjects for our themes. This is not true. Any subject is a suitable subject as long as it is treated with perception and good taste. Among topics about which John McPhee has written are firewood, oranges, Monopoly, and the malt for Scotch whiskey. When A. J. Liebling was assigned by the *New Yorker* to write about France in World War II, he wrote about his trip to catch a seaplane to Paris. Later, when he went to Reno to get a divorce, he wrote about the city of Reno and all the people who were waiting there for divorces.

You may retort that McPhee is a professional writer and therefore better able to write interestingly about seemingly unpromising subjects than the rest of us, and this is partly true. Most of us do not share McPhee's talent. But all of us have lives to live, duties to perform, places to go, people to meet, things to buy, movies to see, magazines to read, meetings to attend, votes to cast, food to eat, pleasures to enjoy, and annoyances to endure. Topics for themes are inherent in much of our everyday experience. When you are looking for a subject for a theme, consider what you have been doing lately: conversations you have had; places you have been; remarks you have overheard; incidents you have seen. If you can remember a conversation that interests you, the subject of that conversation may become the subject of a theme. A camping trip you take might suggest a theme about the wilderness, or slums you encounter might suggest a theme about poverty. Even what appears to be the dullest life contains enough material for any number of themes. But often we do not recognize that material because we fail to use our senses. To find good subjects and to write well about them after you have found them, follow the advice of Henry James: be one of those on whom nothing is lost. Listen to what you hear; look at what you see; feel and taste and smell the world around you.

Getting Under Way

Once you have found your subject and narrowed it to manageable size—and we will discuss how to do this and most of the other matters we mention here in later chapters—you are an author in search of a beginning. All successful essays, no matter what kind or of what length, have beginnings, middles, and ends. The beginning sets forth the topic: it is the first incident in the story, the statement of the problem, the formulation of the argument. The middle develops the action or the idea. The end is the conclusion—the final act in the narrative, the completion of the explanation or the argument. As a general rule the more you know about what you are going to say in your essay, or at least the line you want to follow or the end you want to reach, the easier it will be for you to find your beginning. But different people write in different ways, and here are some of the ways that good writers conduct their business.

Some writers begin with no plan: knowing the subject about which they are going to write, they sit down at the typewriter or with pencil and pad and let the words flow and see what comes of it. If this is the way you choose to work, you had better be a master at revision. You are probably going to write the way most people talk, which is very loosely and often at random. Think of how you converse with an acquaintance you meet on campus or how you start a telephone conversation with a friend. You say *How are you?* and *I'm fine* and *Isn't it a pretty day?* and *Wasn't that a hard test we had?*—none of which conveys any information that both people do not already know. There is no harm in putting this sort of conversation into a narrative if you cut it out before you write the final draft of your essay. It is all right to ramble about bald eagles and striped bass as you warm up in trying to write an essay on the dangers of forest fires, but these extraneous matters must be deleted before the theme is finished. From beginning to end every sentence should bear on the subject and convey some information about the subject to the reader.

Another way of writing, which is the opposite of just letting the words come, is to work from an outline. This method involves planning the whole theme in great detail before the first word is written. The theme topic is divided into subtopics; the subtopics are further divided, and the subsubtopics are put into order: some to form the beginning and some to make the middle and some to compose the end. In some very strict outlines each main entry in the outline will become the topic sentence of one of the paragraphs in the essay, so if you follow this kind of detailed outline, you always know where you are. Writing this way is like traveling from Minneapolis to San Antonio with the help of a road map. If you follow the map and check the road signs, you know exactly where you are starting and exactly where you are going and exactly how and when you are going to get there. At any stage along the way you can pinpoint your position and know how far you have traveled and how far you have left to go. This method probably works best when you are explaining technical procedures or developing carefully constructed arguments. The drawback here is that when you follow an outline diligently you are likely to deprive your writing of spontaneity, and you may prevent yourself from discovering new dimensions of your subject as you write.

A third method, which we will examine more closely in the next two chapters, is a combination of the two methods discussed above. You list all the facts you can discover about your subject, and you try to put those facts into an order. You divide the important points from those which are less important and try to find a pattern within the facts: which should come first, and which are likely to make the best conclusion. But you do not make a formal outline. Instead you determine the place where you are going to start, the general direction you propose to take, and where you think you will arrive when you are finished. This method is less like traveling the interstate than following a compass and your own instincts through the woods. Though you know your beginning and your probable route and your likely end, as you work you find new aspects of your material and sometimes details and facts that you overlooked when you made your original list.

Whatever method of composition you use, do not allow yourself to get locked into a specific idea or plan or approach. Working with an outline would appear to be the safest way to write, but an outline that appears to be perfect may prove to have serious flaws when it becomes the basis for a theme. Writing is the final proof of any plan because it is the final proof of thought. Sometimes we believe that we know a subject thoroughly or know absolutely what we think about a topic, but when we are required to write what we think, gaps appear in our memory and our research and our logic. Therefore, if you realize when you are writing your theme that you are not making total sense or that your prose seems awkward or fragmented, reexamine your plan. Very likely that plan is at fault. If you are following one of the other methods we have discussed and your theme falters, you may have begun at the wrong place or you may have wandered away from your subject. In most cases, in order to correct failures of structure and design, you have to look back from the point where the mistake becomes obvious. When things go wrong in your writing, check your original concept and the development of your theme up to the point you have reached. Never be reluctant to change radically or even to discard what you have already done. No plan, no approach should be considered sacred.

Writing Grammatically—and Well

So far we have talked mostly about the structure of themes, but good themes also require good writing. Structure is the way sentences and paragraphs are put together to form a suitable design. If the sentences and paragraphs are not well written, no structure, no matter how good, can turn the bad sentences into a good essay. Sentences should, first of all, be grammatical. If you are to be properly understood by your reader and if your reader's mind is to move with the flow of your prose, all your sentences will need subjects and predicates, your verbs must agree in number with their subjects, and you will have to be conscious of the varieties of sentences and the uses of modifiers and the cases of pronouns. Correct grammar comes first. And good sentences must be formed into good paragraphs, each of which states and develops an idea and leads into the paragraph that follows.

When you are planning your writing, you can usually maintain your own personality. With a unified mind you choose a subject, gather facts, select details, plan an approach. But once you start writing, you have to become slightly schizophrenic. One part of your mind cranks out the words and the sentences and the paragraphs; another part of your mind reads what is being written to see whether the writing actually says what you want it to convey. Often the part of the mind that is writing wants to be lazy. Sometimes we are inclined to write badly because writing badly is easier than writing well. When this happens, the part of you that is looking over your shoulder has to be firm. Go back and do it right, says the critical part of your brain. And the creative part sighs and starts over again. Every minute we are engaged in the task of writing we must demand the absolute best of ourselves.

Correct writing is essential to any kind of essay, but it does not guarantee an engaging theme. To make our writing attractive, we must make an appeal to our readers: if possible—and it usually will be possible, no matter how special the subject—we must show how the subject about which we are writing has a bearing on their lives. We do this by simplifying technical terms and by using concrete examples. People who might ordinarily stop reading at the sight of the word *arrhythmia* will probably want to learn about the causes and dangers of irregular heartbeat, which is what arrhythmia means. An essay on inflation might begin not with statistics but with a man and woman trying to balance their budget: after they have paid mortgage and automobile and charge-card installments, they realize they do not have enough left for food and clothes. The weather is an interesting topic to us because we live in it. We are interested in airplanes because we fly on them. We build with stone, we burn coal, we eat fish, and we wear shoes. Everything in the universe has a relationship to people, and as writers we must find and use these relationships.

Considering the Audience

Remember that whatever you write is written for someone, and your consideration of your audience helps to determine your tone. The effect of the intended audience on what we write and what we say is obvious on a fundamental level. If you are invited to speak to the graduating class of Thomas

Jefferson Junior High School on the topic "Rock Groups I Have Seen," you probably will not need to know much about the theory of music. Descriptions of groups you have heard and concerts you have attended will be enough, and these can be offered in the language of junior-high students. If you were writing a theme on rock, your instructor would expect you to tell something about the music, the way it is constructed, the instruments used to play it; or you might write about it as a social or cultural phenomenon: in either case you would use language different from the language you used at Jefferson Junior High. If you took your subject to an audience at the Juilliard School of music, you might want to fit rock into the history of popular music, and you had better know the difference between a flatted fifth and a minor seventh.

The different ways in which we write for different audiences are easily seen as long as those audiences are clearly defined. Physicists write one way for other physicists, another way for the membership of the PTA. The author of an article about the Bahamas in the *Encyclopaedia Britannica* gives you facts and figures. The author of a brochure for a travel agency tells you how beautiful the beach is and how bright the sun is and how much fun you will have when you go there. People who write for the *National Enquirer* write a simpler and more sensational prose than those who write for the *New York Times*. An essay you write for a history course will not be written in quite the same way as an essay for a course in sociology. You should be sensitive to the different requirements of different courses and instructors and the varying needs of varying audiences. But always write everything as well and as clearly as you can: explain whatever needs to be explained; simplify whatever needs simplification; never condescend; always maintain respect for your readers.

Tone is a reflection of the author's attitude toward his or her subject; to see how audience influences tone, think of the subjects that can be approached and the ways they can be discussed, depending on who is involved in the discussion. Catholics can tell other Catholics Polish jokes about Pope John Paul; Jews can tell Jewish jokes at the synagogue; blacks can tell jokes about blacks to one another. If we mix the ethnic groups, the jokes will probably be taken as insults because we can no longer be sure of the attitude of the speaker. We must be careful that whatever tone we use will not inadvertently offend some of our readers. But your first audience is always yourself, and your first step in establishing the tone of an essay is to determine what you think about your material.

For example, consider a date you may have had when you were young during which everything went poorly. You wore the wrong clothes, spilled ice cream in your date's lap, lost a filling out of your front tooth, and had to leave before the party was over. There are at least two ways of remembering all this: you may think it is an image of the disaster your social life has been until this day; or you may think it a funny incident of your childhood which always gets a laugh when you tell people about it. If you write about this material, the tone of the theme will be sad, perhaps even bitter; or the tone of the theme will be comic. The vocabulary you use, the details you include, the emphasis that you give various incidents will be determined, at least in part, by your attitude; and these words and details and incidents will indicate whether the reader should laugh or be sad.

Establish your tone as exactly as possible, keeping within the limits of taste and judgment. Natural disasters that claim lives can never be humorous. A bad haircut cannot be made into a tragedy. Depending on our temperament, we can view most things in life with approval, disgust, fear, humor, sorrow, pity, or any of a dozen other attitudes. But, except in the case of narrative, where tone can sometimes make abrupt shifts as the fortunes of the characters rise and fall, your tone should be consistent. It can deepen. A tone of sadness at the death of a dog can turn to deep sorrow when we learn that the dog was an invalid's sole companion. A tone of annoyance at air pollution can become anger as we discover the damage done to the environment by acid rain. But a tone that shifts from joy to anger or from affection to loathing will confuse your reader and spoil the effect of your theme. If you find your tone shifting appreciably, stop, reexamine your topic, and decide what your attitude toward your material really is.

Learning to Read

One of the ways we can learn to write better is to learn how to read. You might object here that you already know how to read, and that is true: you know what words mean and how sentences are put together. You can read a story in a newspaper or magazine or book and tell someone else the substance of what you have read. But there is another kind of reading that you need to master in order to know how writing works and how good writing gets written. Think, for example, about watching a basketball game. Most of us who have never played on an organized team or made a study of the techniques of play understand only a little of what we are watching. The television commentator Bill Russell, a former player and coach, watching the same game we think we are watching, can tell us not only what is happening at the moment but what is likely to happen as the game progresses: which team is going to tire first, which team will have to adjust its defense, which team needs a substitute, which player should shoot more frequently, and which coach should call a time out. Russell knows basketball from the inside, not merely from the sidelines; to learn writing from the inside, we have to teach ourselves to read the way Russell watches basketball. This means we must read the work of other writers as carefully and as critically as we read our own themes when we start to revise them.

Look at the following essay by Steve Nikitas, a professional writer.

In June 1975, I rode a freight train for the first time—the Union Pacific "hot shot" nicknamed "The Triple S" for "SuperSonic Slingshot." It's well known as one of the fastest freights to roam the West, a high-priority cargo haul that runs daily from Salt Lake City to Portland, Oregon, reaching speeds of more than 60 miles an hour, kind of quick for 4,000 tons of train.

My buddy Joe and I rode the Slingshot for 650 miles to La Grande, Oregon, a "division point," where a fast freight will make one of its few stops for a crew change. The yard detective there spotted us riding a flatcar and escorted us from the premises with some terse mumblings about not returning.

Since that initial baptism, I have got it in my blood and in my brain to ride the freights.

I have ridden the Burlington Northern across the North Dakota prairie and then up and over the Rockies via Marias Pass, in Montana; rocketed the eerie full-moonlit Utah desert on the Denver and Rio Grande Western; traversed the Continental Divide in Colorado on its steepest rail crossing; slogged twenty-two hours across Nevada with three hapless hobos on a way freight—a low-priority train—in subfreezing weather (one old man's legs were so stiff we had to pull him up and lower him out of the boxcar); and picked up the Southern Pacific in Louisiana and Texas on what's known as the Sunset route, California-bound.

The romantic "high" that I get when I submerge myself in the world of the freight train is made better by the tramps who still "ride the high iron" out West. They're of another era, out of the mainstream, and welcome young men like me whom they view as inexperienced and in need of instruction. The hobos have adopted a fatherly air, taking me under their wing to show me the ropes so that I can be a better rail rider and perhaps live a little longer in a hard world where adversity stalks.

One instructed me to "listen for the square wheel" as the train rolls into the yard when sizing up prospective cars to ride in or on. "If you hear the ka-thunk, ka-thunk," he warned, "don't get in that car. It'll ride so bad you'll never get to sit down."

A scruffy bum whom I caught out of Grand Junction, Colorado, taught me about riding the auto racks. If you can get inside a new car, you get a comfortable ride but you might get in trouble. I did.

A dignified tramp named Merle instructed me in the fine art of making cold bean sandwiches during a trip over "the hump" (the Continental Divide): "Take two slices of bread, a can of beans, and a can opener."

I'm twenty-seven now, a little older and wiser but still one of those American men with a fascination about the trains, about moving, about escaping from time to time for a few months of rest and relaxation on the road.

                                        —"Riding the Rails" (1981)

Considering Organization and Detail

Understanding why Nikitas's essay is arresting and successful will help us learn to write more effectively. Look first at the organization. The beginning consists of the first three paragraphs, the third of which states the subject of the essay. But the beginning has its own form. What Nikitas wants to do first is to engage our attention, and he does this by starting with a brief anecdote. Now it is good for us to remind ourselves that everything in this essay represents a choice the writer had to make. Once writing gets into print, we are inclined, at least subconsciously, to think of it in the same way we think of birds or rocks—as if it were a part of the natural landscape. But all writing has to be written. Even *Hamlet* did not always exist. Once there was a man named Shakespeare who had an idea for a play and a quill and ink and blank paper. He had to decide how he wanted to begin his play, and he had to make this decision on the basis of his experience as a writer and an actor as well as a reader and observer of plays written by other people.

One way to understand why Nikitas decided to start his essay as he did is to think of other beginnings that he could have written. Suppose he had begun by giving us a series of statistics: how many freight trains run in the United States and how many men are thought to ride them regularly and how much the railroads spend to hire how many detectives to apprehend the hobos. This might be a good opening for a paper on the economics of the railroad business, but "Riding the Rails" is an autobiographical sketch, and numbers have nothing to do with why Nikitas likes to ride on freight trains. Suppose he had started with a description of his childhood infatuation with electric trains and the way he used to pretend he was riding in a toy boxcar. This would be relevant to Nikitas's life, but a childhood dream is too far removed from the reality of riding the rails, which is Nikitas's subject. Nikitas or any writer might consider using a dozen different beginnings before he settles on one that is both pertinent and likely to make the reader want to keep on reading. Our job as learning writers is to compare the ways he might have begun with the way he did begin—and to think of what he did not do as well as of what he did do, of what he left out as well as of what he put in.

Look at the middle of the essay, the four paragraphs that follow the beginning. Having created momentum with the anecdote at the beginning and the statement "I have got it in my blood and in my brain to ride the freights," Nikitas opens his middle section with a paragraph that is mostly summary—a list of some of the places he has been. But notice that even here Nikitas uses concrete details—for example "eerie full-moonlit Utah desert" and "subfreezing weather."

These images of the landscape and the weather help us to understand more fully what Nikitas wishes to convey by making an appeal to our physical senses. To a certain extent we see what he saw, feel what he felt. And the picture of the old man whose legs were so stiff from the cold that he had to be lifted out of the boxcar conveys something of the quality of the particular experience. People who are not skilled writers frequently do not tell us what we want to know. Ask someone what it is like to ride a freight train in winter, and that person might reply: *It's cold,* or *It's uncomfortable,* or *You really do get numb sometimes.* These answers are too general and vague to be of much help. You can get cold skiing or watching a football game or camping or sleeping in an unheated room. But the image of the old man with stiff legs shows exactly what it is like to be cold on a slow-moving freight train.

Paragraph five, the second paragraph of the essay's middle, is another general statement about Nikitas's relationship with veteran hobos, the danger and harshness of the world in which they live, and the good advice they have given him. But in the next three paragraphs, which comprise the rest of the essay's middle, the general statement is supported by specific incidents and by pointed dialogue. Nikitas tells how he was taught to listen for a "square wheel," and warned not to hop a car that had one. He learns of the comforts of riding in automobiles from a "scruffy bum" whom he "caught out of Grand Junction, Colorado." He is instructed in the "art of making cold bean sandwiches" by a "dignified tramp named Merle."

All these are good details, but think once more of what Nikitas knows but does not tell us. For instance, he once got in trouble when he rode in a new automobile, but he does not elaborate on this. His subject is riding the rails, not harassment from the police. Nikitas's scrapes with the railroad detectives are another story. Where do hobos get food or the money to buy it? Where and how do they take baths and brush their teeth and shave and get their hair cut and wash their clothes? Where do they stay, and how do they pass their time when they stop in cities? Do most of them drink? Do they smoke pot? Are they more or less honest than people who live more conventionally? In what ways is Nikitas different from an ordinary hobo? The answers to these questions are doubtless interesting, but they belong in a theme on hobos' way of living. We remind ourselves once again that Nikitas is writing autobiography: his subject is the romance of riding the rails as he has experienced it. Only those details that help to develop this subject get into his article.

The final paragraph is the end of the essay. Nikitas tells us that because he is now twenty-seven, he rides the rails less often, if at all. We get the impression that he has settled into a more ordinary kind of life, but he does not say what. His present mode of existence, the job he has, the place he lives, his wife and children, if any, have nothing to do with riding the rails. What is important to his subject is that the adventure of hopping freight trains still appeals to him and lives in his imagination. The end of the essay marks the close of a period in Nikitas's life. Thus it is a logical place to stop.

Developing the Habit of Writing

The best way to improve your writing is by writing. Thinking about writing helps; reading what others have written helps even more; but nothing takes the place of experience. To get this experience write everything as well as you can. Remember that you are probably going to be writing regularly—letters, business reports, speeches, and so forth—the rest of your life, not to mention your subsequent work in college and perhaps in graduate school. Frequently, when we are writing letters, or papers for classes other than English, we allow ourselves to be lazy and we try to convey our thoughts in loose and haphazard prose. When we do this, we not only fail to gain experience, but we confirm ourselves in bad habits that we should be trying to break. Even when we do our best at whatever we are writing, unless we do more than the minimum of assignments and of correspondence, we will not do enough. This is why many professional writers keep daily journals in which they record as accurately as possible what they see and hear and think and feel.

A journal is not necessarily the same thing as a diary. Many people keep diaries in a kind of shorthand. *Slept late and missed three classes. Afternoon in library. P.M. at the pub with Tommy and Beth.* This is a series of bare facts, the recording of which requires no literary skill. In contrast, a journal entry, using some of the same material, might read as follows:

> Lying in bed when I should have been in class. I was feeling all right—plenty of sleep the night before and no drinking, no drugs. I was awake early. I knew I would have time for a shower, time to get coffee and danish, but my mind seemed blank. But not blank either. I knew that I ought to be going to class, but I couldn't make myself believe that this was important. I may have dozed a while, but most of the time I was awake. I heard the tower clock strike ten. I had already missed biology, but I knew that if I got up and dressed quickly, I could make economics. I knew this was the day we were going to review for a big test. But I didn't move.
>
> I heard voices and footsteps in the corridor. There was the sound of traffic outside my window, cars passing and a truck shifting down. I thought of how it would be on campus: people on the walks, students and professors going to and from class, and people gathering in the commons. How it would be on the campus was so clear in my mind that at first it was almost like I was two places at once—in bed where I really was and on the campus where I should have been. But later I felt alone, cut off from the

rest of the world in a way I had never felt before, knowing
that the day was going on without me, time passing and
everybody else doing what they always did. I felt very separate and a little sad.

We would need to revise this passage if we intended to use
it as part of a theme. Probably we would want to correct the
sentence fragments in the first paragraph and change the
structure and wording of the sentence in the second paragraph which begins "How it would be on the campus," and
make other alterations to tighten and polish the prose. But
the writing is effective nonetheless because the author has
taken the trouble to remember and to write down enough
concrete details to convey to us and to himself when he looks
back at it the essence of the experience.

If writing in a journal every day is more than you are
ready to undertake, at least try occasionally to do some writing that has not been assigned. When you are writing a letter
to your parents or to a friend, try to find the exact detail to
capture someone or something you're describing—a new
friend, or professor, how the campus looks at this time. And
when you are not writing, keep your eyes and your ears and
your mind open. Be aware of the world and receptive to it,
and think about the ways in which you might write about
what you see and hear and experience and think.

Exercises

A. Study the following passages by professional writers. Pay close
attention to vocabulary, sentence structure, and use of detail; see if
you can find a logical explanation for the sequence in which the
ideas are arranged. Find a passage that you think could be improved and rewrite it.

1. Passengers were supposed to be at the plane with their lug-
gage at eight o'clock. Schwed picked me up at an hour I never

had experienced while sober, at the door of the house where I was living, and headed in what I took to be the direction of Long Island because the sun was rising over it. He drove me over one bridge, which was all right, and then around a wild farming country, in which I distinctly saw a hen and on another occasion what I took to be a cow—in one jump more I figured he would have me among the coyotes and Republicans—and then over another bridge, which was all wrong because it landed us in Westchester County. By then I had only an hour or so to catch the plane, so I began to curse, which I do well. The secret of good cursing lies in cadence, emphasis, and antiphony. The basic themes are always the same. Conscious striving after variety is not to be encouraged, because it takes your mind off your cursing. By the time Schwed got me to the landing he felt what a proper swine he was for having gotten up early in the morning to take me to the plane, and if the experience had broken him of volunteering to do favors for people it would have been worth while. I rushed into the dinky frame ticket and customs office they had there, still drooling obscenity, and saw my mother, who had gotten up early in another part of Long Island and come out to see me off. Sucking back four bloody oaths that I could already feel pressing against the back of my teeth, I switched to a properly filial expression, embraced the dear woman, and got aboard the Clipper feeling like Donald Duck.

—A. J. Liebling, *The Road Back to Paris* (1944)

2. The western saloon existed because it filled a basic human need, which it is now hard to imagine. It was a place of comfort, a refuge, even a place of refinement where one could rub elbows with a fellow human being. It was a place where they spoke cow talk, where nesters could commiserate with each other about hails and dry spells. The saloon was a place to dispel the loneliness of a month on the range or two months in the back country with only the sheep for company. There were some people who spent most of their waking and a good part of their sleeping hours in saloons. The saloon was all things to all men. Besides being a drinking place, it was an eatery, a hotel, a bath and comfort station, a livery stable, gambling den, dance hall, bordello, barbershop, courtroom, church, social club, political center, dueling ground, post office, sports arena, undertaker's parlor, library, news exchange, theater, opera, city hall,

employment agency, museum, trading post, grocery, ice cream parlor, even a forerunner of the movie house in which entranced cowhands cranked the handles of ornate kinetoscopes to watch the jerky movements of alluring cancan dancers. A saloon might fulfill none or several of the above functions at the same time.

— Richard Erdoes, *Saloons of the Old West* (1979)

3. I will never forget the feeling I had when my hand touched the lumpy flesh for the first time, nor the first cut I made into this flesh. I looked around me. With me, around the same corpse, were three other young students. They faced the same problem as I, and their honest little-boy faces reflected the same attempt to fight down their horror and disgust. The whole room was filled with such boys, standing about their hideously bedecked tables, former students of Plato and the verses of the *Iliad* who had deserted the disciplines of humanism and now found themselves faced with the necessity to jump down into the foul air of decomposition where analysis takes place.

— Fredrick P. Reck-Malleczewen, *Diary of a Man in Despair* (1966)

4. During World War II Hemingway's career as braggart warrior continued. He wrote his son Patrick that he'd landed at Omaha Beach on D-day, and that during the campaign that followed he would have been taken prisoner several times daily but for using his head and his balls. He told Milton Wolff, in exaggeration (but less, this time), that he'd entered Paris "ahead of anybody" and that he'd been present when the Siegfried Line was "busted." He told Charles Scribner, falsely, that he'd shot a German soldier who refused to respond to interrogating. He wrote Mary Welsh an embellished account of one hectic day when he and two companions came under fire from a German antitank gun. Ernest hurt his head and back diving into a ditch for cover, but in the retelling the antitank gun became a tank, and his injuries the consequence of the explosion of a tank shell, which supposedly left him with a bump on the head, a concussion, and double vision. Most, if not all, of this was exaggeration designed to impress Mary; when Ernest checked in to Lanham's command post immediately after the incident, he did not so much as mention any injury to his head.

— Scott Donaldson, *By Force of Will* (1977)

5. It has always seemed impossible to prevent the English becoming more moral about distresses in Lagos than about distresses in London, and so it was at the end of the eighteenth century. William Wilberforce, the protagonist of the reform, showed no signs of knowing the horrible evils at home. He never seemed to be acutely aware of the sufferings of children in cotton mills, though he did certainly agree that children of twelve ought not to work more than eleven hours a day. He helped to found the Church Missionary Society and also the Society for the Suppression of Vice, and he had no idea of allowing mental liberty to the English poor. Still in fact, however much pity and justice he lacked, he and his friends did fight for the pity and justice they understood. They left too much of horror alone, but they did interfere with horror; pain was a little less prevalent when they had finished. Sincerely or insincerely they did maintain that barbarians must not be made slaves. And they did it with a conviction that this was their Christian duty.

—Charles Williams, *The Descent of the Dove* (1939)

6. Abbot Suger, whose renovation of Saint-Denis is considered the start of Gothic architecture, embodied the spirit of the builders. Determined to create the most splendid basilica in Christendom, he supervised every aspect of the work from fund raising to decoration, and caused his name to be inscribed for immortality on keystones and capitals. He lay awake worrying, as he tells us, where to find trees large enough for the beams, and went personally with his carpenters to the forest to question the woodcutters under oath. When they swore that nothing of the kind he wanted could be found in the area, he insisted on searching for them himself and, after nine hours of scrambling through thorns and thickets, succeeded in locating and marking twelve trees of the necessary size.

—Barbara Tuchman, "Mankind's Better Moments" (1980)

B. Study the following passages describing the same place (Melville's Encantadas are now known as the Galapagos Islands). What audience does each author have in mind—and what is his intended purpose in addressing that audience? Compare and contrast the information that each passage contains; in the same way consider the choice of words in each and the choice of details. Is each effective for the intended audience and purpose?

1. *Galapagos Islands,* an archipelago of five larger and ten smaller islands in the Pacific Ocean, exactly under the equator. The nearest island to the South American coast lies 50 miles west of Ecuador, to which country they belong. The name is derived from *galápago,* a tortoise, on account of the giant species, the characteristic feature of the fauna. The islands were discovered early in the 16th century by Spaniards, who gave them their present name. They were then uninhabited. The English names of the individual islands were probably given by buccaneers, for whom the group formed a convenient retreat. . . .

The total land area is estimated at about 2870 square miles (about that of the West Riding of Yorkshire). The extraordinary number of craters, a few of which are reported still to be active, gives evidence that the archipelago is the result of volcanic action. The number of main craters may be about twenty-five, but there are very many small eruptive cones on the flanks of the old volcanoes. There is a convict settlement on Chatham with some 300 inhabitants living in low thatched or iron-roofed huts. . . . On many of the islets numerous tropical fruits are found growing wild, but they are no doubt escapes from cultivation, just as the large herds of wild cattle, horses, donkeys, pigs, goats and dogs—the last large and fierce—which occur abundantly on most of the islands have escaped from domestication.

The shores of the larger islands are fringed in some parts with a dense barrier of mangroves, backed by an often impenetrable thicket of tropical undergrowth, which, as the ridges are ascended, give place to taller trees and deep green bushes which are covered with orchids and trailing moss *(orchilla),* and from which creepers hang down interlacing the vegetation. But generally the low grounds are parched and rocky, presenting only a few thickets of Peruvian cactus and stunted shrubs, and a most uninviting shore.

—*The Encyclopaedia Britannica,* 11th ed. (1910)

2. Take five-and-twenty heaps of cinders dumped here and there in an outsized city lot; imagine some of them magnified into mountains, and the vacant lot the sea; and you will have a fit idea of the general aspect of the Encantadas, or Enchanted

Isles. A group rather of extinct volcanoes than of isles; looking
much as the world at large might, after a penal conflagration.
It is to be doubted whether any spot of earth can, in deso-
lateness, furnish a parallel to this group. Abandoned cemeteries
of long ago, old cities by piecemeal tumbling to their ruin,
these are melancholy enough; but, like all else which has but
once been associated with humanity they still awaken in us
some thoughts of sympathy, however sad. Hence, even the
Dead Sea, along with whatever other emotions it may at times
inspire, does not fail to touch in the pilgrim some of his less
unpleasurable feelings....

The special curse, as one may call it, of the Encantadas, that
which exalts them in desolation ..., is that to them change
never comes; neither the change of seasons nor of sorrows. Cut
off by the Equator, they know not autumn and they know not
spring; while already reduced to the lees of fire, ruin itself can
work little more upon them. The showers refresh the deserts,
but in these isles, rain never falls. Like split Syrian gourds, left
withering in the sun, they are cracked by an everlasting drought
beneath a torrid sky....

Another feature in these isles is their emphatic uninhabitable-
ness. It is deemed a fit type of all-forsaken overthrow, that the
jackal should den in the wastes of weedy Babylon; but the Encantadas refuse to harbour even the outcasts of the beasts. Man
and wolf alike disown them. Little but reptile life is here
found:—tortoises, lizards, immense spiders, snakes, and the
strangest anomaly of outlandish Nature, the *aguano*. No voice,
no low, no howl is heard; the chief sound of life here is a hiss.

On most of the isles where vegetation is found at all, it is
more ungrateful than the blankness of Aracama. Tangled thickets of wiry bushes, without fruit and without a name, springing
up among deep fissures of calcined rock, and treacherously
masking them; or a parched growth of distorted cactus trees.

In many places the coast is rock-bound, or more properly,
clinker-bound; tumbled masses of blackish or greenish stuff like
the dross of an iron-furnace, forming dark clefts and caves here
and there, into which a ceaseless sea pours a fury of foam; over-
hanging them with a swirl of grey, haggard mist, amidst which
sail screaming flights of unearthly birds heightening the dismal
din.... In no world but a fallen one could such lands exist.

—Herman Melville, *The Encantadas* (1854)

C. Look up in an encyclopedia or a guidebook a place that you are familiar with, and then write a description of it that, like Melville's, gives the reader a sense of the feel of the place rather than a statement of facts about it.

2

Thinking about Writing

How can I tell what I think until I see what I say.

—E. M. Forster

Before starting to write, you should think long and hard about your topic, and the more you think about it before you begin writing, the better your theme is likely to be. You should also try to choose subjects that naturally engage your interest, that appeal to your curiosity and imagination. Doing this will be easier in some cases than in others. If your assignment is to write about the mating habits of caribous and you know nothing about caribous in the first place and are uninterested in learning about their procreative inclinations in any event, then you have to make the best that you can of an unpromising situation. But most of the time, not only in this course but in other courses in which papers are required, you will be allowed some latitude in your choice of subject.

Frequently, as a first assignment in English composition, you will be asked to write about one of your own experiences. The instructor will be following the theory that you ought to know what has happened to you as well as you know anything and that you ought to be interested in your own life. E. B. White once wrote to an unhappy college student who had asked him for advice about writing. "Remember," he said to her, "writing is translation, and the opus to be translated is yourself."

To be given the privilege of writing about yourself does not mean, however, that you automatically have a subject for a composition. Though you may not be aware of it, if you have lived eighteen years you have enough material to fill a book. "Anybody who has survived his childhood," Flannery O'Connor observed, "has enough information about life to last him the rest of his days." So the first thing you have to decide is what particular experience, what small part of your life, is going to be the subject of a theme about yourself.

Considering the Subject

Whatever your subject may be, whether it is assigned or you are free to choose it, the best way of beginning your theme is to consider your topic from every angle. Professional writers do not think about their work only when they are in their studies. Whatever project they are working on they keep always in mind: they think about it before they go to sleep at night and while they are in the shower. Many of them carry notebooks so they can jot down ideas whenever the ideas strike them. You too should think about your topic as often and as much as you can: when you are waiting for a bus, or walking alone across the campus, or jogging, or riding your bicycle, mull over what details will fit properly into your subject and where you will begin your theme and what shape you want to give it, what organization will best reveal your material.

One way to approach your material is to ask yourself hard questions about it. Suppose your assignment is to write about the job you had last summer or, if you were not employed then, about any job you have held at any time, or about volunteer work you have done. Probably you will first think about your job in general terms. *I was a checker in a grocery store,* you might say to yourself; *I pulled the merchandise across the scanner or punched out the prices on the register. I shoved things down the counter to the sacker. I took people's money and made change. Or I worked as a gardener in a park. I cut grass and trimmed shrubs. I hauled mulch and spread wood chips. I helped pick up trash after a crafts fair or a concert. Or I waited on tables. I took orders and brought people drinks and food. I kept their coffee cups and water glasses filled. Before I gave them their checks, I asked if there was anything else I could get them.* This is a good way to start, but you are still not ready to write. What you have thought of so far is what everybody already knows about these jobs. For people to read what they already know is not very engaging.

Now is the time to start asking yourself questions in an effort to find the details that are stored in your mind but that have not yet occurred to you. What did you like about your job? What did you dislike about it? What kind of people did you work with? How did your boss treat you? If you were the boss, how would you change the conditions under which you worked? What was a usual day at work like? What duties did you have that you did not expect to have? What, if anything, was interesting about the job? What unusual things happened while you were working? These and other questions that you might think of should lead you to a final question which will define the topic of your theme: What events and details taken from my experience will help someone who has never checked groceries or worked as a gardener or waited on tables understand what these jobs are really like?

Ask yourself each question more than once, and write down the answers as they come to you. Give your mind free rein, but stay on the topic. If you are trying to remember what you liked about your job, it will do no good to say that you did not want to work; that you would have preferred to sleep until noon every day and spend the rest of your time playing tennis and visiting with friends and listening to music. Regret at having to work is not a relevant part of your theme describing your summer employment. On the other hand some jobs are so disagreeable (dipping sheet metal in acid in a galvanizing plant) or so tedious (fitting microchips into calculators on an assembly line) that it might be proper to say in your theme that you stayed on the job only because you could not find another and you had to make money. If you are in doubt concerning whether or not a detail is germane to your topic, go ahead and put it down. You will not use all the details you list in any event, and it is better to write down an extraneous thought, which can be rejected later, than to leave out a fact that might fit into your theme.

Getting Started

Here is how one student prepared to write his theme. Harry Mason had worked the 11:00 P.M. to 7:00 A.M. shift in a convenience store. He sold things, mostly beer and soft drinks and snacks and tobacco. During slack periods he straightened the merchandise, swept the floor, and cleaned the glass doors on the coolers. He brewed fresh coffee, which he sold in styrofoam cups, when the urn was empty. At the beginning and end of his shift, he and the person he was relieving or the one who was relieving him checked the cash register. The first thing Harry thought of that he liked about the job was the hours. He liked being awake at night, and he particularly liked the quiet time between 2:00 and 4:00, when he could think or read or write letters to his girl friend. He liked being on his own. As long as he got his cleanup chores done, he could do them when and how he wanted to. He enjoyed talking to some of the people who came in for coffee early in the morning.

The main thing that Harry disliked about the job was his fear of being robbed. His boss had told him not to resist, to hand over the money and do whatever else a robber said. Even so Harry was afraid that somebody who was drunk or strung out on drugs might pull the trigger by accident. On slow nights, even with reading and letter writing, he sometimes got bored. He did not like to clean the grounds out of the coffee urn or to clean the glass on the coolers. Some of the customers were rude to him, and some of the people who came in for coffee early in the morning irritated him.

When he thought about it, Harry decided that these people who hung around the store early in the morning were the closest thing he had to fellow workers. A retired railroad man who liked to talk about steam locomotives and pulling troop trains in World War II came in regularly, as did a disc jockey who appeared to be about Harry's age and who had a frail body and a strong deep voice. Police came, parking parallel in front of the store, taking up space for three cars. Because of days off and shift changes, Harry met a lot of people like these. Some were amiable and some less so; some he liked and some he did not like. One of the police that he particularly liked was a woman. She was a couple of years older than Harry, divorced, and had a nine-month-old baby. Harry wanted a date with her, but he was too embarrassed to ask for one while her partner could hear him.

Harry's job was simple, and he did not have any duties that he had not expected. But no job, he decided, is ever quite like you think it is going to be. One summer he had been a lifeguard, and there was no way he could know beforehand how many ways little kids could misbehave and how close they could come to driving you crazy. In the convenience-store job he was impressed by all the junk he had to keep up with: bottle openers, key chains, ballpoints, combs, fingernail clippers, huggers, funny license plates, bumper stickers and other stuff to go on automobiles. Most of these things were displayed on special racks or cards. They were crowded together and were always turning over, and it seemed to Harry that too much of his time was spent straightening them.

Harry remembered three striking but unpleasant incidents that had happened. He finally had found an opportunity to ask the policewoman for a date, and she had flatly turned him down. One night a drunk had upset the coffee urn. Another night a man tried to pay Harry for a six-pack with a large check that Harry was not allowed to accept, and then the man took the beer without paying for it.

Harry will probably remember other details about his job when he starts to write his theme. But he has thought enough about the job now to make a list of details on which he will base his essay. Here is Harry's list.

Details for Theme on Summer Job

1. What I did
   Worked 11 to 7
   Sold merchandise—mostly drinks, snacks, smokes
   Straightened stock
   Cleaned up
   Made coffee
   Checked cash register
2. Things about the job
   No supervision
   Sometimes bored
   Almost always afraid
   Hated cleaning coffee urn and coolers
   Hated rude customers
   Annoyed at having to straighten junk displays so often

3. People who came in
   Railroad man
   Disc jockey
   Policemen
   Policewoman
4. Interesting times
   Asking for date
   Drunk turning over coffee urn
   Man stealing beer

Narrowing the Focus

At this point in his thinking about his essay Harry has more material than he can use. If he tries to describe in some detail all the things he did on the job and all the people he remembers and all the interesting things that occurred, his theme will not have any form; so much will be included that no event or person will seem to be more important than any other. The essay will have no climax and no point. Now Harry should remind himself of the purpose of his theme. He is writing to tell, as accurately as he can, what his summer job was like. This means what the job was like in general, hour after hour, night after night. Harry needs a moment of excitement to keep the theme from being as dull as the job often was, but the moment of excitement must be related as closely as possible to the rest of the material that is used to describe the job.

Every theme should have a beginning, a middle, and an end; and we will talk more about these elements later. Notice now that in planning his theme Harry is looking first not for a beginning but for an end. There is no law of composition that says he has to do this. Under other circumstances, when he is writing about other subjects, he might think first about his beginning or look for some idea or detail to use in the middle of his theme. But every essay must have a controlling idea or thesis, some aspect of the subject toward which or around which the author can build. In considering which moment of excitement to use as an anchor for the rest of his theme, Harry thinks first of the policewoman. She was attractive, all right; he would still like to have a date with her. And he still gets embarrassed when he remembers how she looked at him as if she were undecided whether to laugh or put him under arrest before she gave him a cold *No, thank you.* But in all the time he worked at the store, she was the only person Harry asked for a date. She had almost nothing to do with the routine of his work. The incident would probably fit into a theme about Harry's love life, but he properly decides not to use it in a theme about his job.

When the drunk upset the coffee urn, coffee and coffee grounds ruined a display of breakfast cereal and splashed merchandise halfway down one aisle. The mess stood out in Harry's memory; and because tending the coffee urn was one of Harry's duties, the incident with the coffee urn struck him as more closely related to the job than the incident with the policewoman. But because it happened only once, Harry cannot see any way to use this incident as a major event in a theme that will give the reader some sense of what his job in general was like. Finally he thought of the man big enough to play tackle for the Dallas Cowboys who put a six-pack of Miller beer on the counter and handed Harry a $263 payroll check. Harry did not have $260 in the register, and even if he had he was strictly forbidden to cash any kind of check, payroll or otherwise. When Harry tried to explain this, the man got furious, called Harry names, took back his check, picked up the beer, and left the store. Harry was scared. His heart had been beating almost as fast as he thought it would beat if he were robbed with a gun. This incident is the best one for Harry to use. It ties in with the fear Harry had of being held up, and Harry felt this fear every single night that he worked at his job.

Now Harry is ready to write. He may want to go back

over his list and mark out the details that he is not going to use. He may want to make an outline. But, as we said in Chapter 1, whatever method he employs, he should remain flexible. Usually, while you are writing, your ideas about what you are saying will be modified: you will discover things that you were not aware you knew and remember things that you did not realize you would remember. These discoveries and recollections may make it necessary for you to alter your plan or change your outline. You should feel free to do this. Nothing should be considered final about an essay until the last revision has been completed. Even then you may have second thoughts that can result in further improvement of your essay.

Exercises

A. Think of two jobs you have held. Make a list of details about each job on which you might base a theme. Which list do you think you might develop into the better theme? Explain your answer.

B. If you have never done any kind of regular work, think of two schools you have attended. Make a list of details about each school on which you might base a theme. Which list do you think you might develop into the better theme? Explain your answer.

3

Writing a Theme

Easy writing's vile hard reading.

—R. B. Sheridan

It is often as much what a writer leaves out as what he puts in that matters.

—Gerald Brenan

Writing is hard work, and because this is so, we often have trouble making ourselves do it. Getting started is the most difficult part. Sometimes we delay the task by making extensive preparations: we clean off the desk, we find fresh paper, we sharpen pencils, we try several different positions and then decide to change chairs. Once we are settled, we are likely to feel a profound need for a Coke or a cup of coffee. We may think of a phone call that must be made, or a person we must talk to, or even a lesson for another course that suddenly must be done. People will do almost anything to get out of writing, so an essential procedure in writing of any kind is to discipline yourself.

Preparing to Write

Find a time and place to write. Where and when do not matter as long as you have a regular place and a regular time. You may be able to work best in a reading room where you are surrounded by people at work, or you may need to be alone. Noise may not bother you, or you may need silence; you may like the morning, or you may prefer the night. Suit yourself, but once you have decided on a place and time, stick to them. If you decide to work in your room from eight to nine in the morning, sit down at your desk at eight and stay there. If you are going to need coffee, get it before you sit down. If you think of other things you need to do, resist the temptation to do them. Frequently, when you are trying to write, the lazy part of you is struggling against your better self. It keeps suggesting other things that you ought to be doing. Do not be seduced. Even if you do not write a word—which is unlikely—make yourself sit at your desk for the full time you have set aside for your writing. Once you have convinced yourself that you are going to keep to your schedule, the writing will come more easily.

Start work on your theme as soon as you have received your assignment. Thinking about what you are going to write, making your list of details, and defining your topic are very important steps; but do not linger over them and thereby seriously delay the actual writing. If you have a week in which to complete your essay, spend no more than two days thinking about what you are going to write and no more than two days writing a first draft of your theme. Take a day off, then look at what you have written. All writing, almost without exception, needs some revision; and having been away from your first draft for a day, you will be able to see better what changes need to be made. Sometimes a few alterations in punctuation and sentence structure, corrections of misspelling, deletion of a few words and phrases to tighten the prose are all that will be required. Sometimes you may find that your theme as a whole simply does not work. You may not have discovered your proper subject; you may have written in too big a hurry. For whatever reason, if your theme seems flat and formless, you will want to write an entirely new version of your essay. This is why you need to leave two days for revision.

Writing the First Draft

When you have done your thinking about your theme and have determined the direction that it is going to take, your next task is to find your beginning. To start properly you must move immediately to your subject. We have already pointed out that much of our conversation has no meaning except in terms of our social relationships. It is all right to talk about the weather or last night's baseball game before you ask somebody for a date or before you try to borrow a book or before you discuss a grade with a professor. Conversation of this sort is a kind of warm-up for the main statement. No harm will be done if you get into your writing by composing irrelevant introductions as long as you recognize where your theme really begins and later cut out all the material that is not absolutely pertinent.

For example, when Harry Mason gets down to the actual writing of his theme, he may think initially of how he got his summer job. Harry's uncle put in a word for Harry with Mr. Pacelli, the owner of the store. Harry went for an interview, and he doubtless remembers most of the questions Mr. Pacelli asked and the answers he gave. He knows that he was nervous because his senior year was almost over and he had been looking for a job for months and had found nothing. Writing a description of the interview might help Harry get to the beginning of his theme, but the theme is about the job and not about how Harry got it. So the conversation with Mr. Pacelli will have to be cut out.

Finding the middle part of your theme in which the main idea is developed is largely a matter of selection. If you have thought about your subject intensely and have made a proper list of facts and details, you will have more material than you can put into your theme. Selecting the details you will use and how you will use them will be a test of whether you have a firm grasp of your subject. For example, as we know, Harry has decided to base his theme on the incident of the man who took the beer without paying. Harry still thinks the overturned urn and the good-looking cop are very interesting, but a pretty woman and spilled coffee will divert the reader's attention from Harry's subject—the nightly routine, edged with fear, which is leading toward the man snatching the beer. In other words in writing the middle we must be careful to maintain focus. No matter how striking they may be in themselves, details and events that direct our minds away from that focus damage the theme. Any good writer will tell you that you will always have to sacrifice some of your best material in order to maintain focus and momentum. "Every article is strong in proportion to the surplus of details from which you can choose the few that will serve you best," as William Zinsser has pointed out.

The ending is the final point or last incident. If you have written your beginning and middle properly, you will probably have little trouble writing your conclusion. The ending does present two major temptations to error: one is to write too little; the other is to write too much. For example the big scene in Harry's theme is the theft of the beer. If Harry ends his theme immediately after this event has occurred, his ending will be underdeveloped. The reader will not have time to comprehend the effect of this scene. If, after he tells us about the theft of the beer, Harry writes another two paragraphs telling how he felt and how he discussed the robbery with his boss and what new thoughts the incident put into his head about the dangers of working in a convenience store, the theme will be too long. All this will dissipate the effect of the main scene. The reader's response to what has gone before will be dulled, and the theme will become flat and lifeless.

Here is the first draft of Harry Mason's theme.

WORKING IN A CONVENIENCE STORE

Last summer I worked at Angelo's Stop-and-Go Market. My shift started at eleven at night, and I was surprised at how much business we did from then till one-thirty or two in the morning. We carried groceries, of course, and I would sell some bread and some canned soup, stuff like that; but mostly I sold beer and soft drinks and snacks and cigarettes. The work was pretty easy. I rang up the sales, made change, sacked the merchandise, and tried to be pleasant to the customers. When the slack period came around two or so, I cleaned the glass doors on the coolers and did a little sweeping and dusting. We sold coffee by the cup, and I had to clean the coffee urn when it ran dry and start it perking again. Making coffee and sweeping floors didn't excite me, but there was a long dead period between two and four. Not many people came in then, and I could get my cleaning done and have plenty of time to read or to write letters.

The time between two and four was the easiest time I had, but in a way it was also the worst time. Convenience stores are perfect targets for robbery. During those hours, when there was practically no traffic on the street and nobody was coming in, I would remember all the stories I had seen in newspapers and on television about convenience stores getting robbed and the people who worked in them being shot or taken hostage. There are some weird-looking characters around at night, which made things worse. Every time a car drove up and some guy would get out and start into the store, I would think: This may be it. After a while I got used to being afraid. As I have said, I could write letters and read books. But the idea that I might get robbed was always with me.

One night a man I had never seen drove up in an old Plymouth Valiant. He parked parallel, across the lines, the way I thought a stickup man might do in order to make a quick getaway. I thought that night, and I still think, he was the biggest man I ever saw. He was wearing a T-shirt, and his arms looked as big as most people's legs. Most people who come in late like that will say hello, but he didn't. He stopped just inside the door and looked around. Then he went to the beer cooler and fooled around there for a while. I was too scared to watch him and see what he was doing. Finally he came up to the counter and set down a six-pack of Miller and handed me a piece of paper. It was a payroll check for $263. I was so frightened that I kept looking at the figure on the check until the man told me to hurry up and give him his money.

I told him I wasn't allowed to cash any checks, and even if I had been, I didn't have that much money in the register. The man's face was flushed. "Listen," he said, "that check's good. Ain't this a goddamn store?" I told him I couldn't cash it. "To hell with it," the man said. He took his check and picked up the beer and left, and I didn't say anything. My heart was beating so hard I could feel the pulse in my neck. I sat down on my stool and breathed through my mouth, and after a while I began to feel more normal.

About four the police who rode that beat stopped for coffee as they usually did, and I told them what had happened. One of the cops was a woman. She was good-looking. Once I tried to date her, but she turned me down flat. She was divorced and had a baby. She looked at her partner and laughed. He laughed too and said: "You're lucky, Harry. The next time you don't take somebody's check, the son of a bitch might kill you."

I was still scared, and I thought the police ought to do more than just laugh about what had happened, but they didn't. They drank their coffee and bought some cigarettes and acted as if nothing out of the ordinary had happened. After that night I was pretty jumpy for a while, but the man never came back, and nobody else ever took anything from me.

Revising the First Draft

The first draft of Harry's theme is fairly good, but it needs revision. The opening paragraph is loose and uncertain because, in trying to establish the basic conditions of his job, Harry tells us things we already know: that the store, which has been identified as a market, carries groceries; that he rang up sales, made change, sacked the merchandise, tried to be pleasant. Seeing that he has stated the obvious, Harry looks for ways to cut and tighten the first paragraph. He also discovers that he mentions the dead period between two and four twice, so he will have to remedy that failing.

The second paragraph is stronger than the first. Harry has found his direction now, and from this point he needs, for the most part, only to tighten his prose. He tries to make his writing more direct by using fewer words to convey the same amount of information. For example "The time between two and four" is revised to read "This slack period." Harry also decides that everybody knows there are "weird-looking characters around at night," so he deletes that phrase.

In the third paragraph there is more tightening up to be done, and so Harry makes more cuts. Mostly these are deletions of extraneous words and phrases, but the reference to "most people who come in late" shifts our attention away from the man who has just entered the store. The shift in focus is admittedly slight, but anything that deflects our attention from the particular man, even momentarily, reduces the dramatic force of the passage. Harry therefore removes the sentence about most people.

Harry sees that the fourth paragraph presents him with a new problem. The scene described here is the most important sequence in the theme, and because it is, it needs to be presented in detail. Now, rather than delete and compress, Harry needs to expand. He must accomplish two things: first, he needs to make the reader visualize the scene as concretely as possible; second, he should hold the scene before the reader long enough for the reader to realize the full importance of what is happening. Harry thinks about his experience and remembers more fully what he did that night. He adds detail. The added detail holds the scene in focus and enables us to see the man more clearly.

Harry now puts each line of dialogue into a separate paragraph. This is the correct way to present dialogue. The division of speeches into separate paragraphs makes the passage easier to read. It also isolates the passage on the page and thereby calls the attention of the reader to the importance of each speech.

In the last two paragraphs Harry needs to cut again. He has allowed himself to be diverted by his memory of the beautiful policewoman. But he probably was not thinking of how pretty she was immediately after he had been badly frightened. And whether or not she was pretty or he had asked her for a date or she was a mother has nothing to do with the incident Harry is describing. On the other hand the fact that she is a woman is significant: Harry perhaps feels, at least subconsciously, that he is more courageous than most women. Therefore her response to what has been for him a bad time is slightly embarrassing. So Harry leaves in the fact that one of the police is a woman, but he cuts all the other details about her.

Harry's final paragraph tells too much. His story has been told, and we should be allowed to stop reading while the main events of the theme are still fresh in our minds. Harry replaces the three-sentence paragraph of the first draft with a single sentence: "For my part I didn't think it was funny."

Just before he makes a clean copy of his revision, Harry decides he will change the title of his theme from "Working in a Convenience Store" to "Working the Night Shift." The new title is better because it was the time Harry worked rather than where he worked that made his experience frightening.

Here is Harry's marked theme after its revision.

THE NIGHT SHIFT
WORKING ~~IN A CONVENIENCE STORE~~

Last summer I worked at Angelo's Stop-and-Go Market. My shift started at eleven at night, and I was surprised at how much business we did from then till one-thirty or two in the morning. ~~We carried groceries, of course, and~~ I would sell some bread and some canned soup, stuff like that; but mostly I sold beer and soft drinks and snacks and cigarettes. The work was pretty easy. I rang up the sales, made change, sacked the merchandise, and tried to be pleasant to the customers. When the slack period came around two or so, I cleaned the glass doors on the coolers and did a little sweeping and dusting. We sold coffee by the cup, and I had to clean the coffee urn when it ran dry and ~~start it perking again.~~ ^{restart it.} Making coffee and sweeping floors didn't excite me, but ~~there was a long dead period~~ between two and four/~~Not many people came in then, and~~ I could get my cleaning done and have plenty of time to read or to write letters.

^{The slack period}
~~The time between two and four~~ was the easiest time I had, but in a way it was also the worst time. ~~Convenience stores are perfect targets for robbery.~~ During those hours, when there was practically no traffic on the street and no-

body was coming in, I would remember all the stories I had seen ~~in newspapers and on television~~ and heard about convenience stores getting robbed and the people who worked in them being shot or taken hostage. ~~There are some weird-looking characters around at night, which made things worse.~~ Every time a car drove up and some guy got ~~would get~~ out and ~~start into the store~~ started in, I would think: This may be it. After a while I got used to being afraid. As I have said, I could write letters and read books. But the idea that I might get robbed was always with me.

Late ~~One~~ night a man I had never seen drove up in an old Plymouth Valiant. He parked parallel, ~~across the lines~~ the way I thought a stickup man might do ~~in order~~ to make a quick getaway. ~~I thought that night, and I still think~~ he was the biggest man I ever saw. He was wearing a T-shirt, and his arms looked as big as most people's legs. ~~Most people who come in late like that will say hello, but he didn't.~~ He stopped just inside the door and looked around. Then he went to the beer cooler and fooled around ~~there~~ for a while. I was too scared to watch ~~him and see~~ what he was doing. Finally he came up to the counter and set down a six-pack of Miller and handed me ~~a piece of paper. It was~~ a payroll check for $263. I was so frightened ~~that~~ I kept looking at the figure on the check until the man told me to hurry up and give him his money.

I told him I wasn't allowed to cash any checks, and ~~even if I had been,~~ anyway, I didn't have ~~that much money~~ $260 in the register. ~~The man's face was flushed.~~ "Listen," he said,

ade myself ce up at man's flushed . His eyes e very red. ooked stoned.

"that check's good. Ain't this a goddamn store?" I told
him I couldn't cash it. ¶ "Then To hell with it," the man said. He
took his check and picked up the beer and left/ and I
didn't say anything. My heart was beating so hard I could
feel the pulse in my neck. I sat down on my stool and
breathed through my mouth, and after a while I began to
feel more normal.

About four the police who rode that beat stopped for
coffee as they usually did, and I told them what had happened. One of the cops was a woman. ~~She was good-
looking. Once I tried to date her, but she turned me down
flat. She was divorced and had a baby.~~ She looked at her
partner and laughed. He laughed too and said: "You're
lucky, Harry. The next time you don't take somebody's
check, the son of a bitch might kill you."

~~I was still scared, and I thought the police ought to do
more than just laugh about what had happened, but they
didn't. They drank their coffee and bought some cigarettes
and acted as if nothing out of the ordinary had happened.
After that night I was pretty jumpy for a while, but the
man never came back, and nobody else ever took anything from me.~~ For my part I didn't think it was funny.

Here is a clean copy of Harry's final draft after he completed revising it.

WORKING THE NIGHT SHIFT

Last summer I worked at Angelo's Stop-and-Go Market.
My shift started at eleven at night, and I was surprised at

how much business we did from then till one-thirty or two in the morning. I would sell some bread and some canned soup, stuff like that, but mostly I sold beer and soft drinks and snacks and cigarettes. When the slack period came around two or so, I cleaned the glass on the coolers and did a little sweeping and dusting. We sold coffee by the cup, and I had to clean the coffee urn when it ran dry and restart it. Making coffee and sweeping floors didn't excite me, but between two and four I could get my cleaning done and still have plenty of time to read and to write letters.

The slack period was the easiest time I had, but in a way it was also the worst time. During those hours, when there was practically no traffic on the street and nobody coming in, I would remember all the stories I had seen and heard about convenience stores getting robbed and the people who worked in them being shot or taken hostage. Every time a car drove up and some guy got out and started in, I would think: This may be it. Although I got more or less used to being afraid after a while, the idea that I might get robbed was always with me.

Late one night a man I had never seen drove up in an old Plymouth Valiant. He parked parallel, the way I thought a stickup man might do to make a quick getaway. He was the biggest man I ever saw. He was wearing a T-shirt, and his arms looked as big as most people's legs. He stopped just inside the door and looked around; then he went to the beer cooler and fooled around for a while. I was too scared to watch what he was doing. Finally he came up to the counter, set down a six-pack of Miller, and handed me a payroll check for $263. I was so frightened I kept looking at the figure on the check until the man told me to hurry up and give him his money.

I told him I wasn't allowed to cash any checks, and anyway I didn't have $260 in the register. I made myself glance up at the man's flushed face. His eyes were very red. He looked stoned.

"Listen," he said, "that check's good. Ain't this a goddamn store?"

I told him I couldn't cash it.

"Then to hell with it," the man said.

He took his check and picked up the beer and left. I didn't say anything. My heart was beating so hard that I could feel the pulse in my neck. I sat down on my stool and breathed through my mouth, and after a while I began to feel more normal.

About four the police who rode that beat stopped in for coffee as they usually did, and I told them what had happened. One of the cops was a woman. She looked at her partner and laughed. He laughed too and said: "You're lucky, Harry. The next time you don't take somebody's check, the son of a bitch might kill you."

For my part I didn't think it was funny.

Exercises _____

Here is a short essay by a professional writer which is based on personal experience and observation.

My parents were products of their time and place, and when they were married early in 1906, the automotive age had not reached Nebraska.

My father farmed with horses and gave them up reluctantly when tractors took over, much later.

As a bride, my mother had her own horse. It was a "buggy" horse. That is, it was not so big and awkward and cumbersome as a draft horse. When she wanted to visit a neighbor or go to town, she'd whistle for her horse and he'd come to the barn.

She could harness him and hitch him to the buggy and be on her way. As a result, she was more independent than were many farm wives.

My parents were married about fifteen years before they bought their first automobile. For my mother, the car did not lead to freedom or open the way to a mobile society.

As the family acquired cars and the "modern" age burst upon her, the private "buggy" horse was displaced. And my mother never learned to drive a car. I never asked why. But I recall that riding in a car made her nervous, and it would have been in character for my father to feel that only men drove cars.

My mother thus had to depend on someone else to take her when she wanted to go anywhere. And since my father often didn't wish to go places, my mother spent a lot more time at home in her mature years.

The automobile, rather than freeing her, confined her more than ever.

—Robert M. Lienert, "Moving Backward" (1980)

A. After carefully reading the essay, answer these questions:

1. Are all the ideas Lienert uses here relevant to his subject?

2. What does the title tell us about the author's attitude toward his material?

3. What does the essay tell us about the personalities of Lienert's mother and father? How is this information conveyed?

4. Make a list of the ideas Lienert uses. Could the essay be improved by changing the order in which the ideas are placed? Explain.

B. Write a theme of about 500 words based on your own experience or the experience of someone close to you.

Considering the Personal Report

Focusing on something that you have done or on something that has happened to you—as Harry Mason does in "Working the Night Shift"—or on something that has occurred to a member of your family—as Robert Lienert does in "Moving Backward"—is not the only way to write from your own experience. Another way is to write an essay on a subject that is *suggested* by something which you have done or seen or heard or read. Most of the time in your writing you will be asked to move out from your own experience and to describe and explain less personal matters. Now consider the following theme by Kathie Thompson.

RUNNING IS THE BEST EXERCISE

Regular exercise is very important to your physical and psychological well-being. Whatever else you do, whatever lifestyle you follow, exercise will make you feel better and make life more worth living. There are a lot of ways to get exercise. My cousin, who works in the city, plays racquetball on his lunch hour. The lady who lives next door to me is very fat. She has an exercycle in her den and she rides it in the afternoon while she watches the soaps. You can swim or play basketball or golf or do just about anything that will keep you moving. But the best way to get exercise is to run, which is what I do.

The reason running is the best exercise is that you can do it almost anywhere. To swim you've got to have a pool and to play golf you've got to have a course, which has to be outside and won't do you any good in the wintertime anyway. But with running, if you're in a city, you can find a park. If you live in a small town or the suburbs, you can run in the streets. You can run whatever is happening, rain or snow if you don't mind a little discomfort now and then. Or if you have a gym with a track in it, you can run there.

I got started running because of a teacher I had in high school. She was a neat person. Really she wasn't a teacher. She was still in college, and she was doing her practice teaching in my school being supervised by my history teacher. Anyway I had history the last class of the day, and some of us got in the habit of hanging around after class talking to Cynthia, which was her name, about politics sometimes and about music and school rules and the kind of stuff you talk about under that situation. Three of us were hanging around talking one day, and Cynthia asked us if we smoked, which, as it happened, we all did. She asked us if we did pot, which all of us also did occasionally. She told us we ought to stop tobacco and pot because it was all bad for your lungs. She told us she jogged every day, and she invited us to run with her. I took her up, and though I suffered at first, as I got in shape I began to enjoy it.

If you are going to run, you'll need some shoes. You can get the right shoes at a sporting goods shop or at a place that specializes in running equipment like The Athlete's Foot or The Athletic Attic. You'll need some shorts, and there are some that are made specially for runners, but any comfortable shorts will do. There are running shirts too, but in warm weather you can just add a T-shirt. Jogging suits made for the wintertime are good, but regular sweat-suits will do. If you are going to run on roads at night, have bright colors so cars can see you.

Learn a few basic exercises to stretch your muscles and do these as a warmup before you run. Then get out and go, and if your legs and body start hurting and you think you can't get enough air, don't worry but try to keep on going because that's all a part of getting in shape. Remember if you get in good shape you'll feel better, and running is the way to do it.

A. Make a list of the ideas in Kathie's theme. Put them in the order that Kathie uses them.

B. Would the theme be better organized if Kathie had used her ideas in a different order?

C. Which ideas in Kathie's theme receive most emphasis? Should other ideas receive more emphasis? If so, which ones?

D. Does Kathie put her ideas in the best possible relationship to each other? If not, how would you change the relationship of ideas?

E. How would you revise Kathie's theme? What words would you change? What sentences would you rewrite? Would you add ideas that Kathie has not included? Would you delete some of the details she has used? Explain your changes.

Kathie has written about a popular aspect of American life today—running is almost a national religion—so she has chosen a good subject. Kathie's theme, which was assigned as a personal report, not as an expository piece or an argumentative essay or something else, works in part because she did not go to the library and find out what Red Smith or Garry Trudeau or James Fixx said about running. Instead she thought about the subject in terms of her own experience and wrote about it from that single perspective. Ford Madox Ford once remarked that "Kipling was perfectly right when he wrote that there are five and forty ways for a writer. There are probably five hundred thousand, every single one of them being right. But to tell the whole truth, he must have added that there is only one best way for the treatment of every given subject and only one method best suited for every given writer." Even though she probably had not encountered this remark, Kathie realized the truth of it, and she found the right way to express her subject. If Kathie continues to run and if she becomes a sports reporter or a free-lance journalist, in five or ten years she might write about running again; and if so she would approach the subject from an almost totally different perspective. But on that occasion she would probably not want to write a piece that is wholly impersonal. She would decide in all likelihood to write again from a personal standpoint.

Each of us sees the world from a vantage that is uniquely our own. Any writer must learn how to choose and maintain the right point of view, just as that writer must learn how to settle on and stick to the right tone for the given occasion. Since the personal angle is the most common of all ways of approaching a subject, we have begun with it. Learning to establish your own perspective and voice is one of the virtues of learning how to write the personal report.

Exercises

A. Consider now a personal report about a subject that any of us could write about—the sounds that a dwelling makes—but would find hard to write about so well as does this author, whether or not we live in an old house.

One way you know a house is by the sounds it makes. Winter is best for this because the world keeps its distance. Inside is everything. You listen to the worn joists and old rafters, the creaky doors and loose floorboards that tell you a house is alive, breathing, recycling its past, and yours.

The house I grew up in tapped out a steady flow of these messages. The shudder of pipes in the morning, steps springing back into place, meant the day was on schedule. When the curtains whispered we knew the wind was blowing hard, and at times the whole place seemed to lean against it, beams and risers straining in unison. Even these chilling sounds told us that all was well, that action was being taken.

In their own curious way, other things entertained: Among the marvels of our house was a china cabinet that vibrated when you walked on a certain spot in the dining room. We demonstrated this magic to visitors.

The mystifying, furtive sighs we heard at night were different from the cranky daytime noises. We listened to the walls, to the secrets of the closets. I don't think we knew where half of these sounds came from, and we resisted doing anything that might silence them. Perhaps they belonged to the previous owners and should not be disturbed.

This "body language" of a house gives predictability: My mother lived alone for the last seven years of her life and rarely did she bother winding the clocks: The house, she claimed, kept time for her.

The modern family has become desensitized to the inner voice of dwellings. The quiet sounds have been replaced by the food processor and vacuum cleaner, the dishwasher and garbage disposer, from which we vainly seek escape by turning up the TV or stereo. Architects don't pay enough attention to this problem. . . . A house should reverberate to its own rhythms.

—David Dempsey, "Low Moans in the Attic.
Oh! A Creak! *Another!*" (1980)

1. Mark the beginning, middle, and end of this essay. Is each the right length in comparison to the other parts? Explain.

2. What, if anything, is gained by comparing old houses to new houses?

3. Why is the expression "body language" put in quotation marks? Is this an effective image? Whether or not you consider it to be effective, try to think of a better one.

4. Trace the author's use of day and night in this essay. How does this help to unify the theme?

5. The basic idea of this essay is very ordinary. List some of the most significant details in the essay and explain how they help to make the essay memorable.

B. To conclude this chapter, let's turn to an essay on a subject that was suggested by the writer's age. In this sequence of *The View from 80* Malcolm Cowley retells a notorious story about life in New York City that entails the compulsions and hazards of old age. The story of the Collyer brothers has been told many times, and a movie was made of it. But no one has told it so succinctly and pointedly as Cowley does here.

> Why do so many old persons, men and women alike, insist on hoarding money when they have no prospect of using it and even when they have no heirs? They eat the cheapest food, buy no clothes, and live in a single room when they could afford better lodging. It may be that they regard money as a form of power; there is a comfort in watching it accumulate while other powers are dwindling away. How often we read of an old person found dead in a hovel, on a mattress partly stuffed with bankbooks and stock certificates! The bankbook syndrome, we call it in our family, which has never succumbed.
>
> Untidiness we call the Langley Collyer syndrome. To explain, Langley Collyer was a former concert pianist who lived alone with his 70-year-old brother in a brownstone house on upper Fifth Avenue. The once fashionable neighborhood had become part of Harlem. Homer, the brother, had been an admiralty lawyer, but was now blind and partly paralyzed; Langley played for him and fed him on buns and oranges, which he thought would restore Homer's sight. He never threw away a daily paper because Homer, he said, might want to read them all. He saved other things as well and the house became filled with rubbish from roof to basement. The halls were lined on both sides with bundled newspapers, leaving narrow passageways in which Langley had devised booby traps to catch intruders.
>
> On March 21, 1947, some unnamed person telephoned the

police to report that there was a dead body in the Collyer house. The police broke down the front door and found the hall impassable; then they hoisted a ladder to a second-story window. Behind it Homer was lying on the floor in a bathrobe; he had starved to death. Langley had disappeared. After some delay, the police broke into the basement, chopped a hole in the roof, and began throwing junk out of the house, top and bottom. It was 18 days before they found Langley's body, gnawed by rats. Caught in one of his own booby traps, he had died in a hallway just outside Homer's door. By that time the police had collected, and the Department of Sanitation had hauled away, 120 tons of rubbish, including, besides the newspapers, 14 grand pianos and the parts of a dismantled Model T Ford.

Why do so many old people accumulate junk, not on the scale of Langley Collyer, but still in a dismaying fashion? Their tables are piled high with it, their bureau drawers are stuffed with it, their closet rods bend with the weight of clothes not worn for years. I suppose that the piling up is partly from lethargy and partly from the feeling that everything once useful, including their own bodies, should be preserved. Others, though not so many, have such a fear of becoming Langley Collyers that they strive to be painfully neat. Every tool they own is in its place, though it will never be used again; every scrap of paper is filed away in alphabetical order. At last their immoderate neatness becomes another vice of age, if a milder one.

—*The View from 80* (1980)

1. Consider the structure of the essay. Does the opening sentence state the topic of the theme? Does the essay stop at the right place? Why? Does the introduction of another vice weaken the ending? Should the story of Langley Collyer be given so much attention?

2. What sort of details does Cowley use in discussing each vice? What details does Cowley deliberately leave out? What is the effect of the following details: gnawed by rats, parts of a dismantled Model T Ford, buns and oranges, better lodging, booby traps? Consider whether each of these details should be expanded, made more or less specific, changed to a different detail, or deleted.

3. Can you suggest any revisions, no matter how small, that might improve the essay?

4

Exposition

Facts which at first seem improbable will, even on scant explanation, drop the cloak which has hidden them and stand forth in naked and simple beauty.

—Galileo Galilei

In description you have to snatch at small details, grouping them so that after reading them you can see the picture on closing your eyes.

—Anton Chekhov

If you are standing on the corner of Tenth and Main and somebody asks you how to get to Forsyth Street, the answer you give, if you know the answer, is an exercise in exposition. For most of us, sooner or later, many of the things in the world have to be explained. We not only need to know how to get from one place to another; we want to know how to cook eggs and how to change spark plugs, how to bench press and how to do needlepoint, how to apply the Pythagorean theorem and how to tune a guitar. We want to know why about a lot of things too: why the Steelers are favored in the Super Bowl and why wolves are good for the ecology, why the Arabs keep raising the price of oil and why Napoleon lost the Battle of Waterloo. We want to know how things work: the electoral college and a gas stove, a back hoe and a food processor, an optical scanner and a ballpoint pen. We want to understand things: the Hegelian dialectic and the Dow theory, the ebb and flow of tides and the structure of *Hamlet*. The thing to be explained can be simple or complicated; the explanation can tell where or when or how or why or any combination of these. But always remember that the principal aim of exposition is *to explain as clearly as possible*. And clarity requires strong organization.

Finding an Organization

One of the best ways to organize material that is palpable, that we can see and touch—which is what we are going to discuss in this section—is in terms of time or space or a combination of the two. For example, your answer to the question of how to get to Forsyth Street might run something like this. *Go to the next traffic signal. Then turn right and go for three blocks. Then turn left and go to the second stop sign. The street after that is Forsyth.* If you think about what you have said, you will see that you have given a series of instructions in a particular order—which is to say, in a temporal sequence even though space is involved.

1. Go to the next traffic signal.
2. Turn right and go for three blocks.
3. Turn left and go to the second stop sign.
4. Go to the next street.

Obviously the only hope anyone has of getting to Forsyth from the corner of Tenth and Main is to follow the above steps *in the right order*. If we decide to pursue step three first and then go back to step one, we may wind up at the packinghouse, we may wind up at City Hall, but one thing is sure: we will not find Forsyth Street. The explanation, to be of any value at all, must follow the temporal sequence according to which the exposition is organized.

Now suppose we are not in town, but in the woods. We come to the top of a high hill and we meet some people who ask us how to get to a place called Blanket Rock. We show them a valley that runs due south. On each side of the valley is a timbered ridge. At the end of the valley is a rock face. Near the eastern ridge a spring emerges from an outcropping at the bottom of the stone face. This is Blanket Rock. These directions are given not in terms of time, but in terms of space: the organizing principle is not a sequence which must be followed, but a relationship of the parts, the details of landscape, to one another.

1. A valley runs south.
2. There is a timbered ridge on the west.
3. There is a timbered ridge on the east.
4. There is a rock face at the end of the valley.
5. A spring emerges from the rock face near the eastern ridge.

Probably the best way to organize this material is to start with the valley, as we have done, and move on toward the spring. But if each of the pieces of information above was written on a card and the cards were shuffled and dealt to the people who want to find Blanket Rock, they could still find it. This is true because the explanation does not depend on a series of steps set forth in a temporal sequence; instead it depends on the relationships in space of aspects of a landscape. But note that the relationship in space must be established and maintained for the explanation to be effective. We cannot say there are two ridges and a valley and a rock face and a spring and not say which is north and which is east and what is next to what else any more than we can give directions on how to get to Forsyth Street without putting them in the proper temporal order.

Many expositions that we give involve not only temporal sequences and spatial relationships but the use of material or equipment. Go, for example, to a cookbook and look at the recipes. You will not find much graceful writing, but if the author of the cookbook has done a proper job, you can learn how to make angel food cake or lobster Newburg. First, the author of the cookbook will tell you what you will need to do the job: how many eggs and how much milk or how much lobster meat. Before you begin the actual cooking, you can gather all your ingredients. This will be a help. It is easier to follow directions if you do not have to stop at every step to find the ingredient that you need. When materials are to be used, nothing should be left for readers to discover for themselves when they are halfway through their project.

Look at the following passage.

Since the days of excise, moonshiners have been forced to hide their stills. Here are some of the ways they have used.

Since cold running water is an absolute necessity, stills are often high up on the side of a mountain near the source of a stream. Water on the north side of a hill flowing west was preferred by many. Some count on the inaccessibility of the spot they chose for protection. Others, however:

build a log shed over the still and cover this with evergreen branches;

bend living saplings over so they conceal the still. The branches continue growing and their leaves provide cover;

find a tree that has fallen over a ravine or gully and build the still under it, adding branches, if necessary, for additional coverage;

find a ravine, dig out its bottom, place the still in, and then set branches and saplings over the top like a roof. They should be arranged so that they blend in with the landscape;

find a cave and cover up the front of it;

find a large laurel thicket, crawl into the center of it,

and cut out a room right in the middle of the thicket big
enough for the still;
    find a large spruce and put the still under its branches
so it can't be seen from a plane.

—Eliot Wigginton, "Hiding the Still," The Foxfire Book (1972)

Considering the Problem

To those of us who have never been in the line of work under
discussion here, the suggested ways to hide a still are intrigu-
ing. But if we went out into the woods to do the actual hiding, we would soon find that what we have in the above
passage is not an exposition, but rather a list of several topics
which might be enlarged into proper expository essays. For
example, it is well and good to say "build a log shed over the
still," but few people, whether raised in the country or in
the city, will know how to construct such a shed without a
good deal of detailed instruction. To build a shed, what tools
will we need? What kind and what size of logs do we need?
How many logs do we need? What is the very first step in
building the shed? And on and on we go, asking questions
that are not answered here. To look at another suggestion, do
you make a clearing in a laurel thicket with an axe or a saw
or some other instrument? How do you cut the laurel in such
a way that there is ample space at the bottom but still foliage over the top? Or, to take one of the simpler methods of
hiding a still, what kinds of saplings bend best? What kinds
are likely to be killed by excessive bending? What kinds have
leaves that will most likely hide the still completely?

Our point is not to criticize the ways of hiding a still that
are listed here. As far as we know, they are all good methods
which have been used by conscientious moonshiners and in
turn discovered by industrious sheriffs and revenue agents.
The passage itself is fun to read, but it is not good exposition
because it assumes too much knowledge on the part of the

reader. Anyone who knows how to build a log shed will probably already know that such a shed can be used to hide a still. Anyone who does not know how to build such a shed has not learned from the passage above how to get his or her still out of sight of the airborne revenuers.

Organizing by Temporal Sequence

Look at the following passage.

Here is the true way to put up posts for a New England fence, learned from sixteen years of hard experience. Or, rather, here are two ways: the fast way and the best way.

The fast way is to go buy however many posts you need. Make sure you buy large ones, 4" to 5" in diameter at the butt, and sharpened so that the taper extends at least a foot. Throughout New England, such posts are normally cedar—though if you find locust, grab them. Meanwhile buy or borrow a soft iron driving maul—not to be confused with a sledge hammer, which has a much smaller head—and a good four-foot iron bar. Lay out your first strand of wire to make a line, or else do it with string. Then you can start driving posts. Take your bar, and drive it into the ground where you want the first post to go. If you hit a small stone, you can drive it on down with the bar. If you hit a big one, or ledge, move.

When you are down about twenty inches or so (usually about four easy whacks with the maul), stop. Then wiggle the bar around with a circular motion until you have a hole sort of like the inside of an ice cream cone, with the top about 4" in diameter. Then pull the bar out, pace off the distance to the next post, and stick the bar into the ground where the post is to go. (That way you won't lose it.) Now go back and shove a post firmly into the first hole. It will easily stand, and you should be able to drive it in anywhere from six to a dozen blows, depending on what the soil is like. And it will be completely tight—no play at all.

When you get to the big corner posts, you can do them the same way—but it won't be any six to twelve blows. If you have a post hole digger, now is when it's useful. It will make you a straight-sided hole about 5" in diameter. Dig one a foot deep. Then work your bar for another foot in the bottom. Plump the 6" corner post in, and drive it with ease.

That's all there is to the fast way. Provided, of course, you remember to brace all corner posts with braces that go right to the base of the nearest line post on either side. Little bitty braces do nothing. You can buy cedar poles for braces, or you can cut your own. Either way, they should be about a foot longer than the distance between your fence posts, and at least 3" in diameter at the small end. Here's how to install them. With a shovel you make a small hole right up against a line post, and shove the butt end of the brace in. Then you lay the smaller end carefully on top of the corner post, and trim it to length with a neat diagonal cut. Then you slide it down the corner post for about a foot, which gets it good and tight, and nail it in place with a tenpenny (3") nail. Rich people sometimes use sixteen or even twentypenny nails.

The best way is considerably more complicated, and also takes more equipment. But it's cheaper, and Robinson Crusoe would like it better.

First learn to recognize all the trees you have. If you don't already know how to chainsaw, learn to. Then start looking for stands of young trees that need thinning. In the absence of cedar, wild cherry or tamarack is best, though both hemlock and white pine will do. Don't bother with trees growing in the open; they taper too fast, and you'll get only one or two posts from a tree. Three to five is what you should be getting. Since you cut the posts six feet long, that means the tree should have eighteen to 30 feet of straight trunk before it gets too small. Cut a bunch.

Another option is to split out posts. Butternut probably works best. If you had some butternut trees nine to fifteen inches in diameter, growing straight and not too many lower limbs, you can make a lot of posts from one tree. You fell it, buck it into six-foot logs, and split each log into fourths or sixths. All it takes is two wedges, a sledge hammer, and a modicum of skill. Butternut is a notoriously weak wood, so you always make large posts. I myself wouldn't dream of sacrificing a good butternut tree just for posts—but where I wanted to thin a fenceline anyway, or where a butternut was growing too close to sugar maples I wanted to favor, I occasionally take one. I've probably made a hundred posts that way. Six trees' worth.

If you're smart, you will have cut all these posts where you can get pretty close to them with a pickup truck, which you now drive out there. Bring your wife (or husband, or unsuspecting houseguest) and an extra pair of ear protectors. Open the tailgate and load the first three or four posts in the back of the truck, with the butt end sticking out. The spouse or guest puts on the ear protectors and climbs in the back of the truck. While he or she holds the first post steady, you sharpen it with your chainsaw. This amounts to cutting a slice off each side the full length of the chainsaw blade, getting the victim in the back of the truck to turn the post 90 degrees, and then cutting off two more slices. The whole procedure takes less than a minute. It leaves, incidentally, a pile of fluffy shavings like giant excelsior, which children find irresistible. Now do the other two or three, have the victim pile the sharpened posts on one side, and load the next batch.

If you're *really* smart, you will have done all this in the spring, and as each post is sharpened, you can also peel it. The four bark points where the sharpening cuts end will pull like Band-aids. I myself am rarely that smart and, to be honest, I think it matters only moderately.

By lunchtime you will have posts enough for a great deal of fence; and if you want to you can start pounding that afternoon. I have. If you're the deferred-pleasure type, though, instead bring them home and pile them under cover for a year. And the next spring, if you have the time, treat them. With a few posts, you just paint the bottom two and a half feet with creosote or whatever. But if you've cut a lot, that gets exceedingly boring—and besides, painting doesn't give deep penetration. The better way is to give them a 24-hour soak. I have usually done this in an old 55-gallon drum, in which I put a mixture of one-third creosote and two-thirds old motor oil. Say, five gallons of creosote and ten of motor oil. Three-thirds creosote would doubtless be better, but creosote is expensive. You can soak about fifteen posts at a time. I strongly advise tying the barrel to a tree, because when it's full of six-foot posts, it is top-heavy; and few things are more annoying than having a barrel filled with used motor oil and creosote tip over on top of you, or even not on top of you. The smell, my wife informs me, does not come out of work pants until the third washing.

Having done all this, you are ready to take your iron bar and your driving maul, and set posts. You will have a double satisfaction when you're done. You can look at your new fence and reflect that thanks to your skill it's going to last two and perhaps three times as long as ordinary fences. And (provided you take care not to count the purchase price of any mauls or chainsaws—which, after all, you still have, and will keep using), you can compute that your posts cost you about 10¢ each. That's chiefly for the creosote.

On the other hand, part of me hopes that you don't do all this—that you go and cut some basswood in the morning, and have it in the ground that afternoon. True, it will rot out as fast as my elm fence around the garden. But after three years it may be time to move a garden, anyway. And what else are young basswoods good for? Besides, you'll be contributing to that sense of variety which I hope New England never loses.

There are two Yale dropouts who are caretaking/renting a house about three miles from our village. They've made a big vegetable garden, and they have fenced it with chickenwire mounted entirely on alders. Skinny alders driven small end into the ground. What's more, it works. A

deer could probably push that fence over with one hoof,
but they don't. Nor do they jump over. I think they're as
pleased and touched by that fence as I am, and wouldn't
hurt it for the world.

—Noel Perrin, "The Perfect Fence Post," *First Person Rural* (1978)

This essay, as you can see, is organized according to a temporal sequence. We are told what tools we will need and how
to use them, beginning with the starting hole for the first
post and proceeding to the bracing of the corner posts. Note
two aspects of Perrin's exposition. His language is clear and
simple. The words that he uses are familiar, and he never
uses a long, high-sounding word when a short plain word
will serve as well. He also employs an image to tell us what
the starting holes ought to look like. Not all of us have driven
fence posts, but all of us know the shape of an ice-cream
cone. Perrin explains something that we might not know in
terms of something that we do know, and this is the way
images should always work in expository writing. Compare
the spikes on Prussian helmets to those on iron fences; say
that the figures of chorus girls in the 1890s resembled Coca-
Cola bottles. But do not say that insulated underwear is
made like the clothes of Chinese workers or that polo is similar to buzkashi, which is a game played by horsemen in
Afghanistan.

Finally consider how Perrin focuses our attention, never
allowing himself or the reader to be diverted from the subject—setting the fence post. He moves in easy but quick steps
from one stage of the process to the next, at once maintaining momentum and holding our interest. In your own writing look for ways that will help you move from one aspect of
your exposition to another so that you too can hold the
reader's attention.

Now consider a more complicated example of exposition
presented in temporal sequence.

During my association with Model T's, self-starters were not a prevalent accessory. They were expensive and under suspicion. Your car came equipped with a serviceable crank, and the first thing you learned was how to Get Results. It was a special trick, and until you learned it (usually from another Ford owner, but sometimes by a period of appalling experimentation) you might as well have been winding up an awning. The trick was to leave the ignition switch off, proceed to the animal's head, pull the choke (which was a little wire protruding through the radiator) and give the crank two or three nonchalant upward lifts. Then, whistling as though thinking about something else, you would saunter back to the driver's cabin, turn the ignition on, return to the crank, and this time, catching it on the down stroke, give it a quick spin with plenty of That. If this procedure was followed, the engine almost always responded—first with a few scattered explosions, then with a tumultuous backfire, that you checked by racing around to the driver's seat and retarding the throttle. Often, if the emergency brake hadn't been pulled all the way back, the car advanced on you the instant the first explosion occurred and you would hold it back by leaning your weight against it. I can still feel my old Ford nuzzling me at the curb, as though looking for an apple in my pocket.

—Lee Strout White, "Farewell, My Lovely" (1936)

The information here is not going to be of any practical value to us unless we are rich enough to collect antique automobiles; but the literary device which White employs can be applied to almost any kind of subject. White starts with an old joke, which you have probably heard. When automobiles first came into use, they broke down frequently, and their frustrated owners were advised by doubters of the machine age to get a horse. White turns this taunt to advantage: inherent in the clear description of how the automobile was started is a horse-to-car comparison. The front of the automobile is "the animal's head." The Ford is treated by White as though it had a personality, a suspicious and stubborn nature which had to be taken into account. His first pulls at the crank were "nonchalant"; he would "saunter" back to the driver's seat, "whistling as though thinking about something else." In the end, car and driver are on good terms. "I can still feel my old Ford nuzzling me at the curb, as though looking for an apple in my pocket."

Everybody's car has its own peculiarities, its virtues and its defects, which often cause us to think of automobiles as being almost alive. The same feeling sometimes extends to bicycles and even to lawn mowers and tape decks. As White's piece shows, a close personal relationship between the author and the thing explained can make the expository essay more interesting. You can write about how the gears on bicycles in general work, or you can write about how the gears on your own bicycle work. In either case you will be able to explain the functioning of the gears, but if you use your own bicycle as an example, any little quirks it might have will add interest to the explanation, and your own feeling of affection or irritation toward the bicycle will enhance the reader's interest in your subject. This is an application of the old principle that people are at the center of earthly existence, and the more we can relate our writing to human concerns, the more effective the writing is likely to be.

Organizing by Spatial Relationship

Consider this paragraph, which has been developed in spatial terms.

> From the fire tower on Bear Swamp Hill, in Washington Township, Burlington County, New Jersey, the view usually extends about twelve miles. To the north, forest land reaches to the horizon. The trees are mainly oaks and pines, and the pines predominate. Occasionally, there are long, dark, serrated stands of Atlantic white cedars, so tall

and so closely set that they seem to be spread against the sky on the ridges of hills, when in fact they grow along streams that flow through the forest. To the east, the view is similar, and few people who are not native to the region can discern essential differences from the high cabin of the fire tower, even though one difference is that huge areas out in this direction are covered with dwarf forests, where a man can stand among the trees and see for miles over their uppermost branches. To the south, the view is twice broken slightly—by a lake and by a cranberry bog— but otherwise it, too, goes to the horizon in forest. To the west, pines, oaks, and cedars continue all the way, and the western horizon includes the summit of another hill— Apple Pie Hill—and the outline of another fire tower, from which the view three hundred and sixty degrees around is virtually the same as the view from Bear Swamp Hill, where, in a moment's sweeping glance, a person can see hundreds of square miles of wilderness. The picture of New Jersey that most people hold in their minds is so different from this one that, considered beside it, the Pine Barrens, as they are called, become as incongruous as they are beautiful.

—John McPhee, "The Woods from Hog Wallow,"
The Pine Barrens (1968)

We begin with the writer and the reader standing on the fire tower at Bear Swamp Hill facing north and looking out over the wilderness. As the exposition continues, we turn as the clock turns, from north to east to south to west, noting the breaks and differences in the landscape—a lake, a cranberry bog—and being told where the view is deceptive—the dwarf forest, the trees that mark streams. The success of this technique depends on McPhee's having established and maintained a point of view. As we have seen, he puts us on the fire tower and keeps us there. But suppose he had begun on the fire tower looking north, then shifted to the dwarf forest in the east where a person standing up can see for miles in every direction. To see the landscape from the dwarf forest might have worked for McPhee almost as well as seeing the landscape from the tower, if he had decided to begin there. But to switch from tower to hill would require us to shift our point of reference and to reorient ourselves a few sentences into the paragraph. If McPhee then had returned to the tower or had decided to show how things look from the cranberry bog, we would have been required to make another shift, and the result would have been chaos. Remember, in short passages of exposition that are developed in spatial terms, a single physical post of observation is usually essential. Establish your point of view at the place from which all else can be most clearly seen and stay there.

Note two other effects that McPhee achieves. By pointing out the Apple Pie Hill tower in the distance, he emphasizes the vastness of the Pine Barrens. From Bear Swamp Hill we can see "hundreds of square miles of wilderness." Hundreds of square miles more extend beyond our vision, and this knowledge enhances our sense of the largeness of what we see. And, by reminding us of our usual concept of the state of New Jersey, McPhee draws a contrast that emphasizes the beauty and wildness of the Barrens. These are small details, but they extend the organization in space: what we can see is only part of a larger woods; and the entire woods is part of a state which is heavily industrialized.

Exercises

A. The following passage is organized in terms of time and written in simple English. Its author assumes the reader has no knowledge of the subject discussed.

> When checking for leaks in a shingle roof, look first for shingles which have bent or curled upward or for nails which have pulled loose. Raised shingles should be pressed down and made to lie flat by applying a liberal dab of asphalt roofing ce-

ment under the raised edge. Loose nails should be tapped back into position, and nailheads covered with the same roofing compound.

When roof shingles are split, cracked or otherwise badly damaged, an effective repair can be made by sliding a sheet of aluminum, copper or galvanized iron under the damaged shingle. This piece of metal should be wider than the damaged shingle, and it should be tapped or forced upward so that it extends well up under the next row of shingles above the damaged one.

In some cases, it may be necessary to pry up the shingle above and remove nails which are in the way. If so, do this chore carefully, lifting the shingle gently so as not to crack it. A warm day when shingles are most pliable is best for the job. When replacing the nails after the metal piece is in position, drive them firmly into place, then cover the exposed nailheads with a dab of cement.

—Bernard Gladstone, *The New York Times*
Complete Manual of Home Repair (1965)

Using the passage above for a model:

1. Write a 250-word theme explaining how to play a game. Suggestions: how to play handball, stickball, charades, kick the can, draw poker.

2. Write a 250-word theme explaining how to make a simple repair. Suggestions: how to mend a torn garment, replace the wire in a screen, fix a leaking faucet, patch a hole in a canoe, paint old wood.

3. Write a 500-word theme explaining how to do something. Suggestions: how to tune an engine, rappel, bake bread, plan a diet, knit a sweater, make camp in the woods, grow tomatoes, find a place to sleep in a strange city, refinish a piece of furniture, backpack in the wilderness, swim the individual medley, hitchhike for long distances, put a saddle and bridle on a horse, paint in oils (or water colors), program a computer, apply for a job, wait on tables or tend bar, get squirrels out of an attic or rats out of a basement, organize a protest demonstration, look for bargains at a flea market.

B. The next two passages are also organized in temporal sequence, but the authors assume some knowledge of their subjects on the part of the reader. Angell's explanation of the slider is comprehensible only to people who already know the rules of baseball. Fisher assumes her readers can make a piecrust and know the right kind and number of apples required to fill it.

1. The chronically depressed outlook of major-league batters was pushed to the edge of paranoia in the nineteen fifties by the sudden and utterly unexpected arrival of the slider, or the Pitcher's Friend. The slider is an easy pitch to throw and a hard one to hit. It is delivered with the same motion as the fastball, but with the pitcher's wrist rotated approximately ninety degrees (to the right for a right-hander, to the left for a southpaw), which has the effect of placing the delivering forefinger and middle finger slightly off center on the ball. The positions of hand, wrist, and arm are almost identical with those that produce a good spiral forward pass with a football. The result is an apparent three-quarter-speed fastball that suddenly changes its mind and direction. It doesn't break much—in its early days it was slightingly known as the "nickel curve"—but a couple of inches of lateral movement at the plateward end of the ball's brief sixty-foot-six-inch journey can make for an epidemic of pop-ups, foul balls, and harmless grounders.

—Roger Angell, *Five Seasons* (1977)

2. So, given the ingredients and the essentials—like pan, stove, oven—one goes calmly about the game, which can become as skilled as eye surgery or Wimbledon, of concocting an apple pie to fit the sensual expectations and requirements of its eaters. It should leave them happy but expectant of the next time and with excellent digestion.

A woman who is eminent in this branch of gastronomical therapy tells me: Peel, core, and slice about six tart apples into a bowl. Sugar them, add a little cinnamon and a jigger of good brandy or bourbon, and stir them well. While they sit, make a light rich dough, and roll it out (never back and forth but *out*). Have the oven at 450°. Line the pan(s), heap in the apples, dot generously with butter. Cover with top crust, seal edges, and cut a slash in the top. Bake fast for ten minutes, and then reduce heat to 350° for about thirty to forty minutes or until the apples feel tender when speared through the peekhole.

She adds a few casual asides to this basically plain procedure: if the apples are too mild, stir a little lemon juice into them;

add a couple of tablespoonsful of cornstarch if you think the
pie will be too soupy . . . and if it runs over, throw salt onto the
juice in the oven; don't mention the brandy if Aunt Jenny, who
is president of the W.C.T.U., asks why the pie is so tasty, since
she wouldn't admit that all the alcohol has long since evap-
orated.

—M. F. K. Fisher, "Apple Pie" (1975)

Use the above passages as models for the following exercises.

1. Assuming that your reader already knows the fundamentals
of cooking, write a 250-word theme explaining how to make a particular dish. Suggestions: making lasagna, preparing a vegetarian
main dish, making and dressing a tossed salad, choosing a wine to
go with trout, using the less popular parts of a pig.

2. Assuming that your reader already knows the fundamental
rules, write a 250-word theme on some aspect of a game. Suggestions: the Texas transfer (or some other convention in bridge), the
two-minute offense, tactics in pickup basketball, the drop lob in
tennis, beating the odds in roulette (or any other game of chance).

3. Assuming some basic knowledge of the subject on the part of
your reader, write a 500-word theme describing a process or activity. Suggestions: playing winning football, working in a mail room,
canvassing for a political candidate, preparing new ground for a
garden, training for a long-distance race, furnishing an apartment,
bidding wisely at an auction, laying brick, skiing the advanced
slopes, running a community-action group, dealing with your land-
lord, developing a part-time business, traveling cheaply in a foreign
country, painting an automobile, organizing and conducting a
yard sale.

C. In the following passages exposition is executed in terms of
space; however, the places described are made significant by their
association with people. The house on Houston Street is important
to White because while he lived in this house he discovered what it
means to be black in America. The building at 7000 Romaine
Street engages Didion's interest because it is the headquarters of the
conglomerate which was once controlled by the late eccentric capitalist Howard Hughes.

1. There were nine light-skinned Negroes in my family:
mother, father, five sisters, an older brother, George, and my-

self. The house in which I discovered what it meant to be a Negro was located on Houston Street, three blocks from the Candler Building, Atlanta's first skyscraper, which bore the name of the ex-drug clerk who had become a millionaire from the sale of Coca-Cola. Below us lived none but Negroes; toward town all but a very few were white. Ours was an eight-room, two-story frame house which stood out in its surroundings not because of its opulence but by contrast with the drabness and unpaintedness of the other dwellings in a deteriorating neighborhood.

—Walter White, *A Man Called White* (1948)

2. 7000 Romaine Street is in that part of Los Angeles familiar to admirers of Raymond Chandler and Dashiell Hammett: the underside of Hollywood, south of Sunset Boulevard, a middle-class slum of "model studios" and warehouses and two-family bungalows. Because Paramount and Columbia and Desilu and the Samuel Goldwyn studios are nearby, many of the people who live around here have some tenuous connection with the motion-picture industry. They once processed fan photographs, say, or knew Jean Harlow's manicurist. 7000 Romaine looks itself like a faded movie exterior, a pastel building with chipped *art moderne* detailing, the windows now either boarded or paned with chicken-wire glass and, at the entrance, among the dusty oleander, a rubber mat that reads WELCOME.

Actually no one is welcome, for 7000 Romaine belongs to Howard Hughes, and the door is locked. That the Hughes "communications center" should lie here in the dull sunlight of Hammett-Chandler country is one of those circumstances that satisfy one's suspicion that life is indeed a scenario, for the Hughes empire has been in our time the only industrial complex in the world—involving, over the years, machinery manufacture, foreign oil, tool subsidiaries, a brewery, two airlines, immense real-estate holdings, a major motion-picture studio, and an electronics and missile operation—run by a man whose *modus operandi* most closely resembles that of a character in *The Big Sleep.*

—Joan Didion, "7000 Romaine, Los Angeles 38,"
Slouching towards Bethlehem (1968)

Using the passages above as models:
1. Write a 150–word essay about a place that has important as-

sociations with your own life. Suggestions: a house, a camp, a playground, a community center, a bus stop or elevated station.

2. Write a 150-word essay about a place that has important associations with the life of another person. This person need not be famous. Suggestions: the White House or a governor's mansion, an athletic arena, a theater or concert hall, a union office, a welfare center.

3. Write a 300-word essay about a place that is important for its personal associations to you and also important for the role it and its proprietors and leaders, if any, play in the life of your community. Suggestions: a park, a clinic, a day-care center, a museum, a tavern, an adult education center, an animal hospital, a cave, a library, the birthplace of a famous person, a post office, a military or naval base, a grain elevator, a railroad siding, a political party headquarters, a store, a factory or mill, a bank, a transient center, a thrift shop.

Using Narrative to Explain

The main rule of narrative writing is that we should *show*, not *tell*. Harry Mason's theme and Steve Nikitas's essay are narratives, and you will remember how Mason revised his theme to give us a fuller visual image of the man who stole the beer, and how Nikitas used concrete details (such as that of the old man so numbed by cold that he had to be lifted from the boxcar) to give us a sense of what riding the rails is like. In most narrative writing we try to be as specific and as concrete as possible. We appeal to the senses: we convey how things look and feel and sound and smell and taste. At the same time we must keep the narrative moving: the flow of events, the sequence of the action, must be supported by details, not impeded by them. We pursue the line of action and try to make the reader see the action as it occurs. Consider this paragraph.

> Sometimes they did go shopping or to a movie, but sometimes they went across the highway, ducking fast across

the busy road, to a drive-in restaurant where older kids hung out. The restaurant was shaped like a big bottle, though squatter than a real bottle, and on its cap was a revolving figure of a grinning boy who held a hamburger aloft. One night in mid-summer they ran across, breathless with daring, and right away someone leaned out a car window and invited them over, but it was just a boy from high school they didn't like. It made them feel good to be able to ignore him. They went up through the maze of parked and cruising cars to the bright-lit, fly-infested restaurant, their faces pleased and expectant as if they were entering a sacred building that loomed out of the night to give them what haven and what blessing they yearned for. They sat at the counter and crossed their legs at the ankles, their thin shoulders rigid with excitement, and listened to the music that made everything so good: the music was always in the background like music at a church service, it was something to depend on.

—Joyce Carol Oates, "Where Are You Going,
Where Have You Been?" (1966)

The pronoun *they* refers here to two teenaged girls, and their movement gives life and form to the passage. They cross the street, they pass through the parking lot, they enter the restaurant, they sit at the counter. The girls become real for us as characters because we are told what they think and feel. They are glad to be able to ignore the boy who speaks to them; they consider the restaurant a "sacred building"; and when they sit at the counter, their shoulders are rigid with excitement. The girls and their actions are further defined by the scene: the cruising cars, the shape of the restaurant building, the flies, the music. Everything is *shown;* nothing is merely *told.* We perceive the girls in terms of their taut slender shoulders, their crossed ankles, their being "breathless with daring."

Sometimes narrative passages are used in forms of writing that are not principally narrative. In such cases the story is usually included to make a point: plot becomes the important element; detail, while still useful, becomes less important. For example, look at the following passage, which begins an essay about acid rain.

> As Mark Zimmerman steered his pickup around the holes in the old logging road, he was filled with anticipation. He was near the end of a trip that he had been promising himself for over a decade. A successful forty-year-old petroleum engineer, Zimmerman had spent most of his working life outside the United States. One of his dreams during his tours abroad had been to fish once again in his favorite lake at the edge of Tenant Mountain near his home town of Glens Falls, New York. He remembered his route perfectly. Every turn in the road looked familiar. But when he came over the last ridge and stopped at the edge of the water, Zimmerman thought for a moment that he must have lost his way. The shape of the lake was as he remembered it, but the water was too clear. Old logs and clean bare rocks were visible on the bottom. But there were no fish to be seen; there were no frogs, no birds along the shore or in the surrounding trees. The lake where Zimmerman had once fished for trout was dead. Acid rain had killed it.
>
> —Michael Lawrence, "Death from the Sky" (1981)

In this passage the author uses a few details: we are told Zimmerman's name and age and profession and place of birth. We see the logs and rocks at the bottom of the clear lake. But no effort is made to create the sense of reality that Oates creates because this essay is expository, not narrative. Zimmerman is not a major character: he is an example. Having engaged our attention, the author turns to the main topic: what acid rain is and where it falls, the damage it causes and what can be done to stop it.

The following passage also appears at the beginning of an expository essay.

The story is told that in the medieval University of Paris the professors were disputing about the number of teeth in a horse's mouth. They agreed that the number could not be a multiple of three, for that would be an offense to the Trinity; nor could it be a multiple of seven, for God created the world in six days and rested on the seventh. Neither the records of Aristotle nor the arguments of St. Thomas enabled them to solve the problem. Then a shocking thing happened. A student who had been listening to the discussion went out, opened a horse's mouth, and counted the teeth.

—Lord Ashby, "The University Ideal: A View from Britain" (1965)

This narrative is spare and factual. The author does not attempt to show us how the professors or the students looked. We are not told their names or ages. We do not see the university campus or the room where the discussion about horses' teeth takes place. The people here exist for us not as real human beings but as figures in what the author properly calls a parable—that is, a story from which a moral or a lesson may be drawn. In this passage the student's behavior illustrates the advantages of the empirical method of inquiry; the professors unwittingly demonstrate the danger inherent in a blind fidelity to tradition. We are not told how many teeth a horse has or what happened to the student who counted the teeth or whether the professors learned anything about scientific investigation from the incident. In using a parable, we need to make the point as simply and as quickly as possible, stopping as soon as the point is made.

Narrative passages are often used to define things that are difficult or even impossible to define except by the use of an image or an example. We say what love is by telling how people in love behave. We explain courage by presenting the actions of the courageous. Or, as in the following passage, the author uses a narrative passage to illustrate a form of superstition.

The fourth form is Improper Worship of the True God. A while ago, I learned that every day, for several days, a $2 bill (in Canada we have $2 bills, regarded by some people as unlucky) had been tucked under a candlestick on the altar of a college chapel. Investigation revealed that an engineering student, worried about a girl, thought that bribery of the Deity might help. When I talked with him, he did not think he was pricing God cheap, because he could afford no more. A reasonable argument, but perhaps God was proud that week, for the scientific oracle went against him.

—Robertson Davies, "A Few Kind Words for Superstition" (1978)

Here, as in the parable, the plot is of supreme importance. We know nothing of the student except that he placed a two-dollar bill beneath the candlestick. But his action tells us much more than we would learn if Davies had attempted to define "Improper Worship of the True God" in abstract or philosophical terms.

Exercises _____

A. Look at the following narrative passages taken from expository essays. What point does each passage make? How much detail does each passage contain? Would more or fewer details make the passage better? Can you determine from the passages the subject of each of the essays from which the passages were taken?

1. There is an old story about two Vermont farmers who lived a mile apart—one west of the village, and the other east of it. Since rural free delivery didn't exist yet, each had to come into town to get his mail. Every weekday for twenty years Eben would finish morning milking and come striding into the village from the west, while Alfred did the same thing from the east. Since both were punctual men, they invariably met in front of the post office at nine a.m., just as the last letters were being

put up. They'd say good morning, go in and get their mail, and stride off home—one west and one east.

One morning during the twenty-first year, however, Eben came stumping out of the post office and, ignoring his usual route, started briskly south, down the state highway. Alfred stared after him for a second, and then called, "Eben, where on earth ye going?"

Eben whirled around. "None of your goddamned business," he snapped. Then he added, visibly softening, "And I wouldn't tell ye that much if ye wan't an old friend."

—Noel Perrin, "Vermont Silences," *Second Person Rural* (1980)

2. Love is an illness, and has its own set of obsessive thoughts. Behold the poor wretch afflicted with love: one moment strewn upon a sofa, scarcely breathing save for an occasional sigh upsucked from the deep well of his despair; the next, pacing *agitato,* his cheek alternately pale and flushed. Is he pricked? What barb, what gnat stings him thus?

At noon he waves away his plate of food. Unloved, he loathes his own body, and refuses it the smallest nourishment. At half-past twelve, he receives a letter. She loves him! And soon he is snout-deep in his dish, voracious as any wolf at entrails. Greeted by a friend, a brother, he makes no discernible reply, but gazes to and fro, unable to recall who it is that salutes him. Distraught, he picks up a magazine, only to stand wondering what it is he is holding. Was he once clever at the guitar? He can no longer play at all. And so it goes.

—Richard Selzer, "Love Sick," *Confessions of a Knife* (1979)

3. I want to tell you a Sacramento story. A few miles out of town is a place, six or seven thousand acres, which belonged in the beginning to a rancher with one daughter. That daughter went abroad and married a title, and when she brought the title home to live on the ranch, her father built them a vast house— music rooms, conservatories, a ballroom. They needed a ballroom because they entertained: people from abroad, people from San Francisco, house parties that lasted weeks and involved special trains. They are long dead, of course, but their only son, aging and unmarried, still lives on the place. He does not live in the house, for the house is no longer there. Over the years it burned, room by room, wing by wing. Only the chim-

neys of the great house are still standing, and its heir lives in
their shadow, lives by himself on the charred site, in a house
trailer.

—Joan Didion, "Notes from a Native Daughter,"
Slouching towards Bethlehem (1968)

B. 1. Write a short narrative passage which helps to explain an abstract concept such as evil, good, love, hate, courage, friendship.
   2. Write a short narrative passage which can serve as the beginning of an expository essay on any subject you choose. Identify
your subject.
   3. Write a short narrative passage which illustrates a general
concept. Some suggested subjects: campus politics, the hazards of
gambling, dating habits today, how to deal with a professor, the
problem with large or small classes, fast-food restaurants, dealing
with a computer, paranoid people.

Choosing Representative Details

John McPhee's piece on the Pine Barrens, which you read
earlier in this chapter, is an example of description used in
expository writing. You will remember that its success depends partly on McPhee's establishing and maintaining a
point of view from which to examine the landscape. Note
also that McPhee names the kinds of trees that can be seen
from the fire tower, but he does not try to describe every tree
in the forest. All good description must use concrete and specific detail; but, as we have seen, writers can seldom use all
the detail that is available to them. Wherever you are reading this, stop and look around. Even if you are in a small
and sparsely furnished room, you will see many more objects
than you could possibly include in an effective description. If
you are in a dormitory, and you are not a particularly good
housekeeper, you may be surrounded by dirty clothes, clean
clothes, toilet articles, books, notebooks, pencils, pens, backpack, newspapers, magazines, candy wrappers, full ashtrays,
beer bottles, soft-drink bottles—the list could go on and on,

and we have not yet considered an individual item of clothing or a single book or any of the furniture.

We are faced with the same problem—an overabundance of available detail—when we attempt to describe a person. There are hair, forehead, eyes, nose, mouth, teeth, chin, cheeks, ears, eyebrows, mustache and beard (if any), all of which can be used in our description—and we have not yet got to the neck of the person we are describing.

We must select a few details that enable the reader to visualize the whole place or the whole human being. A pair of dirty socks on the pillow of an unmade bed, ashes spilled on the stereo turntable, a wet towel dropped on the carpet will afford the reader a sense of a messy room. An elegant and well-kept room might contain a hundred objects, but the impression that the room gives might be conveyed by such details as tables with inlaid leather tops, crystal decanters, a marble fireplace. A sense of people can be rendered by the use of a few prominent physical characteristics: the width of a mouth, or the shape of a nose, or clothing, or the size or shape of a body. And remember that one well-chosen detail which has metaphoric strength can be better than many bland details: a good example is Dorothy Parker's describing a man by saying that he looked like an unmade bed. Study the following examples.

Jubah was in the kitchen, sitting behind the stove, with his razor scar on his black face like a piece of dirty string.

—William Faulkner, "That Evening Sun Go Down" (1931)

Although the old woman lived in this desolate spot with only her daughter and she had never seen Mr. Shiftlet before, she could tell, even from a distance, that he was a tramp and no one to be afraid of. His left coat sleeve was folded up to show that there was only half an arm in it and his gaunt figure listed slightly to the side as if the breeze were pushing him. He had on a black town suit

and a brown felt hat that was turned up in the front and
down in the back and he carried a tin tool box by a han-
dle.

—Flannery O'Connor, "The Life You Save May Be Your Own" (1953)

Each of these passages, by the use of detail, gives us not a
complete picture but a strong physical sense of the person.
The scar on Jubah's face is what you would notice first and
remember most vividly about his appearance, and it suggests
the violence of his temperament. O'Connor uses several details in her description of Mr. Shiftlet, but she does not give
us the color of his eyes or the shape of his nose or the length
of his hair or the kind of shoes he is wearing. Like Faulkner
she shows us what we would notice first and foremost—the
missing arm. Mr. Shiftlet's face is defined for us by the way
he wears his hat. The tilt of his body implies an instability of
character, but the toolbox hints at industry. Even the smallest details work here. If Mr. Shiftlet's hat were black to
match his suit, our impression of him would be changed
slightly. He would appear to be more prosperous and perhaps more reliable. And suppose he were carrying not a toolbox, but a fishing pole or a shopping bag or a bottle of wine
or a dented hubcap. In each case our sense of Mr. Shiftlet
would be altered.

Now consider these descriptions of interiors, two grand
and one seedy:

The armchairs, stately red velvet couches stamped with
crowns in gold and silver thread, faced the wide seaward
windows and wrought iron balconies.

—Graham Greene, *Brighton Rock* (1938)

... Her large drawing room, which, in addition to her furniture and pictures, owned a large part of the London sky
where the clouds prospered: one looked down on the

tops of three embassies and across to the creamy stucco
of a long square.

—V. S. Pritchett, "Tea with Mrs. Bittell," *On the Edge of the Cliff* (1979)

The gas logs strike against the eyeballs, the smell of two
thousand Sunday dinners clings to the curtains, voices
echo round and round the bare stairwell, a dismal Sacred
Heart forever points to itself above the chipped enamel
mantelpiece. Everything is white and chipped. The floors,
worn powdery, tickle the nostrils like a schoolroom.

—Walker Percy, *The Moviegoer* (1961)

In the passage by Greene the large chairs with lush uphol-
stering, the wide windows and balconies that overlook the
sea are sufficient to convey the richness of the whole room.
We know, without being told, that the carpet is thick, the
draperies heavy, the wood surfaces highly polished. In the
description by Pritchett we realize that the flat is elegant and
well appointed owing to its location—and its elevation. The
view from the drawing room—what we can see—tells us something about the drawing room itself. These scenes are visual,
but Percy gives us not only what we can see but also what we
can feel and hear and smell. The gas logs which offend the
eye, the echoes of voices, the odors of old food, the nose-
tickling dust from the floor work with the chipped mantel
and the badly executed religious picture to give us a concept
of the house. We can assume that like the picture the furniture is in bad taste, and like the mantel and the floor it is
chipped and dusty.

Usually description does not stand alone but is a dimension in another kind of writing. We use description to show
what we are talking about, to establish tone, and to support
general statements by specific example. If we are writing
about manatees or Mayan temples, we will help our readers
to understand what we are saying if we make them see the

things about which we are writing. If our subject is carnivals, our attitude toward the subject will be reflected in the details we use to describe the shows and the rides and the people who run them. If we are pleading for prison reform, we can strengthen our case by describing a cell in an overcrowded prison or a ward in a prison hospital. Good writers often enhance description by including elements of narrative. They show ancient worshipers in the temple, shills and barkers and roustabouts at the carnival, prisoners in the cells and the infirmary. The inclusion of people in description lends movement to the writing and helps to relate what is being described to our common human experience. But remember, above all, that good description must appeal to our physical senses. We must choose those details which make our readers see and, if possible, make them hear and smell and feel what is being described. Consider these passages.

> Sixth Avenue lies buried in the drawers, bureaus, boxes, attics, and cellars of grandchildren. There, blackening, are the dead watches, the long, oval rings for the little finger, the smooth pieces of polished wood shaped into a long-chinned African head, the key rings of the Empire State building. And there were little, blaring shops, narrow as a cell, open most of the night, where were sold old, scratched, worn-thin jazz and race records—Vocalion, Okeh, and Brunswick labels.
>
> —Elizabeth Hardwick, *Sleepless Nights* (1979)

> When she married him, he had had the car for eight months. It still smelled like a brand-new car. There was never any clutter in the car. Even the ice scraper was kept in the glove compartment. There was not even a sweater or a lost glove in the back seat. He vacuumed the car every weekend, after washing it at the car wash. On Friday nights, on their way to some cheap restaurant and a dollar movie, he would stop at the car wash, and she would get

out, so he could vacuum all over the inside of the car. She would lean against the metal wall of the car wash and watch him clean it.

—Ann Beattie, "Shifting" (1977)

While waiting for events to develop, I spent my time having a close look at the wasps. A pair of lenses mounted on a frame that could be worn as spectacles enabled me, by crawling up slowly to a working wasp, to observe it, much enlarged, from a few inches away. When seen under such circumstances most insects reveal a marvellous beauty, totally unexpected as long as you observe them with the unaided eye. Through my lenses I could look at my *Philanthus* right into their huge compound eyes; I saw their enormous, claw-like jaws which they used for crumbling up the sandy crust; I saw their agile black antennae in continuous, restless movement; I watched their yellow, bristled legs rake away the loose sand with such vigour that it flew through the air in rhythmic puffs, landing several inches behind them.

—Niko Tinbergen, *Curious Naturalists* (1958)

Exercises

A. Write a short description of a place. Suggestions: your room, a classroom, a movie theater, a newsstand, a gymnasium, a professor's office, the interior of a bus. Choose your details carefully.

B. Reread the passage by Ann Beattie. Here description is partly accomplished by the author's listing what is not in the car. Try to write a similar paragraph in which part of the description consists of things that are not present. Suggestions: a treatment room in a hospital or doctor's office, a subway station, a dressing room at a discount store, a post-office lobby, a fire hall, a swimming pool in winter, a dead-end street.

C. Reread the passage by Elizabeth Hardwick. Write a similar passage in which you describe a place by accumulating many details. Suggestions: a tavern, a hardware store, a housing project, a kindergarten, a dock, a thoroughfare.

5

Argument

If the cultivation of understanding consists in one thing
more than in another, it is surely in learning the grounds of
one's own opinions.

—John Stuart Mill

Argument is the art of persuading others to think what we
think and to believe what we believe. But before we can persuade others of the justice of our opinions, we must first persuade ourselves. If we believe in unilateral disarmament, we
must ask ourselves why. If we are against abortion on demand, why are we against it? If we are for unilateral disarmament and against abortion because our mothers and fathers
and grandmothers and grandfathers have always been for
disarmament and against abortion, we have a reason for
thinking the way we think, but our reason is not likely to
persuade other people to think as we do. Everybody is free to
state a personal preference, but taking a position on an issue
requires an examination of facts. The first step in this procedure is to gather all the facts that we can find about our subject. Then we try to determine which of these facts are more
important than others and how the facts are related to one
another and, when they are seen in a logical relationship,

what they mean. Here is a simple illustration of some of the ways we can investigate facts.

Suppose you go to a grocery store, select a banana (and pay for it, of course), peel it and start to eat it, talk about it to a friend who is eating an apple, and meet another friend who is eating French fries. While engaged in this ordinary series of events, you have used—probably without being conscious of it—several of the methods we commonly employ to discover facts and to establish their relationship to each other. Before you could select your banana, you had to know what a banana is; therefore, you learned, sometime in your past, the *definition* of banana. At the fruit counter you find that some of the bananas are green, some have turned brown, and some, from which you select one, are yellow. You have *classified* bananas into categories according to their degree of ripeness. When you peel the banana, you *divide* it into its two major parts: the peel and the fruit. When you and your friend talk about your banana and his apple, you are *comparing* and *contrasting* the two fruits. When you meet the friend eating the French fries, you recognize an *example* of bad eating habits.

Definition

Everybody knows what bananas are, and the same is true for horses and books and a thousand other things about which we might wish to write. But not everybody can tell you what a supernova is, and we need only to examine the governments of Russia and the United States, both of which call themselves republics, to see that the same word sometimes means different things to different people. So, when we are writing argument, if there is any doubt about what words mean, we should define our terms.

There are two basic methods of definition. The first places the thing to be defined into a general category and then narrows the meaning by moving from the general to the specific. A banana is a long, slightly curved yellow fruit. It has a peel which should not be eaten and creamy sweet flesh which should. Although many definitions will not be as simple as this one, most of the things that you need to define can be defined in the same way. Another means of definition is by using synonyms, but we must always define the obscure term with a word that is likely to be familiar to the reader. For example, we can say a *tome* is a book, or that *tumid* means swollen. But unless our readers already know what a capacitor is, we will not help them much by defining a capacitor as a condenser.

Defining big or technical words is often easier than stating the exact meanings for terms that are in common use. Look at the following passage:

> Among hunters there are four or five types of classic slobs whom everyone knows, such as the sign shooter, and the truculent trespasser who believes there is still a thing called the free hunt, and the daytime drunk with a loaded rifle, and the litterbug, hunters in general tending to be second only to off-road vehicular recreationists as the sloppiest slobs in the great out-of-doors.
>
> —John C. Mitchell, *The Hunt* (1980)

Slob is a word almost all of us use to describe someone else whose behavior we find offensive. Because *slob* has been used to refer to so many different people and actions, we need to define, as Mitchell does, exactly what we mean when we use it.

Even terms that all of us use to mean generally the same thing often need to be defined precisely.

> White lies are . . . the most common and the most trivial forms that duplicity can take. The fact that they are so common provides their protective coloring. And their very triviality, when compared to more threatening lies, makes

it seem unnecessary or even absurd to condemn them. Some consider *all* well-intentioned lies, however momentous, to be white; in this book, I shall adhere to the narrower usage: a white lie, in this sense, is a falsehood not meant to injure anyone, and of little moral import. I want to ask whether there *are* such lies; and if there are, whether their cumulative consequences are still without harm; and finally, whether many lies are not defended as "white" which are in fact harmful in their own right.

—Sissela Bok, *Lying* (1978)

As these passages demonstrate, in most of our writing definition is used in conjunction with other forms of discourse. Mitchell gives us examples in order to achieve his definition. Bok puts her one-sentence definition of white lies in the context of considering lying in general and then tells us how she intends to explore her subject. In argumentation, as well as in most other writing, we will seldom be using a single literary device. Instead definitions and the techniques we describe later in this chapter are used together to enhance and to reinforce one another.

Classification

In classification we sort a group of things into two or more consistent categories, which can be a simple or an enormously complicated procedure, depending on what we are sorting and on the categories we have chosen. Our purpose for making the classification will determine the categories we choose. For example, if we want to plant trees to form a windbreak or a sound or sight barrier, we can begin by putting all the trees in the world into one of two categories: those that stay green all year and those that lose their leaves in the fall. We will want to plant trees that always have their leaves. Having made the first classification, we will need to make other classifications before we plant. We will classify all evergreens according to those that will grow in our climate and those that will not. Then we can classify those that will grow in our climate according to how fast they grow, or according to the density of their foliage, or according to what they cost. We may make all these and still more classifications before we choose our trees.

There are two very important principles to remember about classification: we must always use logical categories and stick to them, and the categories must provide a place for everything we intend to classify. It would be illogical to say that we will classify trees into evergreen trees, deciduous trees, and Christmas trees since we have already included all trees in the first two categories. We cannot say we will classify all trees into elms, oaks, and pines because this leaves no place for the maples and firs and all the other kinds of trees in existence.

Here is an example of classification.

> Most of the literary works with which we are acquainted fall into one of two classes, those we have no desire to read a second time—sometimes, we were never able to finish them—and those we are always happy to reread. There are a few, however, which belong to a third class; we do not feel like reading one of them very often but, when we are in the appropriate mood, it is the only work we feel like reading. Nothing else, however good or great, will do instead.
>
> —W. H. Auden, "Don Juan," The Dyer's Hand (1962)

Division

Division is the opposite of classification. In classification we put all the automobiles in the world into categories. In division we take a single automobile and divide it into engine, chassis, and body. Classification takes all the governments in the world and finds categories into which they will fit. Division separates the government of the United States into executive, legislative, and judicial departments. As we have seen, we can classify trees according to various principles. In division we divide a single tree into roots, trunk, branches, and leaves.

Just as in classification we can break a category into subcategories, in division we can subdivide the major divisions. The legislative branch of the government of the United States can be divided into the House of Representatives and the Senate. The body of an automobile can be divided into fenders and rocker panels and hood and top and all the other parts that compose an automobile body. We can continue making subdivisions until the last single part is accounted for, which is what medical students do when they study human anatomy. But, as is the case in classification, the principles of division must be complete without overlapping. It would be wrong to divide an automobile simply into engine and chassis, thereby ignoring the body, which is a part of the automobile. Just as bad would be to divide an automobile into engine, chassis, body, and valve lifters, since valve lifters are already included as parts of the engine.

Here is an example of division.

> Knowledge about the structure and function of small blood vessels has evolved during the three and a half centuries since William Harvey's discovery of the circulation of the blood initiated the search for the means by which blood passes from arteries to veins. Studies may be grouped into four periods, the first of which established the existence of capillary vessels, perfected methods for observing them, and incorporated them into current medical theories. The second period, extending from the early eighteenth century to 1831 when Marshall Hall published his *Critical and Experimental Essay on the Circulation of the Blood,* was concerned with experimental studies of vessels in living animals. After the enunciation of the cell theory and the development of histology, the third period

was devoted primarily to the study of the small vessels in excised organs, until around 1920 when the modern study of living organs *in situ* began. This fourth period has witnessed continuously evolving methods for the study of living tissue, as well as the *ex vivo* study of blood vessels by electron microscopy.

—Genevieve Miller, "Early Concepts of the Microvascular System" (1981)

Comparison and Contrast

When you decide what movie you will see, what college you will attend, what car or bicycle or pair of shoes you will buy, one way you reach your decision is through a process of comparison and contrast. If you see a film because you like the actors and actresses in the leading roles, you have, whether you have been conscious of doing so or not, compared the actors and actresses in the film you chose to the other actors and actresses who appear in other films that are then available to you. Other people may choose to attend the same movie you attend because they like the subject the movie treats, or because of good reviews of the film they have read, or because they like the work of the film's director. Many people will consider all of these aspects of the movie before they decide to see it, but in each case the decision will have been reached by comparing and contrasting this film with other films that are playing. We compare and contrast colleges according to the courses that are offered, the scholarships that are available, the distinction of the faculties, the friendliness of the students, or whatever other attributes are important to us in our choice of a college. We compare and contrast the price and color and style and quality and fit of shoes before we decide which pair we will purchase. Several rules guide us in our use of comparison and contrast. The things that we compare should be similar, but not identical. We compare movies to movies and colleges to colleges; we do not try to compare a movie to a pair of shoes, but neither will we learn much if we compare the left shoe to the right shoe. We compare the attributes of the things being compared in parallel sequence. In considering movies, we compare acting to acting, story to story, cinematography to cinematography. We do not compare the acting in one film to the story in another. This means that in comparing *Stagecoach* to *The Tin Drum* we can start with the acting or with the story or with whatever suits us. But we should follow the same order in our discussion of each movie: acting, story, direction, photography in *Stagecoach;* acting, story, direction, photography in *The Tin Drum.*

Balance is important in comparison and contrast. If your comparison is brief, you might write one paragraph about *Stagecoach* and another paragraph about *The Tin Drum.* In a longer piece you might devote an entire paragraph or more to the acting in each movie. There is no strict rule to follow here, but if you write one sentence about *Stagecoach* followed by a sentence about *The Tin Drum* and continue to alternate sentences about the two movies throughout the comparison your readers will be annoyed and probably confused by the rapid shifting of attention from one film to the other. If you write three pages about *Stagecoach* before you ever mention *The Tin Drum,* you will be asking your readers to remember too much. Most of us cannot hold three pages of details about the first movie firmly in mind while we read another three pages of details about the second.

Maintaining a balanced view of the things you are comparing is as important as achieving a balanced structure. Obviously some movies and colleges and shoes are better than others, but few things are either perfect or unredeemably bad. Even if you think *Stagecoach* is the worst movie ever made, you should try to look at it objectively and try to find something good to say about it. And even if you admire *The Tin Drum* enormously, you should view it with an open mind and mention any flaws that you might discover. You want to be fair in your comparisons. And if you show your readers that you are trying to be fair, you will increase their confidence in what you have written.

Here is an example of comparison and contrast.

In the first years of this century there was a notable difference between people who lived on farms and people who lived in country towns and villages. Outsiders—city people—did not understand these differences but the town people and farmers were very sure of them. In general, people in the towns saw people who lived on farms as more apt to be slow-witted, tongue-tied, uncivilized, than themselves, and somewhat more docile in spite of their strength. Farmers saw people who lived in towns as having an easy life and being unlikely to survive in situations calling for fortitude, self-reliance, lifelong hard work. They believed this in spite of the fact that the hours men worked at factories or stores or at any job in town were long, and the wages low, and that many houses in town had no running water or flush toilets or electricity. And to a certain extent they were right, for the people in town had Sundays and Wednesday or Saturday afternoons off, and the farmers didn't. The townspeople too were not altogether mistaken, for the country people when they came into town to church were often very stiff and shy and the women were never so pushy and confident as town women in the stores, and the country children who came in to go to High School or Continuation School, though they might get good marks and go on to successful careers later, were hardly ever elected President of the Literary Society, or Class Representative, or given the award as Most Outstanding Student. Even money did not make much difference; farmers maintained a certain proud and wary reserve that might be seen as diffidence, in the presence of citizens they could buy and sell.

—Alice Munro, "Working for a Living" (1981)

Analogy

Analogy is the comparison of things that are similar in some respects but not similar in others. When Shakespeare has Macbeth say that his life has "fallen into the sere, the yellow leaf," he is invoking an old and familiar analogy that compares the states of human life to the seasons. We know that the growth of people is in most ways not at all like the passage of a year, but young people may understand old people better when the analogy is set between old age and winter. In her autobiography Helen Keller, who was deaf and blind, draws an analogy between herself, before she began her education, and a ship adrift in a deep fog. In one of her stories Flannery O'Connor compares the expressions on a woman's face and the transmission of a truck: forward, neutral, and reverse. There is more difference than similarity between people and ships or people and trucks, but in these examples the similarities that do exist help us to understand Helen Keller's handicap and to see the expressions on Mrs. Freeman's face.

Unlike comparison and contrast, analogy works in only one direction. When we compare *Stagecoach* and *The Tin Drum,* we move back and forth between the two films: the comparison extends both ways. *Stagecoach* is like *The Tin Drum; The Tin Drum* is like *Stagecoach.* But analogies are not reversible. Flannery O'Connor can help her readers imagine how Mrs. Freeman looks and even how she thinks by comparing her shifting facial expressions to the forward and reverse movements of a truck. But we would not be likely to visualize a truck if we were given a simple description of Mrs. Freeman. One of the major functions of analogy is to explain things about which we know little in terms of things about which we know a good deal. In the same way analogy is often used to explain abstract concepts in concrete terms. For example, the idea of the unity and interdependence of all people is, for most of us, an abstraction which is put into concrete terms by John Donne's famous analogy. Humanity, Donne tells us, is one. We are bound together as the grains of earth and sand are bound together to form a continent. The death of one person diminishes the rest of us in the same way that a continent is diminished when a clod of earth is washed away.

Some things are so foreign to us and some ideas are so vague and unformed that they can hardly be explained without the help of analogies. Look at the following passage.

> When a disciple asks, "What is Zen?", the master's traditional answer is "Three pounds of flax" or "A decaying noodle" or "A toilet stick" or a whack on the pupil's head. Zen cannot be debunked because its method is self-debunking. In its mondos and koans, ambiguity reaches its metaphysical peak; it is the ultimate evasion. And for precisely that reason it played a vital part in maintaining the balance of extremes in Japanese life.
>
> Taken at face value and considered in itself, Zen is at best an existentialist hoax, at worst a web of solemn absurdities. But within the framework of Japanese society, this cult of the absurd, of ritual leg-pulls and nose-tweaks, made beautiful sense. It was, and to a limited extent still is, a form of psychotherapy for a self-conscious, shame-ridden society, a technique of undoing the strings which tied it into knots.

If between now and the next time you see her, your grandmother hears about Zen and asks you to explain it to her, the passage above will probably not assist either of you much. We are told that Zen is self-debunking, absurd, a kind of hoax, but none of this helps us to fit Zen into our own modes of thought or to relate it to our own cultural background. Now look at the same passage with analogies added, one at the beginning and one at the end.

Zen is to religion what a Japanese "rock-garden" is to a garden. Zen knows no god, no afterlife, no good and no evil, as the rock-garden knows no flowers, herbs or shrubs. It has no doctrine or holy writ; its teaching is transmitted mainly in the form of parables as ambiguous as the pebbles in the rock-garden which symbolise now a mountain, now a fleeing tiger. When a disciple asks, "What is Zen?", the master's traditional answer is "Three pounds of flax" or "A decaying noodle" or "A toilet stick" or a whack on the pupil's head. Zen cannot be debunked because its method is self-debunking. In its mondos and koans, ambiguity reaches its metaphysical peak; it is the ultimate evasion. And for precisely that reason it played a vital part in maintaining the balance of extremes in Japanese life.

Taken at face value and considered in itself, Zen is at best an existentialist hoax, at worst a web of solemn absurdities. But within the framework of Japanese society, this cult of the absurd, of ritual leg-pulls and nose-tweaks, made beautiful sense. It was, and to a limited extent still is, a form of psychotherapy for a self-conscious, shame-ridden society, a technique of undoing the strings which tied it into knots; in a word, Zen was the *tanki* (as the Japanese call their tranquilliser pills) of feudal Japan.

—Arthur Koestler, "A Taste of Zen," *Bricks to Babel* (1980)

After reading the full passage, we still may not have a perfect grasp of Zen, but we can comprehend its elusiveness in terms with which we are familiar: a garden, but one where nothing grows; a rock garden where the symbolism of the stones changes constantly; and, best of all in our drug-conscious society, a tranquilizer pill, a mind-induced Valium.

Often in argument writers use analogy not only to show the unknown in terms of the known, but to try to prove that things which are similar in some respects are similar in all respects. Here is an analogy for the way that kind of analogy works. Suppose we see two cats. A gray one is in full view; a yellow one is sticking his head out from behind a fence. Since the heads of both these animals are clearly similar, we assume that the part of the yellow cat that we cannot see because of the fence must be similar to the same part of the gray animal that we can see. Sometimes such analogies are very effective. If someone in our government suggested that the United States become involved in a military struggle between two forces in the Philippine Islands, most of us would draw an analogy between that situation and our experience in Viet Nam. We could not know how our involvement in the Philippines would come out, but we would be able to see the similarities between the Philippines and Viet Nam, and we would reason by analogy that since the situations were similar in the beginning, our experience, should we become involved in the Philippines, would be similar to our experience in Viet Nam.

This kind of analogy is very useful, but it is also dangerous, because unless we are careful to look at differences as well as at similarities in the elements of our analogies, we may draw what are called *false analogies.* An analogy is frequently drawn between contemporary America and the Roman Empire in its last days. The Romans, we are told, had large welfare programs, civil disorders, a disrespect for authority, and contempt among the youth for tradition and the wisdom of the old. The same conditions prevail in the United States. Since the heads of the two cats are similar, the cat behind the fence—the United States—must be similar to the cat whose whole body we can see—the Roman Empire. Since the Roman Empire fell, the United States must fall too. But if we look more closely at the two governments, we will see differences between them. For example, Rome had few natural resources, the United States has many; Rome's welfare was at least partially dependent on keeping conquered people in subjugation, the United States has no conquered territories; Rome's economy was heavily dependent upon slavery, but the United States has no slaves; Rome's frontiers were defended largely by foreign mercenaries, but the United States uses no mercenaries; Rome was ruled by dictatorship, the United States has a republican form of government. So the validity of the analogy is doubtful.

Even though we must be careful not to draw—or to allow others to draw—false analogies, sound analogies stand among our best devices for exposition and argument.

Examples

We have already said a good deal about the use of examples. We know that abstractions such as love need to be explained by examples such as Romeo and Juliet. Concrete statements often need to be elaborated and reinforced by examples also. If we say the Sun Belt is growing rapidly, we can make our statement more specific by using as an example the number of people who have moved to Houston in the last two years. If we want to prove to a friend how tough a particular professor is, we can give as examples some questions the professor has asked on a test. There are examples to help explain almost everything. Examples should be as concrete and as specific as you can make them, but they should also be representative of the principle or thing they are intended to illustrate. Though sometimes it rains and turns cool in summer, in most places that we know a typical summer day is warm and sunny, and this is the kind of day we should use as an example of a summer day.

Look at the following passage.

> The brown rat is an omnivorous scavenger, and it doesn't seem to care at all whether its food is fresh or spoiled.... All rats are vandals, but the brown is the most ruthless. It destroys far more than it actually consumes.

Now see how much force the passage gains when examples are added.

The brown rat is an omnivorous scavenger, and it doesn't seem to care at all whether its food is fresh or spoiled. It will eat soap, oil paints, shoe leather, the bone of a bone-handled knife, the glue in a book binding, and the rubber in the insulation of telephone and electric wires. It can go for days without food, and it can obtain sufficient water by licking condensed moisture off metallic surfaces. All rats are vandals, but the brown is the most ruthless. It destroys far more than it actually consumes. Instead of completely eating a few potatoes, it takes a bite or two out of dozens. It will methodically ruin all the apples and pears in a grocery in a night. To get a small quantity of nesting material, it will cut great quantities of garments, rugs, upholstery, and books to tatters. In warehouses, it sometimes goes berserk. In a few hours a pack will rip holes in hundreds of sacks of flour, grain, coffee, and other food-stuffs, spilling and fouling the contents and making an overwhelming mess. Now and then, in live-poultry markets, a lust for blood seems to take hold of the brown rat. One night, in the poultry part of old Gansevoort Market, alongside the Hudson, a burrow of them bit the throats of over three hundred broilers and ate less than a dozen. Before this part of the market was abandoned, in 1942, the rats practically had charge of it. Some of them nested in the drawers of desks. When the drawers were pulled open, they leaped out, snarling.

—Joseph Mitchell, "The Rats on the Waterfront,"
The Bottom of the Harbor (1959)

Exercises

A. Study the following passages. List examples taken from these passages of definition, comparison and contrast, classification and division, analogy, and example. Try to improve one of the following passages by adding one or more analogies. Remove all the analogies from one of the following passages and compare your revision to the original. Is your version better or worse? Explain your answer. In which of the following passages do examples seem least important? In which passages do examples seem most important? Explain your answers.

1. I do not think there is any received philosophy of luck but because of its importance in scientific research I shall do my best to clarify the notion.

Consider first "serendipity." The word was coined by Horace Walpole on the basis of a fairy tale set in Serendip—an old name for Ceylon—about the three princes of Serendip who repeatedly make discoveries by accident of things they were not in search of. It is not a word that can very often be used to describe discoveries in science which are being sought, or anyhow discoveries that gratify an expectation. . . .

But what of "luck" in the everyday sense? Clearly a distinction must be drawn between on the one hand a man who having bought a ticket in a lottery draws a winning number and on the other hand a man who finds on a park bench a ticket that bears the winning number. The difference is that the man who bought a ticket did at the same time buy his candidature for a prize and thus made himself eligible for winning. The rest is merely a matter of probabilities. It is boring and pointless to attribute degrees of luck to the ticket holder's fortunes because everyone's good luck must be counterbalanced by someone else's bad luck or negative luck.

The man who found the ticket on the park bench was really lucky because he wasn't a candidate, merely a beneficiary of a casual intersection of world lines. Contrary to popular belief I do not believe that this is an important part of science. Luck is most usually, I believe, the ratification of some covert expectation—the filling of a vacant slot in the mind. A scientist is a man who by his observations and experiments, by his reading, and even by the company he keeps has made himself a candidate for good fortune—has purchased his candidature for a prize. In biochemical terms his brain is bristling with "luck receptors." Unlike Walpole's princes he wants to make the discoveries he does make.

—P. B. Medawar, "Calling Dr. Cooper" (1982)

2. Possibly because of the more or less steady, change-fostered bewilderment that is our modern lot, a good many of

us have developed the habit of jamming one another—and sometimes, for that matter, ourselves—into convenient categories like Young Executive, Welfare Black, Gay, Middleclass Housewife, Hardhat, Hippie, Educated Brown, Gun Nut, Used-car Salesman, etc. The media and the PR industry assist this trend with a zeal born of their veneration for all usable clichés and lumpings, and the categories have the further advantage of being stackable, as in Gay Hardhatted Gun Nut. In regard to us country-dwellers, city types often cherish a classification called Hick, Redneck, Sturdy Peasant, or something on that order which makes them feel more easy of mind when they stray beyond the developments and the junk yards and see actual human beings out here in the fields and pastures and seated beneath the overhangs of crossroads filling stations.

It won't really work, of course, any more than most of the other categories will, stackable or not, for on closer scrutiny the Sturdy Peasants—like, say, Middleclass Housewives—subdivide into so many disorderly groupings that the would-be categorizer is swiftly again dunked in bewilderment.

—John Graves, "One's Own Sole Ground,"
From a Limestone Ledge (1980)

3. Compare our use of the word *progress*, which for many people means a self-congratulatory conviction that we have improved greatly upon the past, and upon the Victorian age in particular. This crush of verbal traffic is always passing a somewhat smaller flow in the opposite direction: here we find the "good old days" crowd who believe that history is running downhill and that we have the unhappiness to exist in a very deplorable present. On the one hand we look down on the past; on the other we look down on the present. In either case we get an easy lift by going where the traffic is going; it's much more fun than to stop dead, face both past and present, and recognize, perhaps with pain, the contradictions within both, and the strange mixture of losing and gaining, or simply the neutral change, by which one age merges into another.

—Robert B. Heilman, "Verbal Traffic and Moral Freight,"
The Ghost on the Ramparts (1973)

B. 1. Write a paragraph in which you define something. Suggestions: democracy, courage, pinball addiction, Chinese cooking, women's rights.

2. Write a paragraph in which you compare and contrast two or more things. Suggestions: brands of beer, college courses, jeans and skirts, houses and apartments, books or paintings or plays or movies.

3. Write a paragraph in which you classify a group of things. Suggestions: wines, bicycles, vegetables, professors, men, women.

4. Write a paragraph in which you divide something. Suggestions: a camera, a newspaper, a place of worship, a piece of jewelry, a sleeping bag.

5. Write a paragraph in which you draw an analogy for something or some event. Suggestions: registration for classes, a bus station, walking the streets of a big city, being interviewed for a job, growing up in (wherever you grew up).

6. Improve any of the paragraphs you have written by adding examples.

Organization of Ideas

So far we have been discussing devices by which we can develop facts and test ideas. In essays that explain and argue, these devices are used—often in combination with each other—to form a pattern of thought and to reach a conclusion. How they are used will depend on the structure of the argument we wish to develop. Suppose we decide to write about the evils of smoking. Before we write, we shall have to put the subject differently—frame it as an argument rather than as a general topic—but our first task, as we said at the beginning of this chapter, is to make a list of as many facts as we can discover about smoking. Here is a list of facts we might gather:

1. Smoking causes cancer.
2. Smoking causes bad breath.
3. Smoking is a waste of time.

4. Smoking causes heart disease.
5. Smoking makes your clothes smell bad.
6. Smoking is bad for your sinuses.
7. The land and energy used to raise tobacco could better be used to raise food for a hungry world.
8. Smokers often burn holes in their clothes.
9. Smoking in public is an infringement of the rights of those who do not smoke.
10. Smokers often start fires in houses and forests.
11. Smoking is expensive.

Obviously some of the facts listed above are more important than others—better bad breath than cancer—and this is significant, but it is not our first concern. When you consider the facts together, you will see that some of them have to do with the effects of smoking on the smoker; others have to do with the effects of smoking on the world in which the smoker lives. We may be able to use all these facts; we may be able only to use part of them. At this point we cannot tell. So we divide the list of facts into the categories suggested above: what smoking does to the smoker and what smoking does to the rest of the world. As we make this division, we should arrange our facts in the order of their importance, which will be another step toward finding the shape of our theme. Here are the two lists.

Effects on Smoker

1. Cancer
2. Heart disease
3. Sinuses
4. Expensive
5. Bad breath
6. Holes in clothes
7. Wastes time

Effects on World

1. Burns houses and forests
2. Infringes on rights of others
3. World hunger
4. Wastes time

As we study the two lists, we see that some of the facts in the right-hand column are complex and will be difficult to develop. Look, for example, at number 2. While it is true that people who do not smoke have a right not to be injured by those who do, it is also true that people who smoke have a right to pursue this activity without being forced to abide by unreasonable restrictions. But what is unreasonable in this case? Where do the rights of one group end and the rights of the other group begin? This is a question that probably will have to be presented by lawyers and experts and decided by judges. If we try to decide it in a short essay, we will either oversimplify the question and thus damage our argument, or we will be forced to go so deeply into the question that the subject of the essay will become civil rights and not smoking. Point number 3 offers similar difficulties. Redistributing food from rich countries to poor countries is a problem that experts are continually trying to solve. We had better leave it alone.

Having decided that we are going to write our theme about the effects of smoking on the smoker, we consider how the facts in the left-hand column might be arranged in a theme. We decide to take the least important points first and move toward the most important points, a procedure that we hope will clinch the argument; and in making this decision we develop an over-all concept of our essay. In essence, we intend to say: *Smoking is an unattractive, expensive, and inconvenient habit; more important, it can and frequently does cause fatal diseases; therefore, since you want to be an attractive person and since you want to live a long and full life, you should not smoke.* You may ask: *Why, if we can prove that smoking often causes fatal disease, do we need to bother with saying that it also gives you bad breath?* The answer lies in any cigarette advertisement in any magazine, in which handsome people do amusing things in beautiful settings. The people will be smoking, and the captions will tell you how delicious these particular cigarettes taste. And there will be a warning that cigarette smoking is hazardous to your health.

Both you and the people who make the cigarettes agree—or are forced by the evidence to agree—that smoking kills many people. But look at what else the cigarette manufacturers are saying in their advertisements. They are saying that it is true that smoking may give you a bad disease; but that you may not get cancer or heart disease, and if you do not smoke, look at all the fun you are missing. See how beautiful these people who smoke are; see what thrilling things these smokers do; see the lives they lead, the places they go, the houses they live in. Isn't it worth the risk if smoking makes you as happy as these people are? Our argument is the opposite of theirs: Don't risk your life for a nasty habit. Notice also that we put the damage that smoking does to your health last and thereby make it the climax, the most important part of our argument. Though they are done mostly in pictures, the cigarette advertisements clearly imply that the health issue is one to be mentioned, because it must be mentioned, and then forgotten. The crux of their argument is the apparent happiness of smokers.

Here, then, are two points to remember about the organization of ideas in essays that argue: Do not neglect your less important evidence—it is needed to support the more important evidence. And always state your most important points at the end of your argument. You may choose to state them at the beginning as something to be proved, but return to them at the end. The last argument you make should ordinarily be your most powerful argument.

Techniques of Argument

To argue successfully, we must know both sides of the subject, and we must be ready to acknowledge any validity we can find in the opposing point of view. It is easy to argue against Hitler's atrocities or for Mother Teresa's ministrations to the poor: agreement on such subjects is so universal that although we may try to explain them, we no longer argue over whether they are right or wrong. But what about the development of nuclear power? Or the legalization of marijuana? Or federal aid to private schools? These subjects may be too complex for you to undertake in a short theme, but they are good examples of the subjects about which we write argument because, whether or not we like to admit it, on each side of these questions there are cogent arguments. If you are going to write a theme that argues against the construction of nuclear reactors to produce power, you need to find out the main arguments that are offered in favor of the construction of nuclear power plants.

When you look into the matter (and we shall discuss how to do such research in the last chapter), you will find that some reputable scientists favor the construction and use of nuclear reactors. They argue that the world requires energy and that sooner or later our supply of fossil fuels will be depleted; that thus far nuclear reactors have proved to be a safe source of power; that accidents such as the one at Three Mile Island have produced no deaths and no dangerous contamination of the environment; that we cannot create a risk-free world: we must take some chances if our civilization is to survive and prosper; and that modern technology will make reactors continually safer and devise harmless methods for the disposal of nuclear waste. You need to know about these views and to mention them in your argument and present evidence to refute them if you can. To ignore them would imply to your readers either that you did not know of their existence and therefore did not know your subject very well, or that you knew of them but had no facts with which to oppose them; and this omission would damage your argument more than if you mention the claims of your opponents and admit that some of them are valid.

For example, for you to maintain that we have enough fossil fuels to last for millennia to come would be poor strategy, just as for you to suggest that we all start heating our dwellings with wood-burning fireplaces—since wood is a renewable resource—and abandon our automobiles and airplanes, buses and subways in favor of our bicycles and our feet would be frivolous. You will also have to admit that in its present state of development, solar power cannot supply our needs for energy and that windmills have thus far been a distinct disappointment. And you must agree also that insofar as we know, at this time, no serious casualties have resulted from the nuclear accident at Three Mile Island. Having admitted all this, you can use the Three Mile Island accident as a means to shift the focus of your paper from your opponent's arguments to your own. The fact that the Three Mile Island accident—and others of a less serious nature—*did* occur is evidence that such accidents *can* occur, and the safety of nuclear reactors, or the lack of it, is the foundation of your argument. Explosions kill people. Radiation burns, causes cancer, and alters genetic make-up. Radiation released into the atmosphere can contaminate thousands of square miles. You are now well into the presentation of your own argument, and you have used your opponent's arguments as an introduction to your own.

Even when your argument is very strong, you should try to find something favorable to say about the opposing argument. For example, if you are pleading for prison reform, you will not weaken your position by admitting that some people in prison are unsavory characters. Instead, such an admission will demonstrate that you are a reasonable person who sees all sides of an issue. Be calm as you write your argument, and stick to your subject. Many of us feel deeply about the proliferation of nuclear weapons or the destruction of whales or poverty in our cities, and because we feel deeply, we may be inclined to become emotional when we argue about these topics. But we must control our feelings: emotion is the enemy of reason. We may be tempted to dwell on the selfishness and brutality of those who are decimating the whale population, but our argument will be better if we explain why maintaining the whales is important to us and to future generations.

Never make personal attacks on those who hold the position opposite to yours. Anyone who wants to furnish nuclear weapons to countries that do not yet have them would certainly appear to be a fool, but nothing is to be gained by calling him or her that. Instead give reasons to show that whenever another country gets nuclear weapons, the danger of nuclear war increases. Just as bad as calling your opponents names is to belittle them as people or to attack their character. This tactic is called *argumentum ad hominem,* and it has been used against most of us at one time or another. "You are only sixteen, so you don't know what you are talking about." "You never served in the army, so you can't really understand issues of war and peace." Or, in a worse form, it goes like this: "My opponent was arrested for drunken driving when he was eighteen. Later his sporting goods business went bankrupt, and he left the state of Oregon to avoid paying child support. You can't believe anything a man like that says." Attacks like this are tasteless and illogical. The fact that people are young or inexperienced or irregular in their personal relationships does not mean that they cannot think clearly.

Logical and Illogical Reasoning

Look at the following statements.

> All first-year students take English.
> Susan is a first-year student.
> Susan takes English.

> Only those who pass history will be graduated.

Henry will be graduated.
Henry will pass history.

These groups of sentences form syllogisms, and the syllogism is a traditional means of developing logical thought. Entire books have been written about syllogisms, so what we can say about them here will be very sketchy. Knowing a little bit about how syllogisms work, however, will help you avoid fundamental errors in logic.

The first statement in each of the examples above is called the *major premise,* and here are two things to remember about all major premises. They must make statements that are all-inclusive or totally limiting. *All* first-year students take English. *Only* those who pass history will be graduated. If we say *Ninety-nine percent of first-year students take English,* we cannot draw any conclusion from the fact that Susan is a first-year student. She might be among the 1 percent who do not take English. If we say *With a few exceptions, only those who pass history will be graduated,* we cannot be sure that Henry is not one of the few exceptions. The major premise in a syllogism is not reversible. The fact that all first-year students take English does not mean that all who take English are first-year students. The fact that only those who pass history will be graduated does not mean that everyone who passes history will be graduated. Consequently, the second statement in a syllogism, which is called the *minor premise,* must say something about a specific person or thing or group which places that person or thing or group within the meaning of the all-inclusive or limiting statement of the major premise. Otherwise we can draw no conclusions.

Look at the following diagrams of the above syllogisms.

All first-year students take English.

Susan is a first-year student.

Susan takes English.

All first-year students take English.

Susan takes English.

We cannot come to a conclusion, because the all-inclusive statement applies to all first-year students, not to all students who take English.

Only those who pass history will be graduated.

Henry will be graduated.

Henry will pass history.

Only those who pass history will be graduated.

Henry will pass history.

No conclusion because the limiting statement applies to all who will be graduated, not to all who will pass history.

Much of our thinking is based on the syllogism. If you say *It is too bad that my grandfather can't live forever,* you have stated the conclusion of this syllogism: All men must die. My grandfather is a man. Therefore my grandfather must die. Such a formulation, which leaves part of the syllogism unstated, is called an *enthymeme.* Many arguments are pursued by the use of enthymemes and, like syllogisms, enthymemes can be faulty. One way to test the truth of a statement is to cast it into a syllogism. Consider this enthymeme: She is an actress, so of course she's temperamental. Put into a syllogism, the statement reads: All actresses are temperamental. She is an actress. Therefore she is temperamental. But we know that not all actresses are temperamental, so the conclusion is false. Working from a faulty general statement is a very common error in logic. This is true because many of us tend to jump to conclusions, to formulate principles on the basis of too little information.

What we have been talking about so far is called *deductive* reasoning. This means, as we have seen, that we begin with a general truth and apply that general truth to a specific instance. But where do we get our general truths? The answer is by observation—that is, by *inductive* reasoning. Inductive reasoning is what goes on in most laboratories. If you give a cube of sugar to each of seven hundred monkeys and each monkey eats its cube, then from these seven hundred specific instances, you derive the general principle that monkeys like sugar. Much of what we learn from experience is derived by inductive reasoning. We touch fire once or twice or however many times it takes and induce the fact that fire burns. We drop a cup and learn that china breaks. Even when we are taught by someone else that you cannot make a soufflé without eggs, we are learning what someone else learned by inductive reasoning. The inductive process goes awry when we meet two actresses, both of whom are temperamental, and decide on the basis of these two meetings that all actresses, without exception, are temperamental.

The error we make when we base general statements on scanty evidence is called generalizing from a particular. Two temperamental actresses are made to stand for all actresses. A subtler form of this error is generalizing from what may at first glance appear to be a sufficiently large sample. For example, someone may say *All dogs bark at strangers.* Many dogs do bark at strangers, and unless we are paying close attention to what we are reading or hearing, we might accept such a generalization. But if we stop to think of our own experience, of all the dogs we have seen, we will probably be able to remember several dogs who did not bark at strangers unless the strangers yelled at them first—and to recollect some of the dogs did not bark even then. A faulty generalization about groups of people can lead to prejudice and injustice. Perhaps all the Irish people you have ever met have been good drinking companions, and perhaps you know many people from Ireland. Even so you should avoid concluding that all Irish people like to drink. Such a generalization, if universally believed, might damage the reputation of an Irish teetotaler.

Another common error in logic is the *post hoc, ergo propter hoc* fallacy. The expression means *after this, therefore because of this*. Most superstitions are based on the *post hoc* principle. A black cat crosses in front of you and your car runs out of gas. You break a mirror and then lose your watch. You find a four-leaf clover and get an A on a biology test. Folklore tells us that you ran out of gas because the cat went in front of you, that breaking the mirror brought you bad luck, and that finding the four-leaf clover made the questions on the biology test fit the material you remembered. In reality these separate events had no connection with each other. Superstitions are not likely to hurt us unless we take them seriously. But if we assume that jet aircraft affect the weather because we see jets flying overhead and the weather changes, we will mislead ourselves and possibly our readers.

The *post hoc* fallacy is one form of *non sequitur,* which means *it does not follow*. Here are some other types of *non sequitur*. He smokes a pipe, so we know he likes the out-of-doors. Her hair is red, but she has an even temper. She was wearing a dress, so she must have been going to church. Some *non sequiturs* result from a careless use of invalid generalizations. It is not true that all people who smoke pipes like the out-of-doors or that all red-headed people are quick to anger. The statement that a person is going to church because she is wearing a dress depends not on a bad generalization but on linking two ideas that have no necessary connection with each other. Like other logical fallacies, *non sequiturs* can lead to serious misapprehensions. He has been to Russia several times, so he must be a Communist. One of his friends is in prison, so he should not be trusted. These *non sequiturs* are also examples of efforts to establish guilt by association. He is Communist if he visits Russia (guilt by association with a place); and he is dishonest if one of his friends has committed a crime (guilt by association with a person).

Claiming that what you have set out to prove is true without offering evidence that it is true is called begging the question. For example a candidate for public office might say *Every reasonable citizen should reject my opponent's outrageous platform.* Or a member of the educational policy committee might say *Useless courses, such as philosophy, should be dropped from the college curriculum.* As you can see, begging the question is, in some ways, a kind of intellectual name-calling directed at ideas rather than at people. The candidate says that his opponent's platform is outrageous when he should be offering proof that his opponent's program lacks merit. We are accustomed to this sort of rhetoric in political campaigns, and most of us are not deceived by it. But to assert without supporting evidence that philosophy is a useless course is a dishonest assertion. The question that is begged is central to our concept of liberal education. What is meant by *useless* as the word is used here? And what are the criteria by which we judge the value of college courses?

The final point to remember about argument—and about all types of composition for that matter—is that writing is the ultimate test of thought.

Exercises

A. What conclusions, if any, can you draw from the following pairs of statements? Explain your answers.

> Rain falls every day during the rainy season.
> We are in the rainy season.

> Some politicians are dishonest.
> Smith is a politician.

> All presidents live in the White House.
> Jones lives in the White House.

Many mushrooms are poisonous.
Fabian ate a mushroom.

All camels have humps.
That animal is a camel.

Every member of this class is a poor speller.
George is a poor speller.

B. Here is an argument that is pursued by comparison and contrast. Notice how the author defines his argument, the details he uses, and the judgments he makes about Roosevelt and Eisenhower. Look for the evidence he uses to support his points.

Why did Ike dislike Roosevelt? The fact that he came, a plain soldier, from Abilene, Kansas, and Roosevelt came, a wily patrician, from Hyde Park, New York, won't explain their divergence (after all, Harry Truman of Independence, Missouri, and Dean Acheson of Groton and Yale got along fine). The answer lies in chemistry: as Eisenhower once remarked to speechwriter Arthur Larson, anent Roosevelt's love of practical jokes on inferiors, "Roosevelt was essentially a cruel man."

This observation, from a man without a trace of cruelty in his nature, suggests the two inhabited different psychological realms. The contrast shows at the famous wartime encounter in Tunisia of these two giants of recent American political history. President Roosevelt, not yet suffering from fatal illness, debonair, determined, courageous, a sage leader of a still young nation before it became dominant in the world, of a fortunate nation struggling to achieve a dream, meets the foursquare General chosen to head the Allied forces, upon whom he depended for the country's safety and doubtless for much of his own position in history. This military alliance would eventually win America's supremacy the globe around, but that was not known.

Roosevelt had come across the sea to meet with Prime Minister Winston Churchill in late 1943 after the victory in North Africa. Ike, returned from inspecting burned-out tanks, finds him sitting at lunch beside the road. The President looks up and asks him what odds, a year previously, he would have demanded that he would see "the President of the United States" eating in that spot.

At every point in the conversation, Roosevelt, ebullient, asserts his dominance: having, in his own mind, taken over the war, he praises that "Old Tory" Churchill, his staunch ally; he says he wishes the African invasion could have come before the elections of 1942. When the Secret Service suggests they move along for security reasons, Roosevelt reminds Ike of his inferior position: "You are lucky you don't have the number of bosses I have," he remarks. He says nothing directly to show he is pleased with Eisenhower's performance, whereas Churchill, always mindful of a subordinate's feelings, had praised it. Roosevelt is Ike's superior, and he is the sort of superior who often rules by keeping men insecure.

In the bright North Africa light one sees the two men silhouetted against the yellow earth: one with his confident smile, his cigarette holder, his sunken eyes, his urbane voice, his crippled body, facing the other, his khaki uniform worn with hat askew, his happy grin, his taut physical strength and alert mental health. The coddled only child, reared to lead, but whose victory has been achieved only after a cruel struggle against disease, faces the confident man of ordinary expectations, the middle child of a large, struggling family of sons, for whom greatness is still unforeseen. The politician *par excellence*, the master of the devious, the man of irony and wit, faces the honest soldier, bluff, straightforward, an average man, the man not of wit so much as of humor. The chemistry was different.

Both men smiled easily, one with open animal good spirits, one with reflective amusement. One enjoyed testing men to learn the parameters of the human condition; one met everyone with the same good feeling and rigid code of behavior, limiting mine and yours: he resisted any intrusion over the barriers, not just his own but anyone else's. Both were optimists, one that the spirit could survive anything, one that the spirit was good. Both knew how to rule men and get exactly what they wanted, though one used balance of power and one used cooperation.

The ends of both were humane, though one saw himself as superior, one as high-average in a superior position. To achieve his goal, one could pretend to be of modest intelligence, the other could pretend to be a god. Roosevelt, using Ike for their mutual good purposes, understood why Ike would obey orders. Ike had a rational ground for obeying his superior, but he reserved his judgment.

One man liked to get up in the morning, one had painfully to pull himself out of bed; one required courage for each movement, one's courage was natural as breath. Both believed in the strength of God. One merely witnessed God's power, one was forced to feel it. Reality was more cruel to one than to the other, his wider experience bought by deeper doubt. Yes, the laughter was different. There was a different chemistry.

—William Bragg Ewald, Jr., *Eisenhower the President* (1981)

1. State in a sentence or two the terms of the argument which is pursued here.

2. List some details that support the author's position.

3. List some details that support the opposite position.

4. What conclusion does the argument reach? Is the emphasis on the superiority of one man to the other? If not, what is emphasized?

C. To refresh your memory, here are some of the devices for developing thought and some of the logical fallacies we have discussed in this chapter: definition, classification and division, comparison and contrast, analogy, false analogy, faulty generalizations, *post hoc* fallacy, *non sequiturs,* and *argumentum ad hominem.*

Read the following arguments carefully. Give a brief summary of each argument. Do any of the arguments contain fallacies? If so, point them out. What devices for developing thought does each author employ? Write a short theme in which you attempt to refute one of these arguments.

1. We are no more divided from the world than the water itself [in the ocean] is divided. When we damage the world we damage ourselves. If we destroy it we destroy ourselves. A piece at a time, we think, a part at a time, but the world has no pieces and does not come apart. Wherever we put our hands, points of energy will trail off from us like the tails of comets. The tree that falls without sound falls within our hearing.

—Richard Rhodes, *Looking for America* (1979)

2. For women, life is an ongoing good cop–bad cop routine. The good cops are marriage, motherhood, and that courtly old gentleman, chivalry. Just cooperate, they say (crossing their fingers), and we'll go easy on you. You'll never have to earn a living or open a door. We'll even get you some romantic love. But you'd better not get stubborn, or you'll have to deal with our friend rape, and he's a real terror; we just can't control him.

Pornography often functions as a bad cop. If rape warns that without the protection of one man we are fair game for all, the hard-core pornographic image suggests that the alternative to being a wife is being a whore. As women become more "criminal," the cops call for nastier reinforcements; the proliferation of lurid, violent porn (symbolic rape) is a form of backlash. But one can be a solid citizen and still be shocked (naively or hypocritically) by police brutality. However widely condoned, rape is illegal. However loudly people proclaim that porn is as wholesome as granola, the essence of its appeal is that emotionally it remains taboo. It is from their very contempt for the rules that bad cops derive their power to terrorize (and the covert approbation of solid citizens who would love to break the rules themselves). The line between bad cop and outlaw is tenuous.

—Ellen Willis, "Feminism, Moralism, and Pornography,"
Beginning to See the Light (1981)

3. At first sight, the most curious innovation is that much of the world in the twentieth century apparently lives and dies without religion. This seems, at first sight, to be a unique condition. Even imperial Rome had its formal deities.

But, on examination, this concept of a lay world needs several qualifications. First, putting the matter at its simplest, the last two hundred years have been characterised by revival as well as by disintegration, by innumerable new kinds of religious enthusiasm from messianic preaching to mystical healing. Sceptics in the eighteenth century, such as Gibbon, would have been astonished to find that, two hundred years later, religious conflicts such as those in Ireland, the Middle East, Iran, India, the Philippines and the Sudan were both more numerous and more violent than they were in his day. 'Barbarism and religion', whose triumph, during the fifth century AD, Gibbon claimed to be commemorating, have continued hand-in-hand in the twentieth. The overthrow of the Shah of Persia in 1979, for example, was, on the surface at least, the result of a traditional revolt led by conservative holy men in protest against modernisation—an identification of religion with reaction similar to the popular alliance in Spain in 1808 against Napoleon.

The illusion that religion has declined absolutely derived from the creation of large societies of persons in towns with different outlooks from those held in old villages or settlements. The very metaphors of the Christian Church seemed inappropriate in industrial life; and, in many industrial towns, those who went to church and took communion, excluded, in the first generations or two of industrialisation, the factory workers. Professor Pevsner believes that no church designed after 1750 has been in the first rank among leading examples of architecture. But, taking the word in its broadest sense, religion has since fought a very good defensive battle. Methodism, for example, was, in an astonishing degree, able to attract the loyalties of both factory owners and factory workers in much of England, acting as an invaluable source of discipline for work. Catholicism, on the other hand, has become 'a refuge from the pressures of mass civilisation', as well as the inspiration of an international political movement of the first importance, while the century of anticlericalism which began with the French Revolution inspired almost as many articulate defenders of the Church as did the Counter Reformation. Just as industrialism was beginning in Europe, the Protestants also embarked on a world-wide crusade of missionary activities. Catholic countries also redoubled their missionary efforts. By the 1870s, missions had been set up, for example, everywhere in Africa, reflecting almost every sect of Christianity, and that greatly assisted the discovery and charting of that previously unknown continent. It was not a soldier nor a business man nor an agronomist but a missionary, David Livingstone, who first crossed the continent in the 1850s. In the twentieth century, the churches have, if anything, been more active in politics than ever before, even if some of their activities seem extraordinarily questionable on both theological and political grounds. True, the Orthodox Church made no serious defence of itself against communism after 1917, and exchanged its loyalty to the Tsar for an almost equally uncritical one to the Secretary-General of the communist party—though there is a sense now in which religion today forms a real opposition to communism in Russia. The Protestant churches had many martyrs as well as time-servers in Nazi Germany.

Meantime, beliefs in charms, spiritualism, ghosts, demons and other mysteries have contrived to exercise a fitful attraction even among educated people. Astrology's followers are increasing. Odd numbers, magpies, four-leafed clovers, black cats, spilled salt, dropped teaspoons, still exert modest despotisms over rational people. The most learned Englishman of the eighteenth century, Dr. Johnson, insisted on knocking every post as he walked along Henrietta Street. Burckhardt believed that the

religion of the nineteenth century was 'rationalism for the few
and magic for the many', while a modern writer, Geoffrey Grig-
son, estimates that today, in Britain, 'about a quarter of the population . . . holds a view of the universe which can most properly be designated as magical'.

There have also been some instances in the world since 1750
when a sense of religion has been consciously heightened by a
state. A good example of this was what happened to Shintoism
in Japan. Industrialisation initiated not only the beginning of
Japan's rise to industrial strength but the cult of the emperor as
a descendant of the sun.

Every traditional religion has also had, since 1750, heresies,
splits or re-interpretations which, in the end, have probably
strengthened the appeal of those faiths. The eighteenth century, for example, saw a series of innovations in Protestantism,
such as the Methodism previously noticed, which amounted,
particularly in the US, to a second reformation, whose emphasis
was on popular styles of worship.

—Hugh Thomas, *A History of the World* (1979)

4. The Newark police arrested a very interesting woman the
other day—a Mrs. Sophie Wienckus—and she is now on proba-
tion after being arraigned as disorderly. Mrs. Wienckus interests
me because her "disorderliness" was simply her capacity to live
a far more self-contained life than most of us can manage. The
police complained that she was asleep in two empty cartons in
a hallway. This was her preferred method of bedding down. All
the clothes she possessed she had on—several layers of coats
and sweaters. On her person were bankbooks showing that she
was ahead of the game to the amount of $19,799.09. She was a
working woman—a domestic—and, on the evidence, a thrifty
one. Her fault, the Court held, was that she lacked a habitation.

"Why didn't you rent a room?" asked the magistrate. But he
should have added parenthetically "(and the coat hangers in
the closet and the cord that pulls the light and the dish that
holds the soap and the mirror that conceals the cabinet where
lives the aspirin that kills the pain)." Why didn't you rent a
room "(with the rug that collects the dirt and the vacuum that
sucks the dirt and the man that fixes the vacuum and the fringe
that adorns the shade that dims the lamp and the desk that
holds the bill for the installment on the television set that tells

of the wars)?" I feel that the magistrate oversimplified his question.

Mrs. Wienckus may be disorderly, but one pauses to wonder where the essential disorder really lies. . . . I read recently that the only hope of avoiding inflation is through ever increasing production of goods. This to me is always a terrifying conception of the social order—a theory of the good life through accumulation of objects. I lean toward the order of Mrs. Wienckus, who has eliminated everything except what she can conveniently carry, whose financial position is solid. . . . I salute a woman whose affairs are in such excellent order in a world untidy beyond all belief.

—E. B. White, "Mrs. Wienckus,"
Poems and Sketches (1981)

5. This seems to be an era of gratuitous inventions and negative improvements. Consider the beer can. It was beautiful—as beautiful as the clothespin, as inevitable as the wine bottle, as dignified and reassuring as the fire hydrant. A tranquil cylinder of delightfully resonant metal, it could be opened in an instant, requiring only the application of a handy gadget freely dispensed by every grocer. Who can forget the small, symmetrical thrill of those two triangular punctures, the dainty *pffff,* the little crest of suds that foamed eagerly in the exultation of release? Now we are given, instead, a top beetling with an ugly, shmoo-shaped "tab," which, after fiercely resisting the tugging, bleeding fingers of the thirsty man, threatens his lips with a dangerous and hideous hole. However, we have discovered a way to thwart Progess, usually so unthwartable. *Turn the beer can upside down and open the bottom.* The bottom is still the way the top used to be. True, this operation gives the beer an unsettling jolt, and the sight of a consistently inverted beer might make people edgy, not to say queasy. But the latter difficulty could be eliminated if manufacturers would design cans that looked the same whichever end was up, like playing cards. What we need is Progress with an escape hatch.

—John Updike, *Assorted Prose* (1964)

6. I am always entertained—and also irritated—by the newsmongers who inform us, with a bright air of discovery, that they have questioned a number of female workers and been told by one and all they are "sick of the office and would love to get out of it." In the name of God, what human being is *not,* from

time to time, heartily sick of the the office and would *not* love to get out of it? The time of female office-workers is daily wasted in sympathising with disgruntled male colleagues who yearn to get out of the office. No human being likes work—not day in and day out. Work is notoriously a curse—and if women *liked* everlasting work they would not be human beings at all. *Being* human beings, they like work just as much and just as little as anybody else. They dislike perpetual washing and cooking just as much as perpetual typing and standing behind shop counters. Some of them prefer typing to scrubbing—but that does not mean that they are not, as human beings, entitled to damn and blast the typewriter when they feel that way. The number of men who daily damn and blast typewriters is incalculable; but that does not mean that they would be happier doing a little plain sewing. Nor would the women.

I have admitted that there are very few women who would put their job before every earthly consideration. I will go further and assert that there are very few men who would do it either. In fact, there is perhaps only one human being in a thousand who is passionately interested in his job for the job's sake. The difference is that if that one person in a thousand is a man, we say, simply, that he is passionately keen on his job; if she is a woman, we say she is a freak. It is extraordinarily entertaining to watch the historians of the past, for instance, entangling themselves in what they were pleased to call the "problem" of Queen Elizabeth. She was the tool of Burleigh, she was the tool of Leicester, she was the fool of Essex; she was diseased, she was deformed, she was a man in disguise. She was a mystery, and must have some extraordinary solution. Only recently has it occurred to a few enlightened people that the solution might be quite simple after all. She might be one of the rare people who were born into the right job and put that job first. Whereupon a whole series of riddles cleared themselves up by magic.

—Dorothy Sayers, "Are Women Human?"
Unpopular Opinions (1946)

D. Write a 500-word theme in which you present an argument. Suggested topics: abortion, prayer in schools, affirmative-action programs, gun-control laws, college athletics, dormitory rules, leash laws, required courses, drug laws, any rule or set of rules in effect at your college.

Paragraphs

> Just as the sentence contains one idea in all its fullness, so the paragraph should embrace a distinct episode; and as sentences should follow one another in harmonious sequence, so the paragraphs must fit on to one another like the automatic couplings of railway carriages.
>
> —Winston Churchill

Considering Paragraphs

Every paragraph should develop a single idea, a single aspect of the topic about which you are writing. Usually in the first sentence, and almost invariably near the beginning, you should state the idea that you are going to discuss; in the next few sentences you should develop that idea; and at the end of the paragraph you should conclude your consideration of the idea stated in the opening sentence or point the reader toward the next paragraph, if it is to develop a slightly different aspect of the same subject.

Consider this well-written paragraph.

> The wolf is a strong, sensitive, intelligent animal with complex social behavior and lasting family ties. It has a tendency to travel long distances and to seek out vulnerable big-game animals that it can kill and eat with enough

safety and efficiency to maintain its species. All the while, the wolf is subject to any number of stresses from its environment, and must constantly contend with forces tending to suppress its numbers. With minor variations in this mode of living, the wolf has survived and evolved for millions of years in a variety of habitats throughout most of the Northern Hemisphere.

—L. David Mech, The Wolf (1970)

The first sentence introduces the topic, which is the general characteristics of the wolf. The second and third sentences give some details of the wolf's existence. The final sentence concludes the statement that the paragraph makes by telling us that the wolf has been living essentially the same way for millions of years. If we changed the order of the sentences in this paragraph, the paragraph would no longer be effective. Obviously the opening and closing sentences could not be reversed, but the same applies to the two sentences that compose the body of the paragraph. Logic demands that we say what the wolf does before we comment on the difficulties he encounters doing it. It is important that you remember to arrange the details within your paragraph in a sequence that makes sense to the reader and that presents and develops the material in an orderly way.

Exercises

Describe the structure of each of the following paragraphs. Point out the topic sentence. Discuss how the main idea of the paragraph is developed. Find the conclusion.

1. The main reason for carrying a gun, and it was plenty legitimate, was the lonesomeness of the country and the need a man had to take care of himself in case of accidents. If he were off by himself, say, and took after a calf, and his horse stumbled and fell and broke its neck, and he was partly underneath, the

dead horse might lie on him for four days and the worms eat
him up before anybody would find him. With a gun in reach, he
had some chance of summoning help. Or if an old cow got on
the prod and came for him when he was afoot, he might have
to kill her to save himself from her wicked horns. Sometimes
there was a coiled rattlesnake right where he wanted to bed
down the cattle; they wouldn't settle down while the snake was
there, and it was easier to move him with his head shot off than
with it on and working. If there was a stampede, sometimes he
could head it by shooting his gun a few times in front of the
running animals. So most cowboys carried guns, but not primarily for purposes of homicide.

—N. Howard Thorp, *Partner of the Wind* (1941)

2. If motherhood isn't instinctive, when and why, then, was
the motherhood Myth born? Until recently, the entire question
of maternal motivation was academic. Sex, like it or not, meant
babies. Not that there haven't always been a lot of interesting
contraceptive tries. But until the creation of the diaphragm in
the 1880's, the birth of babies was largely unavoidable. And,
generally speaking, nobody really seemed to mind. For one
thing, people tend to be sort of good sports about what seems
to be inevitable. For another, in the past, the population
needed beefing up. Mortality rates were high, and agricultural
cultures, particularly, have always needed children to help out.
So because it, "just happened" and because it was needed,
motherhood was assumed to be innate.

—Betty Rollin, "Motherhood: Who Needs It?" (1970)

3. We continue to share with our remotest ancestors the
most tangled and evasive attitudes about death, despite the
great distance we have come to understanding some of the profound aspects of biology. We have as much distaste for talking
about personal death as thinking about it; it is an indelicacy,
like talking in mixed company about venereal disease or abortion in the old days. Death on a grand scale does not bother us
in the same special way: we can sit around a dinner table and
discuss war, involving 60 million volatilized human deaths, as
though we were talking about bad weather; we can watch
abrupt bloody death every day, in color, on films and television,
without blinking back a tear. It is when the numbers of dead
are very small, and very close, that we begin to think in scurry-

ing circles. At the very center of the problem is the naked cold deadness of one's own self, the only reality in nature of which we can have absolute certainty, and it is unmentionable, unthinkable. We may be even less willing to face the issue at first hand than our predecessors because of a secret new hope that maybe it will go away. We like to think, hiding the thought, that with all the marvelous ways in which we seem now to lead nature around by the nose, perhaps we can avoid the central problem if we just become, next year, say, a bit smarter.

—Lewis Thomas, *The Lives of a Cell* (1974)

Dividing Material into Paragraphs

Before you begin to write a theme, look at your material to see what details best fit together to form paragraphs. For example, if your theme is going to be about flowers, and you have decided that you intend to consider roses, chrysanthemums, and lilies, you already have a basic division of your material into five segments: (1) an introduction, which has to do with flowers in general; (2) a section on roses; (3) a section on chrysanthemums; (4) a section on lilies; and (5) a conclusion which makes a final statement about flowers and which is based on the body of the theme.

If the theme is short, you may want to complete it in five paragraphs, in which case you already have the topic for each paragraph. If the theme is going to be longer, however, you will have to make further divisions. Probably you will still have single opening and closing paragraphs, but you may find that you need three paragraphs to say what you want to say about roses: one about types of roses, another about the cultivation of roses, and a third about the arrangement and display of roses. This, of course, does not exhaust what can be said about roses. If you are writing a very long theme, you might want six or sixteen or sixty paragraphs on roses, in which case your single paragraph on the types would become several paragraphs as you wrote a paragraph about wild roses and a paragraph about creeping roses and a paragraph about rose trees. In any case the principle remains the same: each paragraph states its subject and remains faithful to it. That we can write a single paragraph about roses in general or a single paragraph about the color of the American Beauty rose does not alter the basic method for writing paragraphs.

Study the paragraphs in the following passage.

So gorgeous was the spectacle on the May morning of 1910 when nine kings rode in the funeral of Edward VII of England that the crowd, waiting in hushed and black-clad awe, could not keep back gasps of admiration. In scarlet and blue and green and purple, three by three the sovereigns rode through the palace gates, with plumed helmets, gold braid, crimson sashes, and jeweled orders flashing in the sun. After them came five heirs apparent, forty more imperial or royal highnesses, seven queens—four dowager and three regnant—and a scattering of special ambassadors from uncrowned countries. Together they represented seventy nations in the greatest assemblage of royalty and rank ever gathered in one place and, of its kind, the last. The muffled tongue of Big Ben tolled nine by the clock as the cortege left the palace, but on history's clock it was sunset, and the sun of the old world was setting in a dying blaze of splendor never to be seen again.

In the center of the front row rode the new king, George V, flanked on his left by the Duke of Connaught, the late king's only surviving brother, and on his right by a personage to whom, acknowledged The Times, "belongs the first place among all the foreign mourners," who "even when relations are most strained has never lost his popularity amongst us"—William II, Emperor of Germany. Mounted on a gray horse, wearing the scarlet uniform of a British Field Marshall, carrying the baton of that rank, the Kaiser had composed his features behind the famous up-turned mustache in an expression "grave even to severity."

Of the several emotions churning his susceptible breast, some hints exist in his letters. "I am proud to call this place my home and to be a member of this royal family," he wrote home after spending the night in Windsor Castle in the former apartments of his mother. Sentiment and nostalgia induced by these melancholy occasions with his English relatives jostled with pride in his supremacy among the assembled potentates and with a fierce relish in the disappearance of his uncle from the European scene. He had come to bury Edward his bane; Edward the arch plotter, as William conceived it, of Germany's encirclement; Edward his mother's brother whom he could neither bully nor impress, whose fat figure cast a shadow between Germany and the sun. "He is Satan. You cannot imagine what a Satan he is!"

This verdict, announced by the Kaiser before a dinner of three hundred guests in Berlin in 1907, was occasioned by one of Edward's continental tours undertaken with clearly diabolical designs at encirclement. He had spent a provocative week in Paris, visited for no good reason the King of Spain (who had just married his niece), and finished with a visit to the King of Italy with obvious intent to seduce him from his Triple Alliance with Germany and Austria. The Kaiser, possessor of the least inhibited tongue in Europe, had worked himself into a frenzy ending in another of those comments that had periodically over the past twenty years of his reign shattered the nerves of diplomats.

Happily the Encircler was now dead and replaced by George who, the Kaiser told Theodore Roosevelt a few days before the funeral, was "a very nice boy" (of forty-five, six years younger than the Kaiser). "He is a thorough Englishman and hates all foreigners but I do not mind that as long as he does not hate Germans more than other foreigners." Alongside George, William now rode confidently, saluting as he passed the regimental colors of the 1st Royal Dragoons of which he was honorary colonel. Once he had distributed photographs of himself wearing

their uniform with the Delphic inscription written above
his signature, "I bide my time." Today his time had come;
he was supreme in Europe.

—Barbara Tuchman, "A Funeral,"
The Guns of August (1962)

These paragraphs, as you immediately see, are logical and
coherent in themselves and in their relationship to one another. The first paragraph is a general description of the funeral procession of King Edward VII; the second focuses on
William II of Germany, on what he thinks and feels; the
third paragraph is a flashback which explains why William
feels as he does; and the final paragraph returns us to the
present and to William's position as the most powerful political figure in Europe. If you will examine the passage carefully, you will see that the first sentence of each paragraph
states a topic that is developed in the body of the paragraph
and brought to a conclusion in the final sentence. Each concluding sentence is also a kind of climax that piques our curiosity and helps move us toward the paragraph that follows:
it is morning according to ordinary time, "but on history's
clock it was sunset." Edward, according to William, is Satan.
For twenty years William has "shattered the nerves of diplomats" with his indiscreet public statements. Now that Edward is dead, William's "time had come; he was supreme in
Europe."

In any well-written and well-organized passage the paragraphs are organized according to the author's intention, the
aspect of the material that interests the author, the line the
author wishes to follow. Tuchman's concern is with William
II. Another author might have been interested in Edward.
Edward's death and the spectacle of his funeral might be
used as a point of departure for going back over the dead
king's career. Still another way of dealing with Tuchman's
material would be to focus on George, the new English king.
Then we would be told what he was thinking and feeling

and what motivated him to think and feel as he did. Any of these approaches would be valid. But what we must remember is that we cannot use all of the approaches at the same time. We must have a center, a direction in which we intend our writing to move. One reason that bad paragraphs are written is that we do not know what we want to do in the first place. We let our minds wander on paper; we change direction without warning, and our paragraphs lose their unity.

Tuchman focuses on a character, a figure of historical significance. But much of what we write, though it is usually related to the human condition, is not about specific people and therefore must be organized according to different principles. Look at the following passage.

> Every one has heard people quarrelling. Sometimes it sounds funny and sometimes it sounds merely unpleasant; but however it sounds, I believe we can learn something very important from listening to the kind of things they say. They say things like this: "How'd you like it if anyone did the same to you?"—"That's my seat. I was there first"—"Leave him alone, he isn't doing you any harm"—"Why should you shove in first?"—"Give me a bit of your orange, I gave you a bit of mine"—"Come on, you promised." People say things like that every day, educated people as well as uneducated, and children as well as grown-ups.
>
> Now what interests me about all these remarks is that the man who makes them is not merely saying that the other man's behaviour does not happen to please him. He is appealing to some kind of standard of behaviour which he expects the other man to know about. And the other man very seldom replies: "To hell with your standard." Nearly always he tries to make out that what he has been doing does not really go against the standard, or that if it does there is some special excuse. He pretends there is some special reason in this particular case why the person who took the seat first should not keep it, or that things were quite different when he was given the bit of orange,

or that something has turned up which lets him off keeping his promise. It looks, in fact, very much as if both parties had in mind some kind of Law or Rule of fair play or decent behaviour or morality or whatever you like to call it, about which they really agreed. And they have. If they had not, they might, of course, fight like animals, but they could not *quarrel* in the human sense of the word. Quarrelling means trying to show that the other man is in the wrong. And there would be no sense in trying to do that unless you and he had some sort of agreement as to what Right and Wrong are; just as there would be no sense in saying that a footballer had committed a foul unless there was some agreement about the rules of football.

Now this Law or Rule about Right and Wrong used to be called the Law of Nature. Nowadays, when we talk of the "laws of nature" we usually mean things like gravitation, or heredity, or the laws of chemistry. But when the older thinkers called the Law of Right and Wrong "the Law of Nature," they really meant the Law of *Human* Nature. The idea was that, just as all bodies are governed by the law of gravitation and organisms by biological laws, so the creature called man also had *his* law—with this great difference, that a body could not choose whether it obeyed the law of gravitation or not, but a man could choose either to obey the Law of Human Nature or to disobey it.

> —C. S. Lewis, "The Law of Human Nature,"
> *Mere Christianity* (1952)

The three paragraphs in the passage by Lewis are well constructed, and we need not spend much time analyzing them. In the first two paragraphs the topics are stated in two sentences rather than in one, but that is all right as long as the topics are clearly stated. In the first paragraph we are told that we can learn something from the things quarreling people say. In the body of the paragraph we are told what they say, and the paragraph concludes by telling us that quarrelers from every age group and every walk of life say the same things. The second paragraph shows that when people quarrel they usually do so in terms of the same set of moral rules: nobody could accuse anybody else of having misbehaved if we had no agreement about behavior in the first place. The third paragraph declares its theme in its opening sentence: "Now this Law or Rule about Right and Wrong used to be called the Law of Nature." We are told what people used to mean by the Law of Nature. And then the third paragraph reaches a climax by distinguishing between physical laws, which we all must obey, and moral laws, which we may obey or not according to our inclinations.

Consider the paragraphs in their relationship to each other. Another way of developing Lewis's subject would be to start with the topic that is introduced in the third paragraph. After all, our main interest is in the Law of Nature. Why not start with it and with a general description of what it is? You could start that way, but the method Lewis uses is probably more effective. Usually it is better to proceed from the specific to the general because the attention of the reader is more easily aroused by something that is concrete. Admittedly we could not have put people on the moon without the work of many physicists and mathematicians and engineers. But most of us had rather hear an astronaut tell of his adventures in space than listen to a scientist discuss the theoretical work that made those adventures possible. Consequently a skillful writer who wants to explain the theory of space flight to a general audience will probably begin his essay not with the theory itself but with a reference to a specific astronaut or a specific incident. The writer catches the attention of the reader with an event or a line of dialogue, and the momentum thus developed carries the reader into the more general material that the writer wishes to discuss.

Beginning with something specific such as a story about dogs or the language of argument is not merely a device to snare readers. It is also a logical way of proceeding. As we saw in Chapter 4, we learn through our senses, and because we do, we share a deep psychological inclination to begin with the concrete and move toward the general. Therefore, when Lewis begins with what people say to each other and proceeds from there to make a general statement about the Law of Nature, he is himself following another sort of natural law. He is following a method of mental progression with which we are familiar and which we will probably be able to understand.

Exercises

A. In the following passage a short paragraph follows one that is much longer. What is the effect of the short paragraph? Could it better be part of the longer paragraph? How could the longer paragraph be divided logically into two paragraphs? Would such division make the passage more or less effective? Why?

> I knew them all and some have been my friends over the years, but I saw less of them after 1942 or thereabouts. By that time a few of them were dead and the Second War was scattering the others. I was a deaf man living in the country, hoeing my garden. Some of them I saw on weekly visits to New York, which was still the center of literary life—but it was rather less of a center than before and chiefly one, it seemed to me, for younger age groups. Among middle-aged writers the political arguments of the 1930s—over the New Deal, Trotsky, the Spanish Civil War, and the Russian purges—had left fissures some of which were never to be closed (as for instance the one between Hemingway and Dos Passos). That may be part of a pattern in writers' lives: at first they are happy to roam in bands, then year by year they retire from the herd like old bull elephants. Still, the famous writers of my own age and others who deserved to be famous were reassuring though invisible presences. Pleased by each public sign of recognition, I did what I could to explain features of their work that I thought had been missed. They were our spokesmen, after all, and every glittering success they

made reflected on the rest of us. Fitzgerald was not the only one to feel that we were all playing on the same team.

Now most of the team is gone and the survivors are left with the sense of having plodded with others to the tip of a long sandspit where they stand exposed, surrounded by water, waiting for the tide to come in.

—Malcolm Cowley, "Taps for the Lost Generation,"
A Second Flowering (1973)

B. Write a paragraph using one of the following sentences as your opening sentence. It does not have to be your topic sentence.

1. The college cafeteria is not the best place in town to eat.

2. Once an airplane is off the ground and flying smoothly, most people relax.

3. The day set for our picnic was dreary and overcast.

4. My sister (or some other person), who bailed me out of jail, was the only person who knew I had been arrested.

5. Robert Frost used to say: "Every year I give myself another chance with Shelley and every year I give Shelley another chance with me."

6. To err is human; to forgive is divine—or so people say.

7. A dog (or some other animal) is the best kind of pet to have in the city.

8. Early every morning in the summer, I was awakened by the banging of garbage cans.

9. Grapes (or another fruit) are the best of all fruit.

10. My uncle (or other relative) is the most eccentric member of my family.

C. Using the following passages for models, write a paragraph about a place, a public event, or an incident in your life.

1. Hoboken is one of those improbable towns out of which so many eminent Americans have come. It is squeezed into a square mile of flatland between the rump of the Jersey Palisades and the Hudson River. Who's from Hoboken? I ask, and almost everybody in town has the same answer—Frank Sinatra. A few recall that Hetty Green became "the richest woman in America" by speculating on Wall Street while living in a cold-water flat in

Hoboken which cost her $19 a month. The others do not know, or care, that Alfred Stieglitz, the photographer, came from there too, as well as another Alfred, Kinsey, author of the liberating sex report. And Dorothea Lange.

—Milton Meltzer, *Dorothea Lange* (1978)

2. Alan Shepard finally got his turn on May 5. He was inserted in the capsule, on top of a Redstone rocket, about an hour before dawn, with an eye toward a launch shortly after daybreak. But as in the case of the ape, there was a four-hour hold in the countdown, caused mainly by an overheating inverter. Now the sun was up, and all across the eastern half of the country people were doing the usual, rolling the knobs in search of something to give the nerve endings a little tingle—and what suspense awaited them! An astronaut sat on the tip of a rocket, preparing to get himself blown to pieces.

—Tom Wolfe, *The Right Stuff* (1979)

3. I was saved from sin when I was going on thirteen. But not really saved. It happened like this. There was a big revival at my Auntie Reed's church. Every night for weeks there had been much preaching, singing, praying, and shouting, and some very hardened sinners had been brought to Christ, and the membership of the church had grown by leaps and bounds. Then just before the revival ended, they held a special meeting for children, "to bring the young lambs to the fold." My aunt spoke of it for days ahead. That night I was escorted to the front row and placed on the mourner's bench with all the other young sinners, who had not yet been brought to Jesus.

—Langston Hughes, "Salvation" (1940)

Beginning Paragraphs

As we know, all themes have beginnings, middles, and ends, but not all themes start or develop or conclude in the same fashion. How you construct your theme will depend on the kind of theme you are writing. Some themes tell stories; some explain; some argue; some describe. A letter to an old friend telling of a party you attended or a new person you are dating will begin and proceed in a different way from a letter which tries to explain to your father why you have not attended your chemistry class for the last five weeks. A letter asking for money does not have the same shape as a letter describing the beauty of the campus after a heavy snow. The exact structure of a theme will be determined by your material and the audience for whom you are writing and the effect you wish to achieve.

There are several ways to begin a theme. You can organize your essay as a sequence of events in time, in which case you begin with a paragraph that tells what happened first. You can start with an anecdote, a pertinent or illustrative story that will introduce your subject and engage your reader's interest. You can introduce your subject with a paragraph that focuses on a person, which is similar to starting with an anecdote. You can begin by stating your subject—by saying what the essay is going to be about. You can begin by stating the subject as a problem that will be discussed and, if possible, solved in the middle and conclusion of the essay. You can start with a paragraph that defines exactly what you mean when you intend to discuss a word or phrase that might mean different things to different people.

Here are some beginning paragraphs written by professional writers.

1. Beginning at the beginning in a sequence in time.

There is nothing new about the three martini lunch. More than 150 years ago Americans customarily gulped down three or four drinks with lunch. They drank just as heartily at dinner; a good many took eye-openers at breakfast. But, you say, what about the temperance movement? Weren't those God-fearing Americans of 1820 dry as dust? Not at all. We're talking about life in the United States before the temperance movement, before the WCTU, before Carrie Nation, and even before the idea of prohibition existed. There was a time before all those things when Americans drank as much hard liquor as they could get their hands on as often as possible. The average adult drank about three times as much alcohol in the 1820s as adults do now. And the consumption of alcohol had been growing vigorously. Between 1790 and 1830 the annual amount of hard liquor—primarily whiskey—that an average American drank nearly doubled.

—W. J. Rorabaugh, "A Nation of Sots" (1979)

2. Beginning with an anecdote.

The last time I saw Grandmother, already in the early 1930s, a big pimply youth with a large swastika on his lapel boarded the streetcar in which I was taking Grandmother to spend Christmas with us. Grandmother got up from her seat, inched up to him, poked him sharply in the ribs with her umbrella, and said, "I don't care what your politics are; I might even share some of them. But you look like an intelligent, educated young man. Don't you know this thing"—and she pointed to the swastika—"might give offense to some people? It isn't good manners to offend anyone's religion, just as it isn't good manners to make fun of acne. You wouldn't want to be called a pimply lout, would you?" I held my breath. By that time, swastikas were no laughing matter; and young men who wore them on the street were trained to kick an old woman's teeth in without compunction. But the lout meekly took his swastika off, put it in his pocket, and when he left the streetcar a few stops later, doffed his cap to Grandmother.

—Peter Drucker, *Adventures of a Bystander* (1979)

3. Beginning with a person.

It's midnight on the 87th floor of the World Trade Center. Nerelda Santiago pads her way through empty offices in fuzzy blue bedroom slippers, dusting desks, emptying ashtrays and vacuuming.

"Who has time to stare at the view?" she asks, waving

her yellow dust rag at the skyline glimmering in the distance. "This is the tallest building in New York. I've got work to do."

—Kathleen A. Hughes, "Tidying Up Trade
Center Is a Towering Task" (1981)

4. Beginning with a statement of the subject.

Although it is extremely difficult to alter significantly the genetic endowment of the human species, it is easy to shape the physical and psychological expressions of each individual person. Irrespective of color and size, all human beings possess a biological plasticity which makes it possible to modify their appearance, physiological functions, and ways of life without affecting their genetic constitution. For example, life in high altitudes rapidly brings about changes in the blood that facilitate the intake and utilization of oxygen; life in a very sunny climate results in tanning, which increases resistance to certain radiations; life in an environment contaminated with microbes stimulates the emergence of protective immune mechanisms; life in large urban agglomerations elicits certain types of behavior that decrease the deleterious effects of crowding. These effects are not due to genetic adaptations; they are not transmitted through the genes to succeeding generations.

—René Dubos, "Biological Freudianism" (1974)

5. Beginning with a statement of the subject as a problem.

The word "radical" is frequently used as a meaningless catchall to describe everything from the black-power movement to the use of psychedelic drugs. The overuse and misuse of the word evoke an image distorted by the violent acts committed by fringe groups like the Weathermen in the sixties. Seen through this murky lens, a radical might be a civil-rights worker or a war protester or a bomb thrower; the confusion of violence with radicalism has frequently served as the basis for the indictment of an entire generation.

> —Susan Jacoby, "We *Did* Overcome" (1979)

6. Beginning with a definition of the subject.

Altruism is the performance of an unselfish act. As a pattern of behavior, this act must have two properties: it must benefit someone else, and it must do so to the disadvantage of the benefactor. It is not merely a matter of being helpful, it is helpfulness at a cost to yourself.

> —Desmond Morris, "Altruism" (1977)

Middle Paragraphs

Usually an essay will contain more middle paragraphs than any other kind, and the middle paragraphs do the main work of the essay. Their shape and purpose are determined by the shape and purpose of the essays in which they appear. Middle paragraphs narrate, explain, argue, describe, which means they advance the story or give directions or definitions or offer reasons or tell how things look or sound or smell or taste, as we have discussed in previous chapters.

Here are some middle paragraphs from the work of professional writers.

1. Paragraphs that narrate.

[From a narrative about the Alaskan gold rush]

The first wave brought ten thousand people to Nome. They dumped their belongings on the beach and went quickly inland to search for gold. Except for those who were so disillusioned that they returned immediately to their ships when they found that the beaches of Nome consisted of sand, and not of gold dust, as they had been led to believe. One man was reported to have jumped ashore, grabbed some of the sand in his fingers, and shouted, "I knew it was all a hoax." He then returned to his ship, remarking that he was "glad to get out of the damned country."

—Joe McGinniss, *Going to Extremes* (1980)

[From a collection of essays about William Spooner]

One by one we were taken up to him for a little conversation. When my turn came he put to me a few conventional questions—what School was I reading? Had I a pleasant room? What was the general nature of my interests?—and when these were duly answered he went on to say: 'I hope you will have a happy time at Oxford. I am sure you will. But if you will take the advice of an old man'—I am a little doubtful about that introductory sentence, not at all about the words that followed—'*beware of the lure of men and women*'. This surprising injunction, quickly and quietly uttered, impressed itself indelibly upon my mind, and though I have never been sure what exactly was the warning it was intended to convey, I have always done my best to follow the general line it seemed to indicate.

—John Sparrow quoted in William Hayter, ed., *Spooner* (1977)

2. Paragraphs that explain.

[From an autobiographical essay on the changing roles of women]

I should clarify what I mean by crazy lady. In my youth— which ended about eight years ago—I occasionally had a date with someone who was very straight. Which is to say, square. In most relationships, I tend to be the straight one, cautious, conservative, not crossing on the Don't Walk, but whenever I was confronted with someone even squarer than I was, whenever I was confronted with a relationship where the role of the crazy person was up for grabs, I would leap in, say outrageous things, end the evening lying down in Times Square with a lampshade on my head. I wasn't a patch on Zelda Fitzgerald—I would never have leaped into the Plaza fountain for fear of ruining my hair—but I was in there doing my damnedest.

—Nora Ephron, "Crazy Ladies: 1," *Crazy Salad* (1975)

[From an essay on the purposes of hunting]

Anthropologists inform us that members of our family, the Hominidae, have been meat hunters for at least half a million years and maybe even two million years. And that—a hundred thousand generations within the outside guess—is a far piece of time over which to hone the racial appetite for flesh. There is no clear evidence that either *Homo erectus* or Neanderthal hunted woolly and fearsome game in order to indulge a personal attraction to the great outdoors or to seek diversion from the tedium of a dark and voiceless cave. They hunted in order to eat; and eating, survived.

—John G. Mitchell, *The Hunt* (1980)

3. Paragraphs that argue.

[From an autobiographical essay on the complexity of race and racism]

At the root of the American Negro problem is the necessity of the American white man to find a way of living with the Negro in order to be able to live with himself. And the history of this problem can be reduced to the means used by Americans—lynch law and law, segregation and legal acceptance, terrorization and concession—either to come to terms with this necessity, or to find a way around it, or (most usually) to find a way of doing both

these things at once. The resulting spectacle, at once foolish and dreadful, led someone to make the quite accurate
observation that "the Negro-in-America is a form of insan-
ity which overtakes white men."

—James Baldwin, "Stranger in the Village,"
Notes of a Native Son (1955)

[From an argument about changing attitudes toward the
sexes]

Aggression is not, as I secretly think, a male-sex-linked
characteristic; brutality is masculine only by virtue of opportunity. True, there are 1,000 Jack the Rippers for every
Lizzie Borden, but that surely is the result of social forms.
Women as a group are indeed more masochistic than
men. The practical result of this division is that women
seem nicer and kinder, but when the world changes,
women will have a fuller opportunity to be just as rotten
as men and there will be fewer claims of female moral superiority.

—Anne Roiphe, "Confessions of a Female
Chauvinist Sow" (1972)

4. Paragraphs that describe.

[From a description of a small country store]

Then through the motes of cracker dust, cornmeal dust,
the Gold Dust of the Gold Dust Twins that the floor had
been swept out with, the realities emerged. Shelves
climbed to high reach all the way around, set out with not
too much of any one thing but a lot of things—lard, molas-
ses, vinegar, starch, matches, kerosene, Octagon soap
(about a year's worth of octagon-shaped coupons cut out
and saved brought a signet ring addressed to you in the
mail). It was up to you to remember what you came for,
while your eye traveled from cans of sardines to tin whis-
tles to ice cream salt to harmonicas to flypaper (over your

head, batting around on a thread beneath the blades of
the ceiling fan, stuck with its testimonial catch).

—Eudora Welty, "The Little Store,"
The Eye of the Story (1978)

[From a novel about a man of disorderly habits]

Look at his house: a tall brick Colonial house in north Baltimore. Even this early on a January morning, when the
sun was no more than a pinkish tinge in an opaque white
sky, it was clear there was something fragmented about
Morgan's house. Its marble stoop was worn soft at the
edges like an old bar of soap, and heavy lace curtains
glimmered in the downstairs windows; but on the second
floor, where his daughters slept, the curtains were made
from sections of the American flag, and on the third floor,
where his mother slept, they were lace again, misting the
tangle of ferns that hung behind them. And if you could
see inside, through the slowly thinning gray of the hallway, you would find the particles of related people's unrelated worlds: his daughters' booksacks tumbling across the
hall radiator, which also served as mail rack, sweater shelf,
and message bureau; his wife's League of Women Voters
leaflets rubber-banded into a tower on the living-room
coffee table; and his mother's ancient, snuffling dog
dreaming of rabbits and twitching her paws as she slept
on the cold brick hearth. There was a cribbage board
under the sofa. (No one knew this. It had been lost for
weeks.) There was a jigsaw puzzle, half completed, that
Morgan's sister, Brindle, filled her long, morose, spinsterish
days with: a view of an Alpine village in the springtime.
The church steeple was assembled and so were the
straight-edged border and the whole range of mountains
with their purple and lavender shadows, but she would
never get to the sky, surely. She would never manage all
that blank, unchanging blue that joined everything else
together.

—Anne Tyler, Morgan's Passing (1980)

Concluding Paragraphs

There are many ways to write endings. Some are conclusions in two senses of that word: they are endings for essays, and they are also judgments formed on the basis of facts that have been set forth in the middles of the essays. A theme on solar energy might conclude with a paragraph that says in the future our energy will come from the sun. Another kind of ending is gounded not so much in fact as in speculation and therefore must itself be speculative. No matter how much information we gather on some subjects, our conclusions will still be informed guesses, so they will be written differently from the last paragraphs of themes about which we are certain of our judgment. Some themes end by bringing us out of the past into the present. Nikitas does this in his essay "Riding the Rails." In some endings authors take a look at the future. For example a theme on race relations might show the progress we have made since World War II and end by suggesting what must still be done. Other essays, in which a problem is discussed at length, simply end with a paragraph that assesses the present situation: a theme about violence in our society might end without offering a solution or suggesting what is to happen in the years ahead; the final paragraph would be a description of where we stand now. Some concluding paragraphs round off an essay by referring in the end to something that was mentioned in the beginning. In general our last paragraphs bring our essays to their logical stopping points, and the essay itself helps to dictate its own ending.

Here are some conclusions by professional writers.

1. A conclusion that draws a conclusion.

> Sports are like natural religions. All things human are proper to them. In pushing humans to extremities, they push virtues and vices to extremities, too. The world of

sports is no escape from evil. Nor is it an escape from virtue, excellence, and grace. In sports, we meet our humanity. Assuming one begins with limited hopes, there is more to admire in sports—and in our humanity, and in our nation—than to despise.

—Michael Novak, *The Joy of Sports* (1976)

2. A conclusion that is speculative.

It is over 30 years since the modern era of UFOs began. Only now are the first efforts being made to examine scientifically the mystery UFOs represent. For the first time the phenomenon is being studied by researchers who make no unwarranted assumptions about what they discover and are as ready for negative results as they are for some dramatic breakthrough. But inevitably in the mind of even the most sober researcher is the fascination of being involved in work that could culminate in the most exciting event in human history—mankind's first contact with extraterrestrial intelligence.

—Anthony Feldman, *Space* (1980)

3. A conclusion that brings us out of the past into the present.

[From an autobiographical account of a girl's running away]

We were never, as long as my mother and father lived, to mention that time again. But it was of great importance to them and I have thought about it all my life. From that day on, I knew my power over my parents. That was not to be too important: I was ashamed of it and did not abuse it too much. But I found out something more useful and more dangerous: if you are willing to take the punishment, you are halfway through the battle. That the issue may be trivial, the battle ugly, is another point.

—Lillian Hellman, *An Unfinished Woman* (1969)

4. A conclusion that expresses a hope for the future.

[From an open letter in which the author expresses his belief in the solidarity of man]

I hope this letter finds you strong in the faith. I also hope that circumstances will soon make it possible for me to meet each of you, not as an integrationist or a civil-rights leader but as a fellow clergyman and a Christian brother. Let us all hope that the dark clouds of racial prejudice will soon pass away and the deep fog of misunderstanding will be lifted from our fear-drenched communities, and in some not too distant tomorrow the radiant stars of love and brotherhood will shine over our great nation with all their scintillating beauty.

—Martin Luther King, Jr., "Letter from
Birmingham Jail" (1963)

5. A conclusion that makes an assessment of the present situation.

Who are we kidding? The problem with drinking isn't so much "alcoholism." The problem is death and destruction—of lives, property, relationships. Warped personalities and blunted perceptions may be annoying, but that is inconsequential when weighed against the protection of life—yet there is a parking lot next to every cocktail lounge. I am at an age when I stand a better chance of being killed by a drinking driver than of dying from any other kind of homicide or accident, or cancer, or cardiovascular disease. They are a greater threat to my life than any mugger or terrorist. What would I do without them? Feel safer at places other than work, certainly. Make less money, probably. And, of course, get more sleep at night.

—John S. Hoppock, M.D., "The Costs of Drinking" (1981)

6. A conclusion that refers to the opening paragraph.

[From an essay that discusses the importance of the otter to our ecology]

Research in Georgia shows that the river otter pays a price for its fish diet: it often ingests sizable doses of toxic pollutants which work their way up the food chain from smaller organisms in the water. "Some of the animals we checked contained astonishingly high amounts of mercury, DDT and the industrial pollutants called PCBs," says Richard Halbrook, who did the study. Thus, by keeping tabs on otters and other furbearers, we can tell when our own environment is becoming polluted. Even the turn-of-the-century conservationist, William T. Hornady, couldn't have come up with a better reason for keeping this beguiling furbearer around.

—Bill Vogt, "What Ails the River Otter?" (1981)

7. A conclusion in which the author confesses ignorance as to the meaning of what has preceded.

[From an essay about a man who inadvertently destroys his keys in a leaf-mulching machine while raking his yard]

I do not know the moral of this story.

—Hank Burchard, "The Modern Parable
of the Leaves and the Keys" (1979)

Exercises

A. Study the following passage. Make an outline of the material it contains, and rewrite the passage using as many or as few paragraphs as you judge the material requires.

Infidelity is the single most frequent theme of the music, as in "I Heard the Jukebox Playing When You Called Me on the Phone." It occurs in well over half of the hit songs of the last quarter-century. The first and most frequent reason for unfaithfulness is that another person has stolen away the beloved, though the partner herself is more often blamed than her new lover, and it appears to be most often the woman who leaves home. Although marriage is the common state, love is held, as it is in all our popular music and literature, at the highest premium. In country music, middle-class morality endures, but true love prevails. "Walk On By" is a good example in which the man, in love with his mistress, admits that he'll continue to see her at night though he cannot acknowledge her by day. What is important is that the country lover *loves* faithfully. According to the one left behind, money or a rival or a combination of the two are the usual motives for leaving; according to the one leaving, *love* is the sole motive. Infidelity often plays a role in songs in which one partner has been lured by city life and has fallen prey to its attendant evils: drunkenness, haughtiness, and perhaps a fall into sin. Southern hillbilly music increasingly links the city to a woman, but to the wrong sort of woman—an evil, conniving, emasculating female. Women (and men) who pass marriage by and choose the life of pleasure come to no good end, as songs like "Mansion on the Hill" tell us. In this song the girl has rejected her country lover for a life of riches and now she is lonely and loveless. Rising in the world and acquiring material goods are synonymous with mortal sin and loss of honor. "Pick Me Up on Your Way Down," a man confidently sings to his innocent-turned-glamour-girl.

Country songs tell stories, and they tend to tell the same story again and again. The typical country song protagonist is a grown man, or at any rate, physically mature in most of the songs. His marriage or romance is the impetus for his story. But his crown has already become his cross, and the songs center on his misery. The country hero is surely not in all ways admirable: a tolerant spirit is not his forte; he is suspicious of those who live differently from him, especially those in more fortunate situations, as songs like "Satisfied Mind" show. The song states flatly that a man with riches can't have a satisfied mind. The hero of country songs is sentimental and weak, complains "Excuse Me, I Think I've Got a Heartache." He knowingly allows himself to be cuckolded, sadly inquiring of his wife, "Does my ring hurt your finger/when you go out at night?"

—Katie Letcher Lyle, "Southern Country
Music: A Brief Eulogy," in Louis D.
Rubin, Jr., ed., *The American
South: Portrait of a Culture* (1980)

B. Reread one of your old themes. Write a new opening paragraph for this theme. Write a new final paragraph. Tell why you think your new paragraphs improve your theme.

7

Sentences

Sentences are not different enough to hold the attention
unless they are dramatic. No ingenuity of varying structure
will do. All that can save them is the speaking tone of voice
somehow entangled in the words.

—Robert Frost

The basic parts of a sentence are a subject and a predicate.
The subject is a noun—or something that can be used as a
noun such as a pronoun or a gerund or a phrase or a clause—
and the predicate is a verb. Sentences may, and usually do,
have objects and modifiers; they frequently have conjunctions and relative pronouns. But however many words you
may put together, the words will not make a sentence unless
you have a subject and a predicate. *You win* is a simple sentence. *You* is the subject; *win* is the predicate. If we write *You
win the prize,* we have added an object, *prize.* If we write *You
win the largest prize,* we have added a modifier, *largest.* But
what makes these constructions sentences is the fact that they
have a subject, *you,* and a predicate, *win.* Because it contains
a subject and a predicate, *I decided* is a sentence. But *Observing
the darkness of the sky and believing that rain was imminent, decided
not to go any further that day but to wait until tomorrow to continue
the journey upon which much depended* is not a sentence, despite

its length and complexity, because it has no subject. We will say more about subjects and predicates, objects and modifiers when we discuss the parts of speech in the next chapter.

Sentences by Grammatical Type

As you know, there are different kinds of sentences. A simple sentence consists of one clause, including one subject and one predicate, though both subject and predicate may contain several parts. Here is a simple sentence.

> Isabel hurried into the house.

A compound sentence consists of two or more independent clauses, usually linked by conjunctions or commas or semicolons.

> Isabel hurried into the house and I stepped from behind the tree.

A complex sentence has two or more clauses, in which one clause is independent and the others are dependent or subordinate.

> When I stepped from behind the tree, Isabel hurried into the house.

> or

> When Isabel hurried into the house, I stepped from behind the tree.

A compound-complex sentence has at least two independent clauses and at least one dependent clause.

> When I stepped from behind the tree, the dog barked, and Isabel hurried into the house.

Simple sentences make statements or ask questions. Compound sentences are essentially two or more simple sentences linked together. The details or ideas expressed in a compound sentence are brought into a slightly closer relationship than the same ideas expressed in simple sentences. Complex sentences declare by their structure which of the ideas they contain is more or most important. *When I stepped from behind the tree, Isabel hurried into the house* is not quite the same as *When Isabel hurried into the house, I stepped from behind the tree.* Here we have a temporal relationship. Either Isabel went in first, or I stepped out first, and the other event followed. There is some suggestion in both sentences that one event was the cause of the other. In many complex sentences the relationship between or among the clauses is logical rather than temporal: *Because I was poor, I was frequently hungry.* But there is always a relationship, and you must always try to put the most significant idea in a complex sentence into the independent clause. Compound-complex sentences do in combination what compound and complex sentences do separately: all the ideas are brought into a closer relationship with one another; and some of the ideas are made subordinate to others.

Generally speaking, no theme should be written in sentences that are all of one kind. Obviously, if you are writing about a complicated subject, you will probably use more complex and compound-complex sentences than if you are writing about an uncomplicated subject. A theme about riding a bicycle might be composed mostly of simple sentences while a theme about pornography and censorship might contain mostly complex and compound-complex sentences. In either case the sentences should vary in length, and from time to time you should vary your sentence structure. A theme composed of all long or all short, all simple or all complex, sentences is likely to be monotonous. Still the main thing to remember is that you should use whatever sentence structures best convey the things you wish to say.

Here is a passage that consists largely of simple sentences.

Hogeye, Arkansas, July 28, 1975—Seth Timmons reports that he did not sleep well the other night because of a katydid that sang outside his window all night long after the others had stopped.

Not only that, he says, he has been unable to get his work done lately, for no apparent reason. He believes that he is fortunate to have gotten his hay in, considering the way things have been going.

He is not alone in his condition. For days, the cattle have passed the afternoons huddled motionless in the shade. The cats have lain on the steps in perfect imitation of death and have had to be kicked out of the way by every person going through the door.

The cats, the cattle, and Mr. Timmons are all apparently beset by the same affliction. They are in the clutches of the dog days. This is the time when evil is on the land, when dogs and snakes must be watched with special care and when all living things seem to wilt under some baleful influence.

—Roy Reed, "Cats, Cattle, and People—
Beware of Dog Days" (1975)

Here is a passage that consists of one long complex sentence.

We have all seen it a hundred times, and in dozens of variations: that short sequence of images in which a husband expresses disappointment and distress at his wife's inability to provide him with a decent cup of coffee and seems inclined to seek a better tasting potion outside the home, perhaps even at the bosom of another lady; the anxious consultation, which ensues between the wife and her mother or an experienced and trusted friend, who counsels the use of another brand of coffee; and finally, the idyllic tableau of the husband astonished and surprised by the excellence of his wife's new coffee, demand-

ing a second—or even a third!—cup of the miraculously
effective product.

—Martin Esslin, "Aristotle and the
Advertisers," Mediations (1980)

Here is a passage that consists of one simple sentence, two
compound sentences, and one long compound-complex sentence.

Lumpenproletarians are the displaced persons of the
world, and the broken city slums and shantytowns of the
world are their camps. Fanon called these people the
damned of the earth, and for all his hope that from this
human rubble a new man would arise, damned they remain! The damned of Harlem and the South Bronx, the
damned of Calcutta and Naples, the damned of Singapore
and San Salvador and Manila; all these unskilled, unregi-
mented, but endlessly resourceful masses, laboring here
one day and there another, idle and then not idle, starving
and then not starving, alternating always between today's
hope and tomorrow's despair; all these men, women, and
children, with their eyes like wolves' eyes, constitute a single if ignored human type who may have far more in common with one another (beneath their apparent cultural
differences), than anyone has yet imagined or attempted
to verify. But in their own lives they remain hidden and
unheard, unknown and difficult to know.

—Thomas Belmonte, The Broken Fountain (1979)

In each of the above passages the sentences are constructed
to enhance the tone and meaning the author wishes to convey. Reed's simple sentences express simple ideas and move
slowly as if they too were affected by the heat and lassitude
of dog days. Esslin's sentence reaches constantly forward, re-
fusing to pause in the same way that television commer-
cials—which is what the author is describing—try to say as
much as possible in the shortest possible time. Belmonte's

passage is the most serious of the three, and this seriousness is reflected in the statements made in the two opening sentences and the closing sentence, and particularly in the repetitions of words—"damned"—and of structural patterns— "idle and then not idle, starving and then not starving"—of the long third sentence. The sentences in these passages are very different, but they are all good, because they all work: they enable the author to say what he wants to say about his material.

Sentence Fragments and Run-On Sentences

Two common errors of sentence structure are sentence fragments and run-on sentences, which are also called comma splices. A sentence fragment is a group of words that does not constitute a sentence but that is punctuated as if it does. Fragments often result when a writer puts into separate sentences two or three ideas which belong in the same sentence.

1. May's ambition was to become an engineer. And perhaps to teach in an engineering school. Or to work for a construction company overseas.
2. It is not easy to remember all that happened. The sudden fire that blazed in the stairwell. Our frantic efforts to save the files.

In the first example the second and third sentences are fragments because they do not have subjects. In the second example the last two sentences are fragments because they do not have predicates. Both examples can be corrected by simple changes in punctuation.

1. May's ambition was to become an engineer and perhaps to teach in an engineering school or to work for a construction company overseas.
2. It is not easy to remember all that happened: the sud-

den fire that blazed in the stairwell, our frantic efforts to save the files.

Relative clauses have subjects and predicates, but they are not sentences because they require other independent clauses to complete their meaning. *While I slept, Which you bought, When the holidays are over*—each is obviously a fragment; and if you are dealing with one or two such clauses, you are not likely to think they are sentences. But if you allow your prose to become overly complicated by trying to fit too much information into one sentence, you risk writing a sentence fragment.

> When the first settlers landed in the New World not very well prepared for what they found and ignorant of the customs of the people who were already occupying the land, yet wanting to establish a successful colony because they did not want to go back to Europe, the passage across the ocean being hazardous, and in many cases probably to be greeted, should they return home, with hostility.

There are several clauses in the example above: *When the first settlers landed in the New World; what they found; who were already occupying the land; because they did not want to go back to Europe; should they return home.* But there is no independent clause, and consequently there is no sentence. The easiest way to correct this fragment is to rewrite the passage so that separate ideas appear in separate sentences.

> When the first settlers landed in the New World, they were not very well prepared for what they found, in part because they were ignorant of the customs of the people who were already occupying the land. The settlers wanted to establish a successful colony. They did not want to return to Europe; the passage across the ocean was hazardous, and should they return home, they would, in many cases, be greeted with hostility.

A run-on sentence consists of two or more independent clauses that are not separated by conjunctions or semicolons. Often the clauses are separated by commas as if one or more of the independent clauses were dependent.

1. I went to the corner to wait for Elizabeth, Helen remained at home in case Elizabeth were delayed and tried to telephone us.
2. Jack crossed the bridge first, Hans followed, Gerald, lacking a good sense of balance, turned back.

The first example can be corrected by inserting *and* after the comma or by changing the comma to a semicolon. The second example can be corrected by changing the first two commas to semicolons or by inserting the conjunction *and* after *followed*.

Another frequent cause of the run-on sentence is that the writer uses a conjunctive adverb (such as *moreover, however,* or *therefore*) without showing what part of the sentence—which clause—the adverb is attached to.

Jack decided he would stand firm, moreover, he would not change his mind even if his mother intervened.

This error can be rectified by changing either comma to a semicolon; the change will depend upon the meaning you intend.

The best way to avoid run-on sentences is to remain alert to the difference between dependent and independent clauses, making sure that each clause maintains its proper identity and function.

Though you will see them occasionally in print, run-on sentences should never be used. Good writers sometimes use sentence fragments to accentuate the thing or idea which the fragment contains.

What I wasn't aware of, until I started looking recently,

was how many How To books are being published dedicated to the science of looking good. They are written by
everyone from doctors and nurses to cosmetologists and
Marie Osmond. I have no idea, nor did the beauty books
tell me, how we came to believe that Pretty was the answer. Perhaps the seed was sown, and harvested, by a kind
of Trilateral Commission of cosmetics makers and sports
outfitters. The fact remains that while the world is falling
apart, we are pulling ourselves together "appearance-
wise." Jobs are said to hinge on looking good. And young.
Ditto everlasting love and self-confidence. Do not imagine
that children will believe any different. A 12-year-old, on
whose birth certificate my name appears, recently re-
quested $40 worth of Clinique products. She said she
needed such things as clarifier and toner.

—Margo Howard, "The Vanity Industry" (1980)

A major reason that the fragments "And young" and
"Ditto everlasting love and self-confidence" are effective here
is that the language of the passage is informal and the tone is
ironic. Fragments work less well and appear less frequently
in more formal prose. They should always be used sparingly—and only after you have tried a complete sentence and
are sure that the fragment is more effective.

Exercises

Study the sentences in the following passages. What types of sentences does each author use? Are these sentences the best that could
be written to convey each author's meaning? Explain your answer.
How do the sentences in each passage reflect the author's attitude
toward the material? Choose one passage and try to revise it so that
your version is better than the original. Explain and defend your
revision.

1. Here is a famous American story. A young man decides to
seek his fortune. He believes in the supreme value of self-edu-

cation. He goes to Philadelphia. He is a success in publishing. He is a genius at advertising, including self-advertising. He marries his employer's daughter. He becomes first a civic, then a national celebrity. He goes abroad to represent his country. His autobiography is required reading in the schools. This is the American legend, the life of Benjamin Franklin. Even more it is that of his reincarnation: for all of the above is the summary of the life of Edward William Bok, who followed him a century and a half later.

—John Lukacs, *Philadelphia: Patricians*
and Philistines, 1900–1950 (1981)

2. The dictator is overthrown and more than half the people rejoice. The dictator had filled the jails and emptied the treasury. Like many dictators, he hadn't begun badly. He had wanted to make his country great. But he wasn't himself a great man; and perhaps the country couldn't be made great. Seventeen years pass. The country is still without great men; the treasury is still empty; and the people are on the verge of despair. They begin to remember that the dictator had a vision of the country's greatness, and that he was a strong man; they begin to remember that he had given much to the poor. The dictator is in exile. The people began to agitate for his return. The dictator is now very old. But the people also remember the dictator's wife. She loved the poor and hated the rich, and she was young and beautiful. So she has remained, because she died young, in the middle of the dictatorship. And, miraculously, her body has not decomposed.

—V. S. Naipaul, *The Return of Eva Peron* (1981)

3. In the now-filthy kitchen of the big house the shelves with the everyday dishes are in confusion. Bottles of pills for innumerable ailments are stacked beside thimbles and shoelaces. It is too difficult for my mother to climb the stairs constantly and put things away. Tubes of Ben-Gay and rubbing alcohol attest to pain. In a cut-glass bowl I find nearly two thousand dollars of uncashed checks (social security and dividends) which I force them to sign and then deposit in the bank. This is only a preliminary to the horror that I come upon one day soon after my father's death. My mother is in the kitchen, quite happy at the

sink scrubbing something in a red dishpan. It is ten- and twenty-dollar bills that she has washed furiously in strong detergent. Now she hangs them to dry in the dish drainer and over the towel rack.

—Maureen Howard, *Facts of Life* (1978)

4. Nature knew it must bribe us with an overwhelming instinct to make sexual music together so the earth would not remain a lifeless rock. Whether you believe that evolution brought light in its timeless and tireless work, or that God in His earliest effort said, "Let there be light," *something* brought light long before the Pedernales Electric Co-op or West Texas Utilities Company. With light came heat, without which no life might exist. In time the great hot lump of earth cooled, and the moisture in its atmosphere fell as rain, and water gathered and pooled, and the winds came and helped the water wear away the cold stone. This formed thin coatings of soil, which eventually toddled its way downhill into the water. There the sun kissed this new mixture toward the end of bringing forth original life: microscopic, tiny, jellylike floating cells. These linked together and multiplied themselves and grew the instinct to keep on doing it.

—Larry L. King, *Outlaws, Con Men, Whores, Politicians and Other Artists* (1980)

5. One reason for the reluctance to acknowledge the sheer idea of an American working class has been the claim—and it has some truth to it—that things in America are "different." American workers, it is said, are not so rigidly held into fixed or limited class positions as workers in Europe. That may also explain why the American labor movement has not been nearly so friendly to socialist ideas as the European labor movement. And as I say, there is some truth to these claims, though with the passage of time, less and less truth. Mainly, however, the idea of the working class as a distinct and major presence in American life has not been fully accepted because of our incorrigible nostalgia for an earlier, simpler America where there were few industrial laborers, few large corporations, few immense cities.

—Irving Howe, "Imagining Labor" (1981)

Sentences by Rhetorical Structure

As you can see from the passages we have discussed, there is more to sentence variation than differences in grammatical type and length. Sentences can also be classified according to their rhetorical structure. Most of the sentences we write are *loose*. In a loose sentence the most important facts are stated first and the details come later. *Evelyn missed her plane, even though she was usually prompt and had packed her bag the night before.* That Evelyn missed her flight is the significant part of this sentence. The rest of the sentence gives us more information, but if we stopped reading after the first four words, we would still know the principle message the writer wished to convey. We can write this sentence another way, which is called *periodic. Even though she was usually prompt and had packed her bags the night before, Evelyn missed her plane.* In this kind of structure the major point of the sentence is stated at the end. Periodic sentences are slightly more dramatic than loose sentences. They make us wait for the main piece of information, and because they are an inversion of the way that we usually think and talk, they are more formal than loose sentences.

Frequently, as is the case with Evelyn's missing her plane, it will make little difference whether a given sentence is periodic or loose. *Susan moved restlessly from the chair to the couch, from the couch to the door.* Or *From the chair to the couch, from the couch to the door, Susan moved restlessly.* Which of these versions you might want to use in an essay is a matter of choice, as long as you remember to vary your rhetorical as well as your grammatical structure. But there are other situations in which the use of periodic sentences gives us a definite advantage. Consider this passage.

> The movement of his entire existence, therefore, was inward now, towards the centre. Darwin withdrew gradually

toward stillness although when he was young, he had been all activity; he had expressed himself in the physical world, imposing himself on it as a hunter and collector. The intensity with which he had formerly looked outwards was refocussed. It turned toward what he was learning and gathering, leaving what was sometimes no more than a token energy for the duties and obligations that pressed upon the social self. The shape of his life and his identity would have looked like a series of concentric rings if it were considered as a single unified phenomenon and laid out in diagrammatic form during the years that led to *The Origin of Species.*

The prose here is grammatically correct, and the paragraph is well constructed; but the sentences are all loose, and as a result the passage is flat and monotonous: nothing impels us to move ahead from one sentence to another. And the ideas in the final sentences are so loosely joined that the reader has difficulty following them. Now look at the same paragraph as it was originally written.

The movement of his entire existence, therefore, was inward now, towards that centre. Darwin, who had been all activity, who had expressed himself when young in the physical world, imposing himself upon it as hunter and collector, withdrew gradually towards stillness. The intensity with which he had formerly looked outwards was refocussed. It turned towards what he was learning and gathering, leaving what was sometimes no more than a token energy for the duties and obligations that pressed upon the social self. If the shape of his life and his identity, considered as a single, unified phenomenon, could have been laid out in diagrammatic form during the years that led to *The Origin of Species,* it would have looked like a series of concentric rings.

—Peter Brent, *Charles Darwin: "A Man of
Enlarged Curiosity"* (1981)

The periodic structure of the second sentence gives energy and focus to the paragraph. Our desire to discover what is being said about Darwin moves us toward the end of the sentence, where we are given the main point the author wishes to make: at this time in his life Darwin is turning inward. The long and complicated modifying clause that begins the final sentence has the effect of making most of that sentence periodic. This structure also moves us forward, and it places the facts to be expressed in a closer relationship than they appear in the loose sentence which concludes the first version of this passage.

We sometimes write compound sentences to create balance between two or more facts or ideas, or to compare one thing with another. *To err is human; to forgive, divine* is not only a cliché but a good example of a *balanced* sentence. Elements that are balanced against each other must have a logical relationship, but this relationship can be established in many ways. Erring and forgiving are part of a larger process: we all make mistakes and some of us excuse the mistakes of others. In *The banks of the river were green, but the land through which it flowed was arid,* the logical relationship is between wet and dry. Parts of a sentence can be balanced in terms of people or time or space or cause and effect or comparison and contrast or even in terms of symbols. Here are two balanced sentences by professional writers.

> The donkey never literally kicked an opponent in the backside, and the elephant has never trumpeted a successful call to anything.
>
> —James A. Kehl, "White House or Animal House" (1980)

> Tradition relates that on rare occasions men were lynched because they erroneously had been supposed to have been the perpetrators of a particular crime with which in fact they had no connection, but tradition adds that each

such victim was known to have performed at least one other act which by itself would have warranted the rope.

—Philip Ashton Rollins, *The Cowboy* (1936)

Balanced sentences give the impression that the author is a fair-minded person who considers all sides of the issues and who sees the interconnections of actions and objects and ideas. Balanced sentences also help us to emphasize and dramatize the relationship between or among facts. Look at the following sentence.

The trucks were loaded with food and medicine; they crossed the border in the morning and came back in the afternoon when they were empty except for an occasional refugee who had managed to hide under a tarpaulin.

Now look at the same words rearranged to make a balanced sentence.

Every morning the trucks crossed the border loaded with food and medicine; every afternoon they returned empty except for an occasional refugee who had managed to hide under a tarpaulin.

Even though we have these sentences out of context—we do not know what border is being crossed or what people are suffering or why the refugees are escaping—the second sentence, with its emphasis on the time of day *(morning* and *afternoon),* gives us an enhanced sense of urgency and drama.

We can shift the emphasis of a sentence by putting the object before the subject or by moving a modifier from its ordinary position. Usually we would write *He would not part with his dog.* But to give more importance to the dog, we can change the structure of the sentence: *His dog, he would not part with.* We would usually write *Almost any kind of music can be heard in Nashville.* Here the emphasis falls on the music. To emphasize the place, we write: *In Nashville, almost any kind of music might be heard.* Look at three versions of the same sentence. (The piece of paper referred to here is President Roosevelt's order naming Eisenhower commander of the Normandy invasion in World War II.)

> Among all his trophies Eisenhower clearly prized that faded piece of framed yellow foolscap.
>
> That faded piece of framed yellow foolscap, Eisenhower clearly prized among all his trophies.
>
> That faded piece of yellow foolscap, framed, Eisenhower clearly prized among all his trophies.
>
> —William Bragg Ewald, Jr., *Eisenhower the President* (1981)

The loose structure of the first sentence puts Eisenhower first and therefore makes him more important than the paper. The second sentence, by putting the object before the subject, shifts the emphasis to the object of the sentence, the paper; and we see in this construction how carefully the words have been chosen to draw attention to the object. Ordinarily alliteration—the repetition of the same initial sound in several words—should be avoided in prose because the repeated sounds call attention to themselves and divert us from the meaning of the sentence. Here, however, the repeated *f*'s in the words *faded, framed,* and *foolscap* invite us to pause and consider the importance of the document. In the third sentence another shift in structure is made to emphasize the paper even further: *framed* is moved out of its ordinary sequence and placed after the noun it modifies. To see the effect of all this, read the sentence aloud. The pause created by the alliteration becomes even more pronounced as a result of *framed* having been moved out of its usual position.

Now consider the following passage.

> As I look back on the trip now, as I try to sort out fact
> from fiction, try to remember how I felt at the particular
> time, or during that particular incident, try to relive those
> memories that have been buried so deep and distorted so
> ruthlessly, there is one clear fact that emerges from the
> quagmire. The trip was easy.
>
> —Robyn Davidson, *Tracks* (1981)

Probably what we first notice here is the force of the short
second sentence. Rearrange these two sentences in your
mind. Think how much would be lost if the author had
begun "I can see that the trip was easy as I look back on it.
. . ." In the original passage the effect of a periodic sentence—
the building to a climax—is accomplished in two sentences.
This is an important point: often the effect of one sentence
will depend on the construction of the sentence that comes
before or after. Notice also that the first sentence is itself a
periodic sentence and the series of clauses that precede the
main statement are balanced. They evoke from the reader a
response similar to that produced by a balanced sentence.
This effect of tightness, of succinctness, of considering one
fact or idea against another is enhanced by repetition. The
opening clauses are bound together by the repeated use of
"As I" and "try" and "so." Repetition is employed more frequently in prose than alliteration, but like alliteration it
should be used sparingly. If we repeat ourselves in every
paragraph, the emphasizing and unifying effect of repetition
will be replaced by a sense of monotony.

As the passages above demonstrate, rhetorical patterns of
sentences are often mixed. We write not only in loose and
periodic and balanced sentences but in combinations of these
three, and the effect of one sentence can be made to carry
over into another. The way you write your own sentences in
your own essays will depend, as does every other aspect of
your writing, on what you want to say. Keep in mind the
important points you wish to make and construct your sen-

tences in such a way that they emphasize these points and give variety to your writing.

Exercises

Study the following passages. Classify each sentence according to its rhetorical structure: loose, periodic, balanced, or a combination of these. Find examples of sentences that work particularly closely with each other. Find examples of alliteration and repetition. Rewrite one of the passages by changing the rhetorical structure of some of the sentences. Defend your revision.

1. A girl stood before him in midstream, alone and still gazing out to sea. She seemed like one whom magic had changed into the likeness of a strange and beautiful seabird. Her long slender bare legs were delicate as a crane's. . . .

She was alone and still, gazing out to sea; and when she felt his presence and the worship of his eyes her eyes turned to him in quiet sufferance of his gaze, without shame or wantonness. Long, long she suffered his gaze and then quietly withdrew her eyes from his and bent them towards the stream, gently stirring the water with her foot hither and thither. The first faint noise of gently moving water broke the silence, low and faint and whispering, faint as the bells of sleep; hither and thither, hither and thither: and a faint flame trembled on her cheek.

—James Joyce, *A Portrait of the Artist
as a Young Man* (1916)

2. The mourners themselves had begun to gather for the vigil the night before, showing up wrapped in blankets and goosedown and otherwise giving evidence of having made detailed preparations for the coming event; they were, after all, representatives of a generation that, like no other, had an appreciation of *equipment*, not least for occasions, such as this one, of self-testing. They listened intently to the detailed instructions of the master of ceremonies for insuring comfort through the ordeal ahead; then, with the sober air of those who are discharging an important obligation, they attended to the relaxing of their bodies. Finally, at two P.M. the vigil began. Against a background, remarkable in itself, of ten full minutes of air si-

lence unprecedented in television history, the network cameras began focusing on the hordes of mourners. Perhaps the most striking aspect of the events the cameras were to record that day was the nearly uniform look on the faces of those in the crowd, expressions bespeaking self-approbation to a degree that neither the ostentatiousness of grief nor the prayerfulness attendant on this occasion could in the slightest mask. (Self-approval is, anyway, one of the least easily concealed of human feelings partly because, like any other form of love, it tends to bring a sheen to the eye.)

—Dorothy Rabinowitz, "John Lennon's Mourners" (1981)

3. The first of the great commercial marriages in America in the postwar years had been between advertising and television, as the networks offered national advertisers an extraordinarily attentive national audience; the second great marriage had come in the late fifties and early sixties, as Madison Avenue, seeking ways to reach the American male, discovered live sports as a prime vehicle. Professional football had been the first triumph, with results so exceptional that advertisers immediately began casting about for other sports. Eventually handsome television contracts reached even the fledgling National Basketball Association. The connection gradually changed the nature of NBA ownership, and the structure of its economics. The old owners had been men of limited income, promoters and arena proprietors who stayed one step ahead of the bill collector. Their revenues were what they could draw from live fans. These new owners were primarily young self-made multimillionaires, in it for the tax writeoffs. Ego gratification was often more important to them than making money.

—David Halberstam, The Breaks of the Game (1981)

4. One of the things commonly said about humorists is that they are really very sad people—clowns with a breaking heart. There is some truth in it, but it is badly stated. It would be more accurate, I think, to say that there is a deep vein of melancholy running through everyone's life and that the humorist, perhaps more sensible of it than some others, compensates for it actively and positively. Humorists batten on trouble. They have always made trouble pay. They struggle along with a good will and endure pain cheerfully, knowing how well it will serve

them in the sweet by and by. You find them wrestling with foreign languages, fighting folding ironing boards and swollen drainpipes, suffering the terrible discomfort of tight boots (or as Josh Billings wittily called them, "tite" boots). They pour out their sorrows profitably, in a form that is not quite fiction nor quite fact either. Beneath the sparkling surface of these dilemmas flows the strong tide of human woe.

—E. B. White, "Some Remarks on Humor,"
Essays of E. B. White (1977)

5. Bats have long been considered undesirable creatures and regarded as symbols of doom and darkness; they have been indelibly associated with haunted houses and blood-thirsty horror stories in the Dracula tradition. No other group of mammals seems so shrouded in folklore, mystery and misinformation. The Angel of Death and the Devil are often portrayed as having bat's wings. A demented person is said to be "batty" or to have "bats in his belfry." A person with defective eyesight is said to be "blind as a bat." A person making a hurried retreat is said to be going like a "bat out of hell." Bats appear along with spooks and goblins at Hallowe'en and are reputed to attack women and get tangled in their hair. Some of our less desirable elderly citizens may be referred to as "old bats." And then there is Batman, about which perhaps the less said, the better.

—R. L. Peterson, "The Incredible
World of Bats" (1981)

8

Words

It should be our faith that everything in this world can be expressed in words.

—Oscar Wilde

Proper words in proper places make the true definition of a style.

—Jonathan Swift

Considering Words

Even the most skillfully constructed sentences will not convey your meaning unless you use the proper words. Keep your vocabulary as simple as you can. Frequently you will have to use large or even obscure words to say what you want to say, and you should not be afraid to use them. But if you have a choice between a big word and a little word, it is almost always best to use the little word. As we shall see, small words tend to be concrete and specific; large words tend to be general and abstract. It is better to say rain, if you mean rain, than to say precipitation, because precipitation denotes not only rain but snow and hail and sleet. Obviously there will be circumstances in which the word *precipitation* will convey exactly what we mean. If you are writing about all the moisture that has fallen on a particular place during a particular time, you will either have to say precipitation or name separately all the forms that moisture falling from the sky can assume. But unless you are trying to be funny—and not very funny at that—you would not come home having been drenched by a thundershower and say "I was caught in the precipitation."

There are simple words to designate the objects and actions and qualities to which we refer most frequently in our writing: *man, woman, boy, girl, tree, brick, river, cake, street, house, bus, beer, candy; walk, see, burn, sleep, cook, lose, kiss, drink, talk, dress, sit, read, think; cold, blue, narrow, tight, fast, straight, soft, salty, slowly, brightly, loudly, easily, shyly.* Sometimes we abandon these words and others like them in an effort to make our writing sound more intellectual or profound. In this kind of prose *pencil* might become *writing instrument,* in which case a precise six-letter word is replaced by a seven-letter word and a ten-letter word that in combination can mean not only pencil but pen and typewriter as well. We have used more space and made our meaning less clear. Say *scarce* rather than *in short supply; now* rather than *at this point in time.*

Clichés, which are trite or wornout expressions that have lost their freshness and power through overuse, are often long-winded as well as stale. This is true of *in short supply, at this point in time,* and hundreds of similar phrases. Often clichés are similes: *hot as fire, green as grass, tight as a tick, slippery as an eel, fast as lightning.* Because we have heard and seen these and other phrases like them frequently, they are usually the first expressions that come to mind when we are searching for a comparison. But through overuse they have lost their power to inform or to persuade. Sometimes lazy writers put clichés in quotation marks, which is a way of saying *I know this is a cliché, and since I have indicated that I know it is, I expect you to forgive me for having used it.* This only calls attention to the original error and makes it worse. If a cliché is the only comparison you can think of, then do not make the comparison. To write *The coffee was very hot* is better than to write *The coffee was as hot as fire.*

Viewed abstractly, no word is superior to any other word: *mud* and *benevolence* and *onomatopoeia* are equals in the democracy of the dictionary. But in a specific context, one word is better than all the other words to help you say what you want to say. After you have trained yourself to write economically and not to use clichés and not to use big words when small words will do as well, you are still obligated to try to find the best possible words for the sentences you are writing. To help yourself do this, try to be aware always of what words really mean. Many words *seem* to mean the same thing: *dirt, soil, earth, ground; talk, speak, converse; generous, charitable, unselfish.* But almost every word in English has shades of meaning that make it different from every other word. When we refer to the planet on which we live, we call it earth. We write of the grounds of an estate, the dirt tracked in from outside, the sample of soil to be analyzed.

We talk to or converse with each other, but *converse* is the more intimate word, and we would never say that we converse to an audience, though we can speak to one. When we say hello, we are speaking, but we are not conversing or talking. *Discourse* is nearer to *speak* than to *talk* or *converse.* It is usually used to describe significant communication on a serious topic: The professor discoursed on the uses of political power. *Discourse* can also be used ironically: He could not pass a bar without discoursing on his formula for martinis. In that sentence the irony of discoursing is reenforced by the use of *formula* rather than a less pretentious word such as *recipe*. *Descant* is a more formal word than *discourse:* it means to comment expansively on a subject; it also means a kind of music. You will probably seldom, if ever, find a context in your writing in which to use it, but see how perfectly *descant* works in these lines by William Butler Yeats.

Speech after long silence; it is right
. . . .
That we descant and yet again descant
Upon the supreme theme of Art and Song.
                    —"After Long Silence" (1932)

Descant is a good word to use in connection with art and song, but you would not descant on batting averages or bus schedules or blueberry pie. If you bear in mind the different shades of meaning that most words convey, you can more easily choose an exact word from among all the other words that mean roughly, but not precisely, the same thing.

Exercises

Find synonyms for the italicized words in the following sentences. See if one of the synonyms will make the meaning of the sentence in which it appears clearer or convey more precisely the emotion that the author wishes to communicate. In each case try to say why the word you choose—either the one used by the author or the one you substitute for it—is the best word to use in the particular context in which it appears. Consider not only the exact meaning of the word but the connotations, the overtones of the word as well.

1. So long as you are not actually ill, hungry, frightened, or *immured* in a prison or a holiday camp, spring is still spring.

—George Orwell, "Some Thoughts on the Common Toad" (1946)

2. Between the marriage elms at the foot of the broad lawn, there hung a scarlet canvas hammock where Andrew Shipley *squandered* the changeless afternoons of early June.

—Jean Stafford, *The Catherine Wheel* (1952)

3. In the Southern Archipelago I had met *strange* people and *stranger* fish, but none so moving as the dying shark whose *nobility* was lit by a torch and *descried* by the tongues of the *mean* and the *mediocre*.

—Sven Berlin, *Jonah's Dream* (1964)

4. [John] Huston is a lean, rangy man, two inches over six feet tall, with *long* arms and *long* hands, *long* legs and *long* feet.

—Lillian Ross, *Picture* (1952)

5. [Maimed war veterans] were dispersed throughout the city and might be expected at any shopping center of the suburbs. For a *dead* and *atrocious* certainty they awaited you at this *particular* and *affluent* corner, which for that reason seemed not to be a street at all, but a pit or arena.

—Shirley Hazzard, *The Transit of Venus* (1980)

6. Only she herself knew that at the centre of her heart was a hard little *place* that could not feel love, no, not for anybody.

—D. H. Lawrence, "The Rocking-Horse Winner" (1933)

7. The will to win in Americans is so strong it is painful, and it is *unfettered* by any of the polite *flummery* that goes with cricket.

—A. J. Liebling, "Depression Kids" (1943)

8. The houses were white as *bones* in the moonlight; the quiet streets stretched out on either side like the arms of a *skeleton,* and the faint sweet smell of *flowers* lay on the air.

—Graham Greene, *The Heart of the Matter* (1948)

Choosing the Right Word

Your choice of words will help you to establish the tone of your essay, which is a reflection of your attitude toward your material—how you feel about your subject. If you are writing a theme about the president of the United States and disapprove of his policies, you might want to replace the simple word *president* with *that hotshot in the White House.* If so, you break the rule that says: Be simple and economical. You are trading economy for feeling: whether to do this, whether you gain more than you lose, is the kind of decision that you have to make every time you write. Sometimes the choice is easier because it can be made between or among two or more words: *politician* or *statesman, author* or *writer,* or *journalist* or *hack.*

Occasionally you can use colloquial or slang words—*pill pusher, flophouse, jock*—but this will depend on the level of formality on which you are writing as well as on tone. Some language that we see used regularly on the sports page is almost never used in editorials. The language you use in a letter to a friend is not the same as the language you use in a letter to a prospective employer. The language in a theme about the organization of the United Nations would usually be more formal than the language in a theme about the difficulties of staying on a diet or the virtues of jazz.

You choose your tone; you choose the level of formality on which you wish to write; and once you have made these choices, stay with them. Do not start on a humorous note and then, halfway through the theme, turn serious. Do not drift from a formal approach to one that is informal or vice versa. If you find, after you have begun to write, that you have made the wrong choice either of tone or of level of formality, do not try to patch up what you have already done. Admit your mistake and start over again. This will save you time in the long run.

Sociologists, government bureaucrats, and educational theorists are notorious for writing inflated and often indecipherable prose. In a federal government report an elevator operator is referred to as "a vertical motion engineer." Malcolm Cowley, a critic and writer, tells of a sociologist who used 160 words to say that rich people live in big houses and that poor people live in small houses; and therefore by studying an aerial photograph of a city, you can determine where the rich and the poor people live. Here is a paragraph by a pair of educationists.

> Professionals' resistance of bureaucratic rules is experienced most often when the professional thinks that adherence to bureaucratic norms will lead to violation of

professional group norms. He may well incur his colleagues' wrath but he will simultaneously gain his superiors' support. Professionals' rejection of bureaucratic standards and supervision results from conflict between professional training and socialization with its commitment to high ideals, received outside the employing organization in contrast with problems the employing organization must regularly confront. Specific to the public school setting, Beckor reports that conflict arises when principals reject teachers' need for independence. Corwin also finds that attempts to bureaucratic control of professionally oriented high school teachers leads to conflicts between teachers and administrators. The professional's conditional loyalty to the bureaucracy results from his greater identity and commitment to a professional rather than to an organizational career.

> —Harold Cox and James R. Wood, "Organizational Structure and Professional Alienation: The Case of Public School Teachers" (1980)

Translated into conventional English, here is what the passage says.

School teachers are professionals. They have learned the best ways to do their jobs through professional training and by discussing their work with other people. Principals are bureaucrats who know less about teaching than the teachers. When principals try to enforce rules that prevent teachers from doing their work in the way they think it should be done, teachers try not to obey the rules. The teachers are more loyal to their work than to the principal. This often causes friction between the principal and the teachers.

The pretentious and vague language of the original paragraph stands like a wall between the writers and the reader. We want to understand what Cox and Wood are saying, but we have to change their big words into smaller, more specific words before we can be sure of what the authors mean. And once we have made this change, we discover that the authors were themselves confused by their own language. Translated into plain English, the second sentence of their paragraph says: A teacher who resists the rules of the principal will please the principal and displease other teachers. This is the opposite of what the paragraph as a whole says and probably the opposite of what Cox and Wood thought they were saying. But in the same way that good writing is a test of logical thought, bad writing is likely to lead us into errors of logic.

Exercises

A. Study the following passage.

> The "plaint" is a traditional form of lovesong, in which a complaint about how much unrequited love hurts is addressed to a courtly lady to persuade her to bestow her favour. In a sort of relative deprivation argument, the poet may urge that the amount of pain that unrequited love brings measures the positive pleasures of requited love.
>
> This literary imagery interferes with social analysis. In fact, people in love avoid pain and seek pleasure like others; they give up hopeless unrequited loves just as insurance companies abandon the hulks that go to the bottom. Common empirical observation shows that by and large love is great fun, most people claim to have happy marriages, love of children gives some of life's deepest satisfactions, and rationality in other spheres, like consumption, often starts from premises laid down by love. It is a family's joint utility function, that is a joint utility of people who love each other, which is maximized in the market—children for example hardly ever maximize their own utilities by trade and barter in the market.
>
> —Carol A. Heimer and Arthur L. Stinchcombe, "Love and
> Irrationality: It's Got to Be Rational to Love You Because
> It Makes Me So Happy" (1980)

1. What language, if any, in the passage above seems to you to be clear and effective? Why?

2. What language, if any, should be revised to make its meaning clearer?

3. Can you find simpler and clearer words or phrases to substitute for the following: "common empirical observation," "maximize their own utilities," "relative deprivation argument"?

4. How can you determine the tone of the above passage?

B. Read the following passage carefully.

It is now a documented fact that a major shift in the value of children took place at the turn of the past century: from "object of utility" to object of sentiment and from producer asset to consumer good. Economically, a child today is worthless to his or her parents. He is also expensive. The total cost of raising a child—combining both direct maintenance costs and indirect opportunity costs—was estimated to average between $100,000 and $140,000 in 1980 (Espenshade 1980). In return for such expenses, a child is expected to provide love, smiles, and emotional satisfaction but no money. In fact, the contemporary parent-child relationship in America can be considered a prototype of a non-market-exchange relationship. Parents cannot even expect significant public support for their expenses. While in all other major industrial countries a system of family allowances grants children at least partial monetary value, in America income-transfer programs remain inadequate and mostly restricted to female-headed, single-parent households below a certain income level. The actual value of a $750 tax deduction for each dependent child is determined by the family's tax bracket. For low-income families, the deduction is minimal (Keniston 1977; Kamerman and Kahn 1978).

—Viviana A. Zelizer, "The Price and Value of Children: The Case of Children's Insurance" (1981)

1. Consider these two sentences from the middle of the passage. "In return for such expenses, a child is expected to provide love, smiles, and emotional satisfaction but no money. In fact, the contemporary parent-child relationship in America can be considered a prototype of a non-market-exchange relationship."

In which sentence is the language clearer? Which sentence is easier to read? Try to rewrite one of the sentences so that the language of both sentences is equally clear.

2. Make a list of vague and/or jargon phrases in the above pas-

sage. Try to find new words and phrases that will make the author's meaning clearer.

3. Rewrite the last two sentences of the paragraph in simple
English.

Viewing Words Grammatically

Words come first in our use of language, and we must agree
about what words mean if we are going to communicate
with one another. But it is not enough to agree on the meanings of words: we must also agree on the ways that words
should be put together to form phrases and clauses and sentences and paragraphs. Every language has its own grammar,
which consists of the rules according to which words should
be used.

Nouns

As you know, nouns are words that name things. The names
of ordinary things such as *trees* and *houses* and *subway cars* are
called common nouns; nouns that refer to specific people or
things are called proper nouns, and they begin with capital
letters: *Muhammad Ali; Albany, New York; Baker Street; the
Dallas Cowboys.*

Concrete nouns are names of things that you can see or
feel or hear or smell or taste—things that you can learn about
and identify by the use of your senses: *ice, carrot, lamp, dog,
needle, sidewalk.* If they refer to objects with which we are familiar, concrete nouns can make pictures in our minds. Say
carrot and we can see a carrot; let us read *lamp* and we can see
a lamp. We will not all see the same carrot or the same
lamp, but each of us sees a carrot sufficiently similar to everybody else's carrot not to be fooled if someone should say
carrot and hand us an egg. The noun *carrot* gives us a grip on
reality, a tool with which to deal with the rest of the world
by referring to a specific identifiable thing.

Abstract nouns are a different matter. We know that a carrot is orange, not purple; we know that a lamp is designed to give light and that a needle has a sharp point. But think of such words as *honor* and *patriotism* and *courage* and *love*. You cannot know these nouns by your senses. They have no color or taste or shape or feel or sound or smell. This does not mean that the word *honor* has no definition simply because you cannot describe it in physical terms, but the meaning of *honor* is harder to define than the meaning of *carrot*. Does honor consist in picking fights or in turning the other cheek, in not cheating on exams and stopping there or in reporting your friend whom you have seen cheating?

Because they cannot be tested by physical measurements, dealing with abstract nouns is difficult. Nobody can hand you an egg and make you believe it is a carrot. But somebody might hand you hate and make you believe, for a while at least, that it is love. You should not be fearful of abstract nouns: they are necessary to our language. They name some of our noblest instincts and some of our most deplorable attributes. But you must be careful in using them and in ascertaining how others are using them: abstract nouns are sometimes used to bring out the best and the worst in us. People have died for what they thought was love and have killed for what they thought was honor. Either way the noun was involved.

A collective noun is a word in singular form that designates a group of things: *crowd, troop, flock.* Some nouns are collective depending on how they are used. *School* is collective when it refers to a number of fish, but not when it refers to a building. *Club* is collective when it refers to the membership, but not when it refers to the place where the membership meets. Generic nouns are similar to collective nouns: they identify all members of a class or category. If you say *The robin flies south in the fall,* you mean all robins, not just one, so in that usage *robin* is generic. For many centuries *man* has been used as a generic noun meaning all people: male and female, young and old. Many people now object to this usage because of its sexist implication.

The principle to remember when you are using nouns is that you should give everything as precise a name as possible. A dog is a member of the canine family and canines are animals; so it is technically correct to call a dog an animal or a canine. But your reader will understand you better if you write dog when you mean dog. Usually we will say *car,* not *conveyance; snow,* not *precipitation; grass,* not *vegetation.* Still there will be times when you want to refer to wolves as well as dogs; to rain as well as to snow; to trains as well as to cars. *After the fire the slope was bare of vegetation. The pilgrims approached the shrine in a variety of conveyances. Dogs are the only canines I know well.* Do not hesitate to use general nouns when they suit your purpose.

Exercises _____

A. Underline all nouns in the following passages.

1. In his last years, when he was bedridden, [Allen] Tate kept photographs on his wall of John Crowe Ransom and T. S. Eliot, which he liked to point out to visitors: "Those were my two great teachers." His indebtedness he discharged in part by the help he gave, both practical and literary, to writers of younger generations. These number literally in the dozens. Only a few of their names are Robert Lowell, John Berryman, Joseph Frank, Karl Shapiro, Howard Nemerov. He was not a farmer, or hunter, or teacher, or doctor, or lawyer who happened to write; he was before anything else a member of the profession of letters, a profession that he helped to define for the twentieth century both by his critical writing and by the example of his life—by the jobs he held, and the terms on which he held them, and by the jobs he turned down, though he needed the money.

—Robert Buffington, "Allen Tate:
Society, Vocation, Community" (1982)

2. First is Jefferson, the center, radiating weakly its puny glow into space; beyond it, enclosing it, spreads the County, tied by the diverging roads to that center as is the rim to the hub by its spokes, yourself detached as God Himself for this moment above the cradle of your nativity and of the men and women who made you, the record and chronicle of your native land proffered for your perusal in ring by concentric ring like the ripples on living water above the dreamless slumber of your past; you to preside unanguished and immune above this miniature of man's passions and hopes and disasters—ambition and fear and lust and courage and abnegation and pity and honor and sin and pride—all bound, precarious and ramshackle, held together by the web, the iron-thin warp and woof of his rapacity but withal yet dedicated to his dreams.

—William Faulkner, *The Town* (1957)

1. List several common nouns from the above passages.
2. List any proper nouns you find.
3. List all the abstract nouns.
4. List all the collective nouns.
5. List any generic nouns you can find.
6. What kind of noun is each of the following words as it is used in the passages above: *nativity, miniature, rapacity?*

B. Use each of the following nouns in a sentence. Use each one so that it conveys your meaning most accurately: *animal, structure, impediment, frill, gravel, larceny, legume, shame, pleasure, bootlegger.*

Verbs

Like the noun, the verb is an essential part of speech: verbs say what things do. Everything is in some kind of motion: birds fly; dogs chase cars; people walk and scratch their heads; put in the sun, ice changes into water. Change and momentum are constants of life, and there is a verb for every alteration. Knowing these verbs, understanding how to use them properly, adds a new dimension to our ability to deal with reality. In a small and admittedly imperfect fashion our comprehension of nouns and verbs brings us to a distinction between space and time. The carrot in the vegetable bin occupies a few cubic centimeters of our mundane environment; the carrot when it is being eaten participates in a temporal sequence.

There are very few, if any, really abstract verbs, and in this respect at least the verb is easier than the noun to deal with. If you say *Tom steals, Tom lies, Tom cheats, Tom murders,* you may be slandering Tom, but the verbs stand for specific actions. A verb such as *agitate* allows some leeway of interpretation on the part of the speaker or writer, but it is not so easy to misuse as an abstract noun such as *patriotism,* and there are few such verbs in the English language.

The verb is grammatically and rhetorically by far the most complicated element of English. If you want your writing to be clear and effective, you must remember, whether consciously or subconsciously, the many rules that govern the use of verbs. To cite a simple example, verbs must agree with their subjects in number. We say *Tom runs* and *Horses run.* Both Tom and the horses are doing the same thing, but if you have a plural subject, you use a plural verb; and if you have a single subject, you use a singular verb. At this point you might say that violating the rule of agreement would not keep us from understanding one another. Saying *Horses runs,* though incorrect, is still not the same as calling books chairs. The faulty agreement might grate on some ears, but all of us would still be sure of the speaker's meaning.

But would we? Since the noun and the verb do not agree with each other, they are saying different things. We have to decide which one to believe, and we cannot believe both. Either the verb is telling the truth and one horse runs, or the noun is right and two or more horses run. The sentence cannot contain both meanings. The fact that most people would probably choose to believe the noun does not alleviate the damage caused by the grammatical error. By violating the principle of agreement between subject and verb, we have allowed doubt to enter into what ought to be a statement of utter clarity.

Consider the matter of tense. If we had only the simple present tense, all you could say would be such things as *Tom runs; Ice melts; Wood burns; Elvira plays tennis.* Adding the simple past *(Tom ran; Ice melted; Wood burned; Elvira played tennis)* helps, but you can see that the distinction between past and present is not sufficiently specific to cover much of what we want to convey in any given situation.

The simple future *(Elvira will play tennis)* is different, however, from the simple present and the simple past because to form it we have to use what is called an auxiliary verb, a verb used to form other tenses. In the simple future the auxiliary verbs are *be, have, could, ought,* and *may.* See what happens when we add an auxiliary verb to the simple present: *Elvira is playing tennis.* The addition of the auxiliary verb *is* changes the tense from simple present to progressive present—that is, the action is in progress as the words are being written or said.

In addition to progressive tenses we have perfect tenses, so called because the action they describe has been completed ("perfected"). As we have seen, if we say *Elvira plays tennis,* she may or may not be playing at this moment, but the action is not completed: playing tennis is something that Elvira does and will, we may assume, continue to do until we are told otherwise. If we say *Elvira has played tennis,* we have used the present perfect tense, and the particular action to which we refer has been completed. Elvira may play tennis again, but that is another matter. The action described by the use of the present perfect tense is a completed action.

An example of the past perfect is *Elvira had played tennis.* Here again the action described is complete, but what, you might ask, is the difference between the past perfect and the present perfect? Both describe completed actions that have taken place in the past. Put the two clauses into sentences and you can see the difference. *Elvira has played tennis for many years, so she is a good player. Elvira had played tennis for many years, so she was a good player.* The difference is a completed action in the present—*has played*—and a completed action in the past—*had played.* The future perfect also describes a completed action, but, of course, one that is completed in the future. *By the time she is twenty-five, Elvira will have played tennis for many years.* A precise use of tenses enables you to communicate with your reader without chance of misunderstanding as to when an action is occurring.

Most of the sentences that you ordinarily write or speak do not consist of only a subject and a verb. You would probably not say simply *I pay* or *I have paid.* More likely you would say *I pay my rent on the first of every month* or *I have paid three installments on my automobile note.* It is also true that good writers are not continuously conscious of the grammatical forms they are using. If you are at home with language, you do not have to remind yourself to use the simple present in one sentence and the past perfect in another. But being at home with language means that through reading and writing and study you have allowed these forms to sink solidly into your subconscious.

You may have noticed that Elvira has been the subject of all the sentences that we have written about her—which is another way of saying that all our statements about Elvira have employed the verb in its active voice. In each case Elvira acts: Elvira does something. But in the sentences *The fence was jumped by Tom, The text was studied by Tyrone, The egg was fried by Yvonne,* the verb is in the passive voice. The meaning is generally the same: either way we make the statement, an egg gets fried and Yvonne does the frying. But in *Yvonne fries an egg* our first concern is with Yvonne. Yvonne is the subject of the sentence, and as such Yvonne (both the word and the person the word names) draws our first and strongest attention. Yvonne is more important than the egg. Just the opposite is true in our perception of *The egg is fried by Yvonne.*

Here the egg gets top billing, which in most cases would not be logical. Under most circumstances the active voice is stronger and more persuasive than the passive. *A prominent source said that the flood victims were suffering severe hardships* is more effective than *It was reported by a prominent source that severe hardship is being suffered by the flood victims.* But the passive construction *Yvonne was hit by a car* is better than the active *A car hit Yvonne.* The person is more important than the automobile and should come first in the sentence.

In the use of verbs, as in the use of nouns, be as simple and precise as you can. Do not say in two or three words what you can say in one. *I decided* is better than *I reached a decision. Simon fired the gun* is better than *Simon caused the gun to fire.* Use *say* rather than *articulate; walk* rather than *ambulate; think* rather than *cogitate.* Make a habit of using the active voice rather than the passive. *Stargell hit a home run,* not *A home run was hit by Stargell.* Use verbs that help to describe the manner of an action when they can be used exactly. *He slinks,* rather than *He moves in a furtive skulking manner. She nudged her date,* rather than *She poked him gently to get his attention.* As in every other aspect of your writing, try to use verbs so that your writing will be direct and your meaning clear.

Exercises

A. Underline all the verbs, including auxiliary verbs, in the following passages.

1. A few miles up the road is a town called Nicholasville, where motel owners won't even answer the door after what they consider a decent hour. When I stopped a man on the street and asked him why this was, he said he was the chief of police and offered to rent me a bed in his house.

I went back to one of the motels, went into the office, turned on the light, picked a key off the desk and located a cabin by myself. The next morning it took me 20 minutes to find somebody to pay—and then I was told I wouldn't be welcome there in the future because my car had a license plate from Louisville. They don't care much for city boys, specially when they're roamin' round late at night.

—Hunter S. Thompson, *The Great Shark Hunt* (1977)

2. I ... watched him head toward the door, a wonderfully set-up fellow in dirty white duck trousers, sandals, and a pale-blue short-sleeved silky sport shirt that stuck to the damp pectoral muscles and almost popped over the brown biceps. His head, with a white gob cap stuck on it, was thrust forward just a little bit, and had the slightest roll when he walked, and his arms hung slightly crooked with the elbows a little out. Watching the arms hanging that way, you got the impression that they were like weapons just loosened and riding easy and ready in the scabbards. He didn't knock, but walked straight into the Boss's office. I retreated to my own office and waited for the dust to settle. Whatever it was, Tom was not going to stand and take it, not even from the Boss.

—Robert Penn Warren, *All the King's Men* (1946)

Using a dictionary, find synonyms for all the verbs in one of the above passages. Substitute your synonyms for the verbs that the author used. For example, in the Thompson passage we might say *open* rather than *answer* the door. Do any of the verbs you found give the reader a stronger sense of action or a more precise idea of what is going on than the original? Do any of your verbs weaken the action or blur the meaning? Which of your substitutions seems to you to be the best? Which is the worst? Please explain your answers.

B. Supply verbs for the following sentences. In each case several different verbs will do. For example in the first sentence of these instructions we might have said *furnish* or *give* or *provide* rather than *supply*. Try to find verbs that specify action and that seem to convey most closely the meaning you think the sentence should have.

1. The candles _____ on the now deserted table.
2. The dog _____ at the intruder in spite of Emily's command.
3. The rabbi spoke well, but the professor _____ his speech.

4. I _____ down the stairs in an effort to stop them.

5. Rain _____ us both before we could find shelter.

C. Look up the following verbs in your dictionary and use each of them in a separate sentence: *fustigate, rusticate, hebetate, permute, etiolate*. Then change the verb in each sentence to a more familiar word or set of words in an effort to make the sentence easier to understand without altering its meaning.

For example one meaning of *negotiate* is to move through, to cross, to surmount.

The girls *negotiated* the swift river without difficulty.

The girls *crossed* the swift river without difficutly.

Which of your sentences lose precision and power by the use of simpler verbs? Which are improved? Defend your answers.

Adjectives

Adjectives are called modifiers because they limit or qualify nouns or words used as nouns; modifiers help us to be precise. If your dog runs away and you go looking for him, it will not do much good to ask the first man you meet whether he has seen a dog. Most of us see many dogs every day, so we need to know what kind of dog, and this is where adjectives come into use. If you say *black dog,* you have limited the dog to the extent that you have excluded from your conversation all white, red, brown, gray, or any other color except black dogs. Since black dogs appear in various configurations, you can further limit the category of black dogs by saying *small black dog,* or by saying whether it is short-haired or fuzzy; its tail is cropped or long; its ears are floppy or stiff; it is all black or has a white spot near its muzzle. All of these details will help make your description of your dog more precise.

Adjectives are similar to nouns in that those which are concrete are some of the best and most useful words in our language. We have already spoken of colors employed as adjectives. Numbers are good modifiers: three apples, a dozen eggs, one hundred thousand people. *Cold, hot, wet, dry, live, dead, hard,* and *soft* are all adjectives which furnish specific information about the nouns they modify. The qualities that concrete adjectives represent are subject to verification. If someone says to you *I have three bicycle seats,* the speaker may be lying, but the falsehood will not reside in the language. The adjective says *three,* and you can count the bicycle seats if you want to. The same is true when you are told that *the coffee is hot* or that *the shirt is wet* or that *the spider is dead.* You can taste the coffee, feel the shirt, examine the spider.

So far, so good, but human experience is not limited to hot coffee and black dogs and dead spiders. We also have to deal with a world of ideas and values and judgments, and there adjectives become abstract. Robert Frost said that at the beginning of his career as a poet he trusted adjectives very little, and he came to trust them less the more he wrote. Other authors have said the same thing. A major reason for this distrust is that abstract adjectives sometimes assert what cannot be proved and what in some cases the author does not even believe. We can know whether a car is green or whether a bed is soft, but an apple is good or not depending on what kind of apples a person likes.

If we use *good* to modify people, the issue becomes more complex. If Jim owes you money and will not pay, you probably will not describe him as good. But if Jim gives some money to a beggar, the beggar will call him good. Who is right? *Good,* as you can see, is an imprecise word, the use of which depends, among other things, on the opinions and values of the speaker and the knowledge the speaker has about the thing of which or person of whom he speaks.

Or take as an opposite example the word *obscene.* In its old and narrow sense *obscene* designated a failure to observe common standards of conduct and decency. It applied in most cases to things that you should not do and should not say. It is a word with a bad sound and an unsavory reputation, and it is meant to condemn whatever object it modifies. Now we speak not only of obscene books but of obscene profits, obscene politicians, obscene laws (as distinct from obscenity laws), obscene university administrations, obscene automobiles. In other words obscene has become a word we use about anything that we violently dislike, and our use of it is an effort to persuade others to agree with us. There is, of course, nothing wrong in trying to persuade other people to share your point of view; but it is dishonest and perhaps dangerous to argue not with facts but with a kind of name calling; and this is what we do when we make loose use of modifiers which have firmly established connotations that are favorable or otherwise. Certainly some profits are exorbitant, some politicians are dishonest, some laws are unjust, some automobiles are wasteful. But by calling all these things obscene we deprive the word *obscene* of the specific meaning that it once had, and we deprive our listeners and readers of their right to have a reasonable argument put before them.

Like nouns, which they modify, adjectives should convey meaning as precisely as possible. Therefore look first for concrete adjectives; if they will not serve your purpose, do not hesitate to use whatever abstract adjective will help you say what you want to say. You will more often need to say *black dog* than *predatory dog,* but in some cases it will be essential that you say the dog is predatory.

Remember that modifiers of all kinds, especially adjectives and adverbs, are frequently dispensable. As William Zinsser says, "the adjective that exists solely as decoration is a self-indulgence for the writer and an obstacle for the reader." The first rule is to avoid a succession of adjectives (which are often repetitious); the second, to determine whether the adjective you choose is essential or superfluous.

The tendency to use nouns as adjectives is growing. To say *August weather* is idiomatic and appropriate, but to write the

resource development commission chairman is to use the mutilated
and obscure language of bureaucracy. The English language
is rich in adjectives—and verbs; don't make a habit of using
nouns for either.

Exercises

A. Underline all the adjectives in the following passages.

1. Two young girls in red came by and two young soldiers in
blue met them, and they laughed and paired and went off arm-
in-arm. Two peasant women with funny straw hats passed, grave-
ly, leading beautiful smoke-colored donkeys. A cold, pale nun
hurried by. A beautiful woman came along and dropped her
bunch of violets, and a little boy ran after to hand them to her
and she took them and threw them away as if they'd been poi-
soned.

—Katherine Mansfield, "Miss Brill" (1923)

2. She loved hospital work. The better we got to know her,
the more we heard about her life on those wards, in those various patients' rooms. She was a keen observer. She had a natural
sense of the dramatic—the critical, revelatory moment in a particular chain of events. Her ears were sharp, were sensitively re-
sponsive to what was being spoken and why. At times a
preacher, a hectoring one at that, she could also be a silent, attentive listener.

—Robert Coles, *Flannery O'Connor's South* (1980)

3. It is perhaps a reflection on the severe morality of that
period that despite Yetta's relatively tolerant attitude toward
sex, Sophie and Nathan felt constrained to live technically
apart—separated by a mere few yards of linoleum-covered hallway—rather than moving in together into either one of their
commodious rooms, where they would no longer have to enact
their formal charade of devoted companions lacking any carnal
interests. But this was still a time of wonderful wedlock and
cold, marmoreal legitimacy, and besides, it was Flatbush, a place
as disposed to the extremes of propriety and to neighborly

snooping as the most arrested small town in the American heartland.

—William Styron, Sophie's Choice (1979)

1. In each of the passages above, change four adjectives, substituting words of your own choosing. Try to make the meaning of each passage clearer and more precise as a result of your changes. Where do you think your changes have been most effective? Where have they been least effective?

2. Examine the passages carefully and choose four adjectives from each that you think might be deleted. Would removing these adjectives make the author's meaning more or less complete and precise? Explain your answer.

3. In the following phrases which of the adjectives are most concrete? Which most abstract? Which convey meaning most effectively? Which least effectively? Give reasons for your choices. "Cold, pale nun"; "beautiful woman"; "wonderful wedlock"; "funny straw hats"; "commodious rooms"; "cold, marmoreal legitimacy."

4. Define the moral and cultural attitude that is inherent, but not openly stated, in the use of "arrested" in passage 3.

B. At least one thesaurus lists the following pairs of adjectives as synonyms. With the help of your dictionary try to determine the most exact meaning of each word. Use each adjective as precisely as possible in a sentence. Test your results by seeing whether the synonym could be substituted for the adjective you have used without changing the meaning of the sentence. If it can, you need to use adjectives with more precision (write a sentence for each word—ten in all): *displeased, disconcerted; malevolent, malign; tempestuous, vehement; recalcitrant, insurrectionary; lush, luxuriant.*

C. Give each of the following sentences three different meanings by suggesting three different adjectives for each blank. For example, in the sentence "The _____ man engaged our sympathy," we might suggest *ragged* and *injured* and *lost.* In each case we would still sympathize with the man, but the reason for our sympathy would be different.

1. The smell of her _____ perfume lingered in the room.

2. His _____ face stared back at him from the mirror.
3. The _____ photographs were confiscated by the secret
police.
4. The _____ father looked sternly at his children.
5. The _____ crowd cheered for the vocalist.

Adverbs

Adverbs modify verbs, adjectives, or other adverbs. They
usually, but not invariably, end in the suffix *ly*—e.g., *slowly,
majestically, usually, invariably*—and most of the time they limit
the words they modify by telling where or when or how
something exists or something happens, or by showing the
degree of the quality described.

Lucy walked *south.* (where)
The mail came *early.* (when)
The burglar moved *rapidly.* (how)
The house was *very sadly* neglected. (degree)

Partly because they modify several different parts of
speech—verbs, adjectives, and other adverbs—we find in adverbs difficulties that are not usually found in the use of adjectives. Adjectives generally fall into place alongside the
nouns or phrases or clauses they are meant to modify. If you
want to say *I am looking for a small black dog,* you put *black* in
front of *dog,* and *small* in front of *black.* Adverbs, however, can
appear almost anywhere in many sentences. You might say
Excitedly I wrote to my parents, or *I wrote excitedly to my parents,* or
I wrote to my parents excitedly. In each case the adverb *excitedly*
attaches itself to the verb *wrote,* and the clarity of the sentence does not suffer.

On other occasions the improper placement of an adverb
can confuse the meaning of the sentence. *The horse I was riding furiously leaped into the creek.* Here the adverb is placed between two verbs, and it is impossible for the reader to know
whether *furiously* should modify *was riding* or *leaped.* If you say

The horse I was riding leaped furiously into the creek, or *The horse I was furiously riding leaped into the creek,* the meaning in either case is clear. What the sentence says is partially defined by the placement of the adverb. Then there are some words that are either adjectives or adverbs, depending on how they are used, and the shifting of such a word in a sentence can change the meaning drastically. For example:

> Only I drive my automobile at night.
> I drive my automobile only at night.
> I drive only my automobile at night.
> I drive my only automobile at night.

In cases of this kind be very careful, because *only,* being at different times both an adjective and an adverb, can modify nouns and verbs and adjectives and adverbs. It will modify whatever you put it near; consequently, when you change the position of *only* in the sentence, you change the meaning of the statement you are making. The first sentence says *I am the only person who drives my automobile at night.* The second sentence says *Night is the only time I drive my automobile.* The third sentence says *My automobile is the only one I will drive at night.* And the fourth says *At night I drive the only automobile I own.* The difference in meaning results from using the same words in different relationships with one another.

Adverbs ask questions. *How are you? Where is the house you want to rent?* In these constructions *how* and *where* are adverbs that inquire, rather than tell, in what condition and in what location. Conjunctive adverbs connect clauses in sentences. *You may go to the game; however, you will have to buy a ticket. Her coat was very expensive; therefore, she wanted to take good care of it.* *However* and *therefore* are adverbs that connect the first clause with the second, and in each case the adverb modifies the whole clause in which it appears. In *No, I don't want any okra, no* is an adverb which modifies the entire sentence. *O'clock* is an adverb which tells when. *It is six o'clock.* As is the case with adjectives and their objects, two or more adverbs may modify the same word or group of words. *She ran swiftly, softly, and carefully toward the highway.* But we should be wary of overusing modifiers; with a more precise verb than *ran* we could do without the three adverbs.

Because they are modifiers, abstract adverbs, like abstract adjectives, are subject to abuse. If we say *The dancers moved gracefully,* the adverb *gracefully* is open to a certain amount of interpretation, depending on our standards; but we can know in any event that the dancers are not falling on the floor and tripping one another.

What if we are told that *The economist spoke stupidly* or *The musicians played beautifully* or *The dean gave handsomely to the endowment fund?* With the use of *stupidly, beautifully, handsomely,* you leave the area of the concrete and demonstrable and enter into the realm of opinion. Your view of how the economist spoke and of how the musicians played and of how generously the dean gave will depend upon your own economic theories, your own taste and sophistication in music, your own notion of the norms of charity. In such instances our use of adverbs reflects our own opinions and values. We mean to be honest, but the fact that others may disagree with us deprives the modifiers of the specificity that more concrete adverbs possess. Even worse is the case of someone who deliberately uses modifiers to twist reality and to suppress truth. Think of the dictator who maintains that his country is democratically governed, or of the loan shark who says he will treat you fairly, or of the seller of shoddy merchandise who claims that his wares are expertly made. Modifiers, both adjectives and adverbs, provide those who can manipulate our language with a subtle and sometimes effective means by which to lie.

In the final analysis adjectives are more likely to be misused than adverbs, because most writers use adjectives more frequently than they use adverbs. And, as we saw when we discussed the necessity for agreement between subject and verb, when agreement is lacking we instinctively believe the noun. And the authority of the noun extends—if only slightly—to its modifiers. The real power of the adjective is seen when we say *Bad Tom, wicked Tom, obscene Tom* as opposed to *Tom behaves badly, Tom conducts himself wickedly, Tom lives obscenely.* The condemnation of the adjective attaches directly to Tom himself: the adjectives say to us that in his primary nature Tom is bad, evil, obscene. The denunciation of the adverb is of the form of the action: Tom is behaving badly, evilly, obscenely. Since it is Tom's behavior of which the adverb speaks and not his essential self, we have some hope that Tom the man might yet reform.

Exercises

A. Underline all the adverbs in the following passages.

> 1. A few light taps upon the pane made him turn to the window. It had begun to snow again. He watched sleepily the flakes, silver and dark, falling obliquely against the lamplight. The time had come for him to set out on his journey westward. Yes, the newspapers were right: snow was general all over Ireland. It was falling on every part of the dark central plain, on the treeless hills, falling softly upon the Bog of Allen and, farther westward, softly falling into the dark mutinous Shannon waves. It was falling, too, upon every part of the lonely churchyard on the hill where Michael Furey lay buried. It lay thickly drifted on the crooked crosses and headstones, on the spears of the little gate, on the barren thorns. His soul swooned slowly as he heard the snow falling faintly through the universe and faintly falling, like the descent of their last end, upon all the living and the dead.
>
> —James Joyce, "The Dead" (1914)

> 2. Typically enough, the struggle between the father and the teen-age son was now crystallizing: the boy who had been conspicuously precocious and a source of pride with his public recitations was inexplicably becoming an embarrassing dunce. Clifford tried, without success, to persuade his father to let him change from the study of Spanish—recommended by L. J. [Clif-

ford's father] because "someday we are going to do a lot of business with South America"—to French, which seemed to the son to be "the language of the poets." Accordingly, Clifford failed Spanish, and algebra as well. L. J. was nonplussed that his bright and obedient son, always eager to please and to placate him, appeared now to be turning into an unrecognizably stupid, lazy, pimply, willful, and useless youth. He alternated between calling him an idiot and a bum.

—Margaret Brenman-Gibson, *Clifford*
Odets, American Playwright (1981)

1. Replace two of the adverbs in passage 2 with adverbs that you have selected. Do you think you have improved the passage? Explain.

2. Joyce repeats two of his adverbs. Find synonyms for these adverbs and substitute your synonym for one of the repeated words. Do your substitutions make the passage more or less precise? Is one of your substitutions better than the other?

3. In each passage try to find a verb that will take the place of both the original verb and the adverb that modifies it. Do your substitutions improve or damage the passages? Explain.

B. At least one thesaurus lists the following pairs of adverbs as synonyms. With the help of your dictionary try to determine the most exact meaning of each word. Use each adverb as precisely as possible in a sentence. Test your results by seeing whether the synonym could be substituted for the adverb you have used. If it can, you need to employ adverbs with more precision (write a sentence for each word—ten in all): *inadequately, scantily; greedily, ravenously; splendidly, superbly; respectfully, reverently; tenderly, lovingly.*

C. Give the following sentences three different meanings by suggesting three different adverbs for each blank.

1. I take cream _____ in my coffee.
2. When the doorbell rang _____ I jumped.
3. The elusive fugitive escaped _____ from the police.
4. The lady _____ scolded the embarrassed man.
5. The professor spoke _____; the students listened _____.

Pronouns

Next to verbs, pronouns are the most complicated words in the English language, but they make writing crisp and help us to avoid what might become a painful repetition of the same noun. Because we have pronouns, we do not have to speak or write Anton's name every time we wish to refer to him. We may say *Anton moved to Spokane. He promised to write, but so far he has not written.* You will notice that in those sentences *he* has a single function: to stand for *Anton.* The pronoun *he* says nothing about its antecedent *Anton.* Like all other pronouns *he* is a neutral word. The noun or words used as a noun to which a pronoun refers may be loaded with moral significance or emotional appeal, and the pronoun will assume the coloration of its antecedent. But the same pronoun *he* is used whether you are talking about Anton or St. Francis of Assisi or Adolf Hitler. Nouns and verbs and modifiers sometimes plead cases. Pronouns do their work without prejudice or opinion.

Pronouns must be used correctly. They follow their own rules with a consistency almost like that of the law of gravity. You are free to violate it by walking out a third-story window, but the law will continue to work and the consequences are likely to be severe. A pronoun will affix itself to the first and nearest antecedent it can find. It will not matter what you had in mind when you wrote the sentence. The pronoun will perform its function, and the sentence will say what the laws of its construction require it to say, just as the force of gravity will pull everything to the ground. If you are talking to Tom's sister and the only subject of your conversation is Tom, then whenever you use or Tom's sister uses the pronoun *he,* you know it refers to Tom, for Tom is the only possible antecedent for the pronoun. But what if you are writing about Tom and Jack and Jeremiah? You might say *Tom was running, but Jack and Jeremiah were drinking beer. Jack decided to go for another sixpack. He got in his car and set out.* Jack should not be driving, but the use of the pronoun is without fault. Jack is the one to whom you want *he* to refer, and because *Jack* is the nearest noun agreeing in case and gender with the pronoun, *Jack* is in the proper place in the sentence to be the antecedent for *he.* The correct use of the pronoun makes the intended meaning clear.

But suppose someone writes: *Tom was running, but Jack and Jeremiah were drinking beer. Jack decided to go for another sixpack. In the meantime he was breathing heavily and his legs were tired.* Now, if you want to stop and figure out what the foregoing sentences mean to say, you can probably do so. Grammatically the antecedent of *he* is once again *Jack.* But if you read the passage the way it is written, it makes no sense. Jack is going to get beer. We know that Tom has been running, so we can deduce that it is Tom who is panting and feeling weary in the legs. By misusing the pronoun we say one thing when we mean another thing, thereby disrupting the orderly progress of the writing and causing the readers to have to dig out the meaning for themselves. Take an example that is even worse: *Tom was rounding the track for the third time. Jack was running up the dormitory stairs with a sixpack. Jeremiah stood at the window looking at the moon. He was breathing heavily and his legs felt tired.* The meaning here is beyond the grasp of even the most patient reader. Unless Jeremiah has a serious problem concerning moonlight, he is not the one who is panting. Yet *Jeremiah* is the antecedent of *he,* and if we search beyond Jeremiah to see what other reference *he* might have, we are at a loss to know whether it is Tom or Jack who pants and is tired.

A moment ago we used the terms *case* and *gender,* and these are the aspects of pronouns that make them more complicated than nouns. In the English language nouns are not inflected, which is to say that when you use the word *table,* it is always spelled and pronounced the same way, no matter how it is used or where it appears in a grammatical construction.

We say *The table stands in the room,* and *The coat is on the table.* But we say *He is in the room,* and *The coat is on him.* When the pronoun is the subject of a sentence or clause, it is in the nominative (subjective) case; when it is the object of a preposition as in the second sentence above, or a direct object or indirect object, it is in the objective case and in some instances the form changes. There is still another case, the possessive. *That is his coat,* or *Her dignity was impressive,* or *Its pages were torn.*

Gender, as our examples of the use of the possessive pronoun indicate, has to do with the sex of the antecedent. Since all inanimate nouns in English are neuter, and since most of us have a reasonably good sense of the difference between male and female, there is very little confusion about gender. *He stands in the room. I gave the book to him. That is his book.* In the feminine gender the possessive and objective forms are the same. *She stands here. I gave the book to her. That is her book.* In the neuter *it* and *its* do all the work. *It is here. I sat on it. Its wheels are gone. Who* and *whom* and *I* and *me,* of course, have the same form for both male and female, but they make up for this convenience by being treacherous in matters of case. One reason for this is that *who* and *whom* are often used in questions where the form of the sentence is inverted. *Whom did you see?* Turned around, the sentence reads *You did see whom. Whom* is the object of the verb *see* and is, therefore, in the objective case. *I* is frequently used incorrectly when the first person pronoun is part of a compound object. People who would never say *He gave the boomerang to I* will sometimes say *He gave the boomerang to Jack and Jeremiah and I.* Being an object of the preposition *to, I* should be in the objective case.

Who and *whom, whose, which, that,* and sometimes *what* are called relative pronouns when they are used to introduce relative clauses. *Whose, that, which,* and *what*—unlike *who*—are not inflected (which is to say they do not change endings or forms regardless of grammatical position or function): therefore they cause no difficulty. Whether to use *who* or *whom* is determined by the use of these words in the clauses in which they appear. *Tom is the man who owes us money. Who* is the subject of the clause. *Tom is the one whom I saw running. Whom* here is used as the direct object of *saw.* A greater problem with *who* and *whom* arises when a clause is the object of a preposition. When we say *To whom did Tom give his money? whom* by itself is the object of *to.* If we say *Tom gave it to whoever would take it, whoever* is the subject of the clause which in its entirety is the object of the preposition. However, since *whoever* follows *to,* we are sometimes tempted to put it in the objective case.

Demonstrative pronouns—*this, that, these, those*—are usually used correctly in sentences; but perhaps more than any other words they tempt lazy writers to express themselves imprecisely. The problem is that a demonstrative pronoun frequently refers not to a single word as an antecedent, but to one or more statements or ideas. For example, *Tom should pay me the money he owes. That I believe with all my heart.* The antecedent of *that* is the sentence which precedes it. But look at the following paragraph.

> Debt is a bad thing. Those who owe money are likely to have feelings of guilt. Those who have lent money are sometimes deprived of things they need or want because they cannot collect what is owed them. If people borrow from banks they must pay high interest, and if they fail to pay they will find themselves in court. People who default on loans are sometimes sued. I do not intend to sue Tom because litigation is expensive. This is why Tom should pay me.

What, exactly, is the antecedent of *this?* The answer is everything and therefore nothing. In the general statement about debt some of the ideas apply to Tom's situation and others do not. We cannot look to the sentence immediately preceding *this* because if we do not intend to sue Tom, the high cost of litigation is not a compelling factor in his case. He may or may not be feeling guilty. We may or may not be deprived. Admittedly the paragraph is not very good. The bad use of the pronoun makes it worse. A pronoun without a proper antecedent is an imposition on the reader, who has to stop and search out the meaning that the writer should have made clear in the first place. In some instances the meaning is never found.

The main thing to remember about pronouns is that each pronoun must refer unmistakably to its antecedent. Whenever there is any doubt concerning the reference of a pronoun, you must rewrite your sentence so that the doubt is removed. Sometimes, in order to do this, you will have to use the noun again, but it is always better to repeat the noun than to let stand a pronoun whose reference is vague. Remember too that pronouns have case and gender. Pronouns that are the objects of verbs and of prepositions will always be in the objective case.

Exercises

A. Underline all the pronouns in the following passages.

1. She kept uphill of him and behind the beacon jacket, tracking him warily, stopping when she got close, not daring to let her breath sob out on a wind that might carry the sound to him. It was hard not to pant for breath. She thought: When did I get so old and fat—a middle-aged huntress in a ratty apron, puffing uphill with the grace of a runaway tractor?

—Joanne Greenberg, *Rites of Passage* (1972)

2. Now as they went their way, he entered a village; and a woman named Martha received him into her house. And she had a sister called Mary, who sat at the Lord's feet and listened to his teaching. But Martha was distracted with much serving; and she went to him and said, "Lord, do you not care that my sister has left me to serve alone? Tell her then to help me." But the Lord answered her, "Martha, Martha, you are anxious and

troubled about many things; one thing is needful. Mary has chosen the good portion, which shall not be taken from her."

Luke 11:38–42, Revised Standard Version

1. In the passages above find four pronouns in the nominative case. Find four in the objective case. Find four in the possessive case. Justify the use of each case by explaining the use of each pronoun in the sentence in which it appears.

B. Furnish a pronoun for each of the blanks in the following sentences.

1. I send this letter to _____ it may concern.
2. I send this letter to _____ will take the time to read it.
3. This letter is very important to Jennifer and Helen and _____.
4. _____ pickles are sweeter than those.
5. _____ and _____ received _____ degrees yesterday.

C. In the following passages locate all the pronouns. Underline any pronouns that seem to you to be poorly used. Tell how you would change the faulty pronoun, or rewrite the passage to make the intended meaning more clear.

1. Swimming is my favorite sport, but since no indoor facility is available to me, I can only swim when the weather is warm. In my part of the world, spring comes late. I find this inconvenient and so does my sister. This is one reason that I want to move to Florida.

2. John saw many fish in the clear water. He ran back to get Kathy, but she had left camp. Her compass and her map were also missing. He believed he knew where she had gone, and his first inclination was to follow her. But he was tired and he wanted to fish, and he found this disheartening.

3. Those girls, whoever they may be, are always at the basketball games. They always have dates, but none of them seems to have a regular boyfriend. When the teams come onto the floor, everyone cheers, and they talk excitedly to their dates who usually respond just as excitedly. Then the girls settle down to watch, which sometimes they do and sometimes not. I find this very curious.

9

The Research Paper

Research is the process of going up alleys to see if they are blind.

—Marston Bates

The art of research is that of making a problem soluble by finding out ways of getting at it.

—P. B. Medawar

We said at the beginning of this book that you should write about what you know, and we stand by that advice. But since the aim of education is to teach you new facts and ideas, you will be asked to write about matters that are strange to you, and this means that you will have to learn about the subjects or ideas before you can write intelligently about them. The process of gathering information about a topic is called research, and its uses are not confined to the classroom. When you considered going to college, you wanted to know which schools offer the courses that interest you, which schools have the best professors, which are within your price range, and which will give you the best preparation for what you want to do in life. You got this information in part through research.

Doctors and lawyers, professors and journalists, marketing consultants and investment analysts, labor leaders and consumer advocates all spend a great deal of time doing research

or spend a great deal of money having people do their research for them. Doctors need to know the latest treatments
for diseases; lawyers must be familiar with the most recent
precedents that apply to their cases; labor leaders should
have current financial information on the companies with
which they negotiate. If you collect stamps or coins or books
or baseball cards, you must do research to learn the current
values of the items that you collect. If you are a serious collector, you will want to know the history and provenance of
individual stamps and runs of stamps; or if you collect pictures of steam locomotives, you will probably want to know
where the locomotives were built and what they pulled and
where they traveled.

Since it is an unfortunate fact that all candidates for political office are not totally frank about their past performances
and their future intentions, citizens who want to vote intelligently often research the records of candidates and their
qualifications for the offices they seek. If you are curious
about your genealogical background, whether your forebears
include officeholders and horse thieves, you can trace your
family's history by doing research. Horse players research the
bloodlines and track records of horses. Baseball fans study
and compare past and present statistics. Gardeners do research on soil and fertilizers and plants. All of us consult
friends, talk to sales people, and perhaps look at *Consumer Reports* before making a major purchase, whether it be a stereo
system or a car. Whatever our vocation may be, whatever
captures our interest, most of us regularly engage in some
form of research. This is a subject that will repay your study,
and sooner or later you will find that payment includes unexpected dividends.

Finding a Subject

As is the case with all other kinds of writing, the first step is
to find your true subject. If you are allowed to choose your

topic, choose something that appeals to you and about which you are eager to know more. If you are assigned a topic that at first seems dull, do not despair: instead try to find some aspect of the subject that interests you.

The topic, when you initially consider it or when it is first assigned to you, will probably be too big. Given the right to choose, you may decide that you want to write about sea shells or football or the environment or the judicial system or the problems of minorities. These are good topics—so good in fact that shelves full of books have been written about all of them. To choose such a topic is a good way to start, as long as you keep in mind that such large topics must be narrowed. There are thousands of different kinds of shells in the ocean and many different kinds of courts operating at every stage of government. We cannot write about all the shells or all the courts or all the levels on which football is played or about the whole environment, which is the world itself, or about the many different minorities and their many problems. You will need to find a smaller, more specific topic within the larger subject, and you may be able to accomplish this partially before you begin your research. When you think about your project, you might discover that you are most interested in the Supreme Court of the United States or in the shells to be found in the Gulf of Mexico or in college football or in the situation of American Indians. Your subject is still too big for a relatively short paper, but you will be able to narrow your topic further as you learn more about it.

Using the Library

Most of your research will be done in the library. Go to the reference room and look up your topic in an encyclopedia. (If you do not know which encyclopedia to use, ask the reference librarian. Whenever you need help in gathering information, ask the people who run the library. They are trained in the methods of research, and most of them are glad to assist you.) An entry in an encyclopedia such as the *New Columbia* or the *Americana* will give you both more and less information than you need. An article about Indians, for example, will remind you of how many different tribes there are and, consequently, how many different tribal histories and cultures. You will learn something about the religious beliefs and customs of the various tribes: how they organized and conducted their councils; how they farmed and hunted; their gods and how they worshiped; how they buried their dead; and how they initiated their young people into full tribal status. You will read about the relations of various tribes with the federal government and about where they live now and under what circumstances. The encyclopedia will give you a list of books about these native Americans and perhaps refer you to other articles in the encyclopedia; but at this point, having seen the dimensions of the general subject, you ought to define your own smaller topic.

You can approach the definition of your topic in several ways. You may decide first that you are going to confine your research to a particular tribe such as the Sioux, because you have come to suspect that although all Indians, as members of a minority, have some problems in common, each tribe has some particular problems that the other tribes do not share. Or you may discover that as you learned more about Indians from your reading in the encyclopedia, you have become fascinated with some aspect of Indian life. You may want to learn more about Indian art or Indian dances and chants or Indian costumes or food. It will be all right if you change your topic from discrimination against the Indian minority to Indian visual art. But this is the time to make your final decision. You must settle on your topic now and follow it through to the end of your paper. You cannot write an essay that is half about minority problems and half about art.

After consulting the encyclopedia, consider the three main

sources of information on whatever subject you have chosen: newspapers, magazines, and books. For newspaper articles begin by checking the *New York Times Index*. (Remember, if you cannot find this or any other reference book, ask your librarian.) Start with the most recent volume and work back in time; how far back you want to look will depend on your subject. If you are writing about some aspect of the civil-rights movement, you will want to read contemporary accounts of demonstrations or speeches or court decisions. If you are researching the latest treatment for diabetes, an article ten years old may not be of much help.

The principal index for magazine articles is the *Reader's Guide to Periodical Literature*. This index lists each signed article three times: under author, under title, and under subject. You no doubt will use the subject index more than you use the others; but in the course of your research, you may find that one or two people have written extensively on your subject. You may want to look in the author index for articles that bear indirectly on your subject and therefore may not have been listed in the subject index. Here, again, how far back you look for articles will be determined by the object of your research and how complicated it is.

You find books in the library's card catalogue, which commonly will be located in the lobby, not in the reference room. Each card in the card catalogue represents a book in the library's collection. The same card will be filed under title, author, and subject. Each card will show the author and title of the book, the subject(s) covered, number of pages, publisher and date of publication, and other information such as whether the book contains illustrations, charts, maps, tables, bibliography. In the upper left-hand corner of each card you will find a set of letters and numbers. Most libraries have diagrams posted near entries and stairways and elevators that show the general areas in which books are shelved according to the first letters of their call numbers. Individual stacks are labeled according to the full call numbers of the books they contain. The books on the shelves are arranged in numerical order. Finding the proper place in the library for a book you want is no guarantee that you will find the book. If you do not find the book you are seeking, take the title, author, and, of most importance, the call number to the circulation desk. If you are lucky, the book will be on reserve. If the book is out, the librarian will tell you when it is due in and usually will agree to notify you when it is returned and to hold it for you for a day or two. If the book is lost, the librarian will institute a search for it and notify you when the book is located.

Checking Bibliography

Many books and some magazine articles contain notes (footnotes or endnotes) and bibliographies. Notes are commonly used to indicate the source of a specific idea or fact that an author has used in a book or essay. A bibliography is a list of books and articles an author has consulted in doing research for a book or essay. Consequently the notes and bibliography that appear in a book on the subject you are researching will direct you to other books and articles on the same subject. More valuable are indexes and reference books, besides the ones we have already mentioned, which will help you in your research. Here is a partial list of them, with the indexes listed first.

For periodicals:
Humanities Index
Social Sciences Index
Essay and General Literature Index
Biography Index

For book reviews:
Book Review Digest
Book Review Index
Current Book Review Citations
An Index to Books in the Humanities

Now comes the selective list of reference books, with the emphasis on encyclopedias:

Collier's Encyclopedia
Contemporary Authors
Dictionary of American Biography
Dictionary of American History
Dictionary of National Biography
Encyclopedia Americana
New Columbia Encyclopedia
New Encyclopaedia Britannica
Webster's Biographical Dictionary
World Almanac and Book of Facts

To these lists could be added dozens of specialized indexes and reference books. We particularly recommend Oxford University Press's many works of reference, including the *Oxford Classical Dictionary*, the *Oxford Dictionary of Quotations*, and the various Oxford Companions to music, literature, and other subjects.

Making Bibliographical and Reading Notes

Notes on your reading should be kept on index cards. (The most common size is three by five inches, but you may prefer four by six or five by eight.) First make a bibliographical card for each book and article that you consult and find useful. A card for a book should contain the author, title, publisher, and place and date of publication. A card for a magazine article should include author, title, publication, volume number, and inclusive page numbers. A card for a newspaper article should contain the author (if the article is signed; otherwise alphabetize it under the article's title: do not use the word *Anonymous*), the periodical, and the date (no volume or page numbers). Be sure that the newspaper's location is shown clearly: hence *New York Times* but Greensboro,

N.C., *Daily News* or Lexington, Ky., *Herald-Leader* (for combined Sunday edition). Be sure that the name of the newspaper is correct: the *Times* of London is not the *London Times.* Do not include the location for such newspapers as the *Christian Science Monitor* and the *Wall Street Journal.*

In taking reading notes, use an individual card (extra cards if necessary) for each idea or fact or quotation. If you are in doubt about whether a fact or idea will be useful when you start to write your paper, make a note of it. To write a successful paper you will need more information—and therefore more notes—on your subject than you can properly use; and it is easier to throw away an unused card than to return to the library and reread something on which you should have made a note in the first place. Follow the same principle if you are in doubt about how much of a passage to copy for a quotation. You can cut quotations or paraphrase them when you start writing. Remember that all direct quotations and all indirect quotations (paraphrases) must be cited in your notes. But in all your note-taking be sensible: do not try to record every minute detail, and do not copy an entire paragraph when you know that you will use only one or two sentences from it. You may decide to photocopy long or complicated passages, but do not rely on the copier to do your research or your thinking, and make cards for this material as well as for other sources.

Following Correct Form

Let us now consider the matter of form—the ways in which notes and biographical entries are framed. Your teacher may instruct you to follow the form we use (the latest edition of the *MLA Handbook for Writers*) or that of another stylebook. Whatever system you use, use it consistently and use it exactly. Some of us write better than others. Some of us can do better research than others. But everybody can compose correct notes and bibliographies, and when you fail to do so, you needlessly throw away a part of your grade.

In the next several pages you will find sample bibliographical and reading cards followed by sample footnotes (or endnotes). These are representative examples, and they by no means exhaust the possibilities facing you. For more information on matters of bibliography and footnoting, consult the style manual that your teacher assigns.

Bibliographical notes should be framed exactly as they will appear in your bibliography. When your paper is completed, you will need only to choose the cards for works that you found useful (not merely those which you quoted or paraphrased) and to alphabetize those cards. Preparing the bibliography will then be mainly a matter of copying those cards, making sure that each item of information is correct.

Book by a single author:	Feldman, Anthony *Space.* New York: Facts on File, 1980.
Editors as "author":	Sagan, Carl, and Page, Thornton, eds. *UFO's—a Scientific Debate.* Ithaca, N.Y.: Cornell Univ. Press, 1972.
Article in a magazine:	Mano, D. Keith. "Cosmic Watergate." *National Review,* 32 (5 Sept. 1980), 1094-96.
Unsigned article in a magazine:	"Are 'Flying Saucers' Real? Latest on an Old Mystery." *U.S. News & World Report,* 75 (5 Nov. 1973), 75-76.
Miscellaneous entry:	Savitch, Jessica. NBC Nightly News. 16 Jan. 1982

Here are some sample cards for recording reading notes. You need not write complete bibliographical information at

the head of each card—only enough information to identify
the source clearly.

Book by a single
author:

Hynek, J. Allen. *The UFO Experience.*
The author provides statistics to
"prove" his thesis. See the table
on p. 27, the notes for chaps.
5–10, and app. 1.

Article in an
edited book:

Morrison, Philip. "The Nature of
Scientific Evidence: A Summary."
In *UFO's—a Scientific Debate,* ed.
Carl Sagan and Thornton Page.
"If we are to believe any
hypothesis, however plausible or
implausible, concerning new
events . . . then we must find a
case . . . clearly filled with
multiple, independent chains of
evidence satisfying a
link-by-link test" (p. 280). See
also p. 283: "sufficient reason;
namely, you do not simply multiply
hypotheses, you try to get by with
the least you can."

Article in a
journal:

Krutch, Joseph Wood. "If You Don't
Mind My Saying So." *American
Scholar,* 38 (Summer 1969),
370–75.
"The saucers have already taken
their place with the mystery of
Atlantis, the secret of the
pyramids, and the question of who
wrote the works of Shakespeare"
(p. 370). J. W. K. adds the Loch
Ness monster and the abominable
snowman to the list, concluding:
"Deprived of such harmless
fantasies, many an enthusiast
might fall victim to more
dangerous obsessions" (ibid.).

Unsigned article:

"Spy Satellite or UFO?" *Science
Digest,* 89 (July 1981), 108.

> The gist of this news brief is
> announced in the title. This is
> one of the latest reports on an old
> speculation about the origins of
> UFOs.

Notes can be either written or typed at the bottom of the page (footnotes) or gathered at the end of your paper (endnotes). In either case the form is the same. There are a few fundamental differences in the form of bibliographical entries and the form of notes. The author's or editor's name appears in reverse order in the bibliography, and the main elements of each entry—author, title (including subtitle), and facts of publication—are separated by periods. In the note the author's or editor's name appears in natural order, and the elements are separated by commas rather than by periods. When you return to a source already given in full, either use ibid. (the same) and another page number (if it is different) when the reference immediately follows or use a shortened version of the original note if other notes intervene.

Books by a single author:	J. Allen Hynek, *The UFO Experience: A Scientific Inquiry* (Chicago: Regnery, 1972), p. 27.
Article in an edited book:	Carl Sagan, "UFO's: The Extraterrestrial and Other Hypotheses," in Sagan and Thornton Page, eds., *UFO's—a Scientific Debate* (Ithaca, N.Y.: Cornell Univ. Press, 1972), p. 273.
Article in a magazine:	Don Berliner, "What Were Those 585 Objects the USAF Failed to Identify—and Why the Coverup?" *Science Digest*, 82 (Aug. 1977), 28.
Unsigned article:	"Are 'Flying Saucers' Real? Latest

	on an Old Mystery," *U.S. News &* *World Report,* 75 (5 Nov. 1973), 75.
Miscellaneous entry:	Barbara Rojak, Personal Interview with Jeremy Bernstein, 21 Jan. 1982.
Subsequent refer- ences to material already cited:	Hynek, *The UFO Experience,* p. 247. Berliner, *"What Were Those 585 Objects . . . ,"* p. 76.

Footnotes or endnotes can also be used to amplify a point made in the text by presenting further evidence in the same (or an opposing) vein. For example, when Barbara Rojak refers to scientific explanations for UFO sightings, she states the most common instances of those explanations in her text and then cites an uncommon instance in a note (see note 12 of her paper). In another case Barbara not only gives the source of her quotation in the text but provides a parallel quotation in her note and then cites still another related source in the same note (see her note 18).

One final point: if you are in doubt about whether to cite a source (this applies particularly to paraphrased material), always give that source rather than risk plagiarism.

Surveying the Subject

Barbara Rojak is the daughter of a computer scientist; he is interested in astronomy, and some of his friends are officers in the U.S. Air Force. Before she came to college, Barbara had heard her father and those friends discuss UFOs—un-identified flying objects—but the conversations, though they went on at sometimes tiresome length, never seemed to come to any conclusion. Nobody she had heard discuss the matter was willing to say that UFOs do exist, but neither was any-one able to prove that the strange objects that people claimed to have seen hovering in or descending from the sky are figments of the imagination. Sightings of UFOs had been reported in all parts of the country by women and men from all walks of life. For a long time Barbara had wondered: Are there really UFOs? And if so, what are they? When her teacher assigned a research paper, with students to choose their own topics, Barbara chose UFOs.

She read articles about UFOs in two encyclopedias, but like the conversations in her father's living room, neither article came to any conclusion. Some authorities, people with Ph.D.s and professorships in good universities, believed that UFOs did exist; but there was little agreement among this group concerning what UFOs were or where they came from. Among those who believed in the existence of UFOs, some people thought they came from other planets; others thought they came from another dimension in time; still others thought they were secret weapons devised by either the United States or the Soviet Union. Another group of authorities, who also had Ph.D.s and professorships at good universities, believed that UFOs were natural or manmade objects—cloud formations or weather balloons or even airplanes—that had been observed by excitable people under unusual circumstances.

At this point in her research, Barbara paused to reexamine her subject. Her original idea had been to prove or disprove the existence of UFOs, but the articles in the encyclopedias suggested to her that she might not be able finally to prove anything. Would a paper that offered no final answer be acceptable? Barbara decided that it would, since her teacher had said that the aim of research was not necessarily to prove a point, but to find out what was known about a subject and to put that information in a new perspective. Barbara still hoped that she might discover overwhelming evidence for or against the existence of UFOs, but she began to think that more likely she would write a paper that presented both sides of the UFO argument. Her conclusion would be an effort to discover why so many people found the idea of UFOs so fascinating.

When Barbara looked at the *Reader's Guide* and other indexes and the card catalogue, she was astonished at the amount of material available to her. The library contained hundreds of articles and scores of books on UFOs, more than Barbara could read if she abandoned all of her other classes and spent the rest of the term on her research paper. She was tempted to pick an article or book at random and start reading, but she went through the indexes and the card catalogue again and saw that some books and articles—or rather some authors of those books and articles—seemed to promise more than others. The name of J. Allen Hynek appeared frequently in both the indexes and the card catalogue. He seemed to have written more than anyone else on UFOs. Barbara decided to start with one of his books or articles. Carl Sagan apparently had not written as much about UFOs as Hynek, but since Barbara had read a story about Sagan in *Time* and seen him on "The Dick Cavett Show," she decided to read something by him. As Barbara discovered, Hynek believes in the existence of UFOs; Sagan does not believe in them. Each author cited other sources in his notes and bibliographies. Barbara used these sources to continue her own research. She had found her way into her subject.

Considering Quotations

Barbara discovered that taking notes on her reading was a little more complicated than it had seemed when her teacher explained it. At first she was inclined to copy long passages from books and magazines. As she worked, she learned to paraphrase the material she was reading and to shorten it in the process. Usually she could reduce a paragraph or even a page to one or two sentences. On the other hand she knew that most essays contained some direct quotations and probably her paper ought to have some too, but when should she quote and when should she paraphrase? She began to look for the answer to this question in her reading, and she found that professional writers used direct quotations either because they made points forcefully and succinctly or because they contained information that the writer wished to emphasize. She also realized that good writers paraphrase in order to simplify and to economize.

To try to sharpen her own sense of what to quote and what to paraphrase, Barbara studied the quotations in an article by Paul Restuccia in the *Boston Monthly* that described a meeting of MUFON—an organization of people who believe in the existence of UFOs—on the MIT campus. The meeting lasted for several days and many people read papers. Restuccia used few quotations, but Barbara found the ones he did use so striking that she copied some of them down for use in her own paper. One was from Hynek: "Ufology today is where chemistry was when it was alchemy." Another was from a lawyer named Peter Gerston: "If this material [evidence for the existence of UFOs] were presented in a court of law, it would prove the existence of UFOs beyond a reasonable doubt." Barbara tried to rewrite these quotations and others Restuccia had used to see if she could write a paraphrase that would have the same dramatic force and contain the same information as the quotations themselves. The quotations were better than any paraphrase she could write; and this quality, Barbara thought, could be one test of whether to use a direct quotation. Did it express the material in the most direct and effective way possible? If so, she would consider it for use in her paper.

Still Barbara remembered the warning her teacher had given the class concerning quotations: a paper could not be composed mostly of quotations with relatively few original sentences put in here and there to join the quotations. Such a paper would not really be an essay, but would instead be a compendium of notes that had not yet been integrated. Quotations, like all the material gained through research, must be digested by the writer. Barbara perceived that she would have to study her material until she knew it thoroughly; then, using that material, she would have to make her own statement about UFOs; she would have to find her own beginning, middle, and end; she would use quotations to make important points and to enhance reader interest.

Continuing to study her sources, Barbara learned that one aspect of the art of using quotations effectively is the ability to find, in a paragraph or longer passage, the one or two phrases or sentences that would best fit into the text of her essay. Sometimes this meant cutting material that was engaging in order to maintain proportion and relevance in her own paper. For example she liked this paragraph so much that her first impulse was to use it in its entirety.

> Let me remind you of a few ancient myths; Echo is a mischievous nymph who pined away for love of Narcissus until nothing was left but her voice. Earthquakes occur when a giant, chained underground beneath a mountain, tries to free himself by shaking his bonds. Lightning is a thunderbolt hurled by Zeus or Jupiter. And so on! The rain, the winds, ocean storms—all controlled by or at the mercy of some personalized deity. Man has traditionally tended to construct a myth to explain anything he cannot understand. And this is precisely the way that flying saucers or UFO's came into existence.
>
> —Donald H. Menzel, "UFO's—the Modern Myth" (1972)

Barbara decided that as striking as they were—at least to her—she would have to leave out the myths and settle for the single sentence that made one of the points she wanted to make in her paper: "Man has traditionally tended to construct a myth to explain anything he cannot understand." Sometimes, because they do not fit into the text, good quotations cannot be used at all. A distinguished writer on science, whom Barbara interviewed before she wrote her paper, said of UFOs: "The whole thing reminds me of mixed doubles: you get neither sex nor tennis playing the game this way." Barbara liked the quotation very much: she thought it both original and funny. But she was never able to integrate it into her theme. Every time she tried to use it, it called attention to itself. The wit of the quotation diverted the reader from the logical progress of the essay.

Conducting an Interview

The scientist whom Barbara interviewed was Jeremy Bernstein, a physicist who is a historian of science and a writer on scientific subjects for the *New Yorker* and other magazines. She was fortunate that Professor Bernstein was lecturing on her campus when she was doing research for her paper, and that he consented to talk to her. But there were other people she might have interviewed. Her teacher had suggested to the class that, as members of the college community, they had access to most of the faculty, most of whom were experts on something. Admittedly none of the professors of physics on Barbara's campus was as famous as Bernstein, but one or two of them had studied UFOs and could have helped if Barbara had asked them. Visiting speakers, if they have time to talk to you, and faculty members, who will usually make time to talk to you, are resources that should not be overlooked.

Barbara knew so little about interviewing people when she met Mr. Bernstein that she decided to admit her ignorance and ask him how he conducted an interview for his *New Yorker* profiles. Bernstein said that to have a good interview Barbara needed to make some advance preparations. If she were going to interview a person about his or her life, she should learn something about the person before she went to the interview, if that were possible. He said that an interviewer should not overprepare by reading too much about the subject and trying to remember everything, but if she were going to interview a person about a subject—as she was going to interview him about UFOs—she should learn enough about the subject beforehand to ask intelligent and specific questions and to understand the answers. She could not expect to learn much if she went to Bernstein and said: "Tell me all about UFOs." Some interviewers—particularly those who are inexperienced—prepare questions and write them down in advance so they will be sure to cover the subject and avoid the embarrassment of suddenly running out of things to ask. This is all right, but the interview should never be confined to such questions. Frequently the most productive questions occur to an interviewer during the course of the interview.

Jeremy Bernstein told Barbara that he uses a cassette recorder in his interviews, but that other writers such as Lillian Ross, John McPhee, and William Zinsser do not. Among the objections to the use of a recorder are that the recorder might malfunction and leave the interviewer with no record of what was said; that the writer needs to keep in physical touch with the tools of his trade; that the recorder is likely to inhibit the person being interviewed; and that taking material from a tape is tedious and time-consuming. But when the recorder works—and if you are going to use one, you should be sure that it is reliable—it preserves a complete and accurate record of the interview; the possibility of misquotation is minimized; and the interviewer is not obliged to slow down the conversation, and perhaps to break the momentum of the interview, when the words are coming too rapidly to be recorded by hand.

Whether a recorder or pencil and paper are used, the interviewer should take a few moments to get acquainted with the person to be interviewed. The more comfortable the people involved feel with each other, the more relaxed and productive the interview is likely to be. Bernstein said to have a game plan, and that his game plan is the simplest and best of all: he likes to start interviews at the beginning. If he is interviewing a person, he asks first where and when the person was born. Then he proceeds through the person's early history, always remembering the purpose of the interview, and trying to relate the questions that move from past to present to whatever makes the person worthy of an interview in the first place. (For example, if in this case Barbara were going to write an article about Jeremy Bernstein and not about UFOs, she would start with the beginning of his life; but while she asked questions about where he went to school and how he got along with his parents, she would bear in mind that he is a famous historian of science. At what point in his life did he become interested in science? Were his mother and father interested in science, and did they influence him in his choice of a profession?)

But Barbara was writing about UFOs, and to begin at the beginning of this subject, she had first to establish Bernstein's credentials as an authority on science and then to ascertain that he had studied UFOs. Here is a part of Barbara's interview.

> Q. *I know that you read widely in the sciences, especially the history of science; and I wonder to what extent you follow the news about UFOs.*
> A. Yes, I do a lot of reading about science, partly for the *New Yorker;* and I am generally familiar with this subject, especially with the book by E. U. Condon— the official report for the Air Force.
> Q. *What is your reaction to UFOs?*
> A. The thing that forcibly strikes me is just how boring this subject is. Like any other subject involving paranormal psychology, such as ESP, it just doesn't hold my attention. I don't know of any first-rate scientist, a person who is deeply engaged with the most profound questions involving science today—

such as energy, especially elementary particles, or cosmology (the study of the world's origins)—who takes this matter seriously. A man like Freeman Dyson, a physicist at the Institute for Advanced Study at Princeton who has not only one of the great minds of our time but of any time, is too concerned with the really significant questions about science to have given this matter more than a passing thought. I think that is true of other people in the sciences who are doing important original work.

Q. *Is it just a matter for speculation—or for a series of speculations—not based on real evidence?*

A. Well that is part of it, yes; but I think that the essential answer is this: even if there were UFOs, their existence wouldn't answer—or help answer—any of the most pressing questions about our world.

Q. *What is your own reaction to this issue, aside from your feeling of boredom?*

A. The whole thing reminds me of mixed doubles: you get neither sex nor tennis playing the game this way.

Q. *What engages you personally about science and scientific investigation?*

A. My feeling is that we are stuck in our world—and that as long as we are along for the ride we ought to do everything in our power to make it interesting. UFOs don't make that ride more interesting so far as the deepest reaches of science are concerned, and that is what concerns me, not UFOs.

Even though Barbara got little that she could use directly in a research paper about UFOs, she still learned a good deal from the experience. One thing was that an interview does not invariably produce the result that the interviewer is looking for. Of more importance was that Jeremy Bernstein's candid and tough-minded response forced her to look anew at her subject. She decided after talking to him that the significance of UFOs is probably more nearly cultural than scientific, and her decision helped Barbara focus her attention and conclude that her approach would be mythic, not scientific or psychological or religious, even though these considerations would necessarily play some part in the paper.

Her research was now complete, and so Barbara turned to organizing her material.

Marshaling the Evidence

Once she started to plan her paper, Barbara saw why her teacher had insisted that the members of the class make their notes on cards. The cards, each containing a single fact or idea or quotation, could be divided into groups and subgroups. They could be rearranged and put in order according to different patterns until they became an outline for a paper. Barbara found that her notes could be conveniently divided into four categories: those that supported the existence of UFOs; those that doubted the existence of UFOs; those that made statements about UFOs with which both the believers and the doubters could agree; and those that recounted the history of the UFO controversy. Barbara decided that she would begin her paper with a short history of UFOs. She would follow with a discussion of theories about UFOs with which both sides could agree. She would give the evidence in favor of the existence of UFOs; the evidence against the existence of UFOs; and she would end with her own conclusion. As we have said, she would not be able to use all the notes she had taken. But neither would she find a gap in her material that would force her to return to the library and do more research after she had begun to write.

A Sample Paper: "UFOs—Reality or Myth?"

Here is Barbara's paper.

UFOs—Reality or Myth?

UFOs first captured national attention in 1947 when
there was a rash of sightings reported in the press.
Since that time UFOs have been reported fairly regularly. During the past year or so there have been
various sightings announced in the press—for example
the *New York Times* reported on April 20, 1980, that
a UFO had been spotted in Scarsdale, New York (investigation shows that this strange apparition in
the sky was a small plane equipped with special
lights). On September 14, 1981, the *Times* ran a
story about a Chinese news agency on the mainland
that was swamped with calls about a UFO (it turned
out to be a research balloon). And earlier, on January 15, 1979, *Newsweek* reported a UFO over New Zea-
land. So we see that the UFO phenomenon is not
limited to the United States.

The phenomenon is now thirty-five years old, and
no end is in sight. If one studies the history of
UFO sightings and the general attention that they
have received in official circles (particularly the
U.S. Air Force), in the national press, and by various segments of the public, especially professional
and amateur scientists, one can draw several conclusions that few people would argue with. The first is
that more and more people are inclined to believe
that UFOs are of extraterrestrial origin; the second, that their occupants have good, not bad, inten-

tions. Next comes the inference that as time goes on
more and more reasons are being advanced for their
existence, and in this connection the unbiased observer is forced to decide that the entire phenomenon tells us something (but what?) about the world
that we live in. The first conclusions are essentially factual in nature and can be shown by a study
of statistics;[1] the others are admittedly speculative
in part but still are basically factual, especially
the conclusion involving the motives of various persons and groups who believe that UFOs come from
other worlds (or other dimensions of reality). In
other words, as the years go by, UFOs are appealing
to more and more people for more and more reasons.

In late December of 1966 J. Allen Hynek published
an article in the *Saturday Evening Post* that was reprinted shortly thereafter in the *Reader's Digest* in
abbreviated form. In "Flying Saucers—Are They Real?"
Professor Hynek, a well-known and highly respected
astronomer then teaching at Ohio State University,
writes in part: "During the years that I have been
its consultant, the Air Force has argued that UFOs
were hoaxes, hallucinations or misinterpretations of
natural phenonomenon. For the most part I would
agree. . . . But I cannot explain them all." He goes
on to say: "The Air Force has never really devoted
enough money or attention to the problem to get to
the bottom of these puzzling cases. The UFO evalua-
tion program, known as Project Blue Book, is housed

in one room at Wright–Patterson."² Hynek ends his article by announcing the news that a committee of
distinguished scientists headed by E. U. Condon will
give the matter proper and unbiased consideration.
But the Condon report, although widely heralded in
advance, settled little or nothing—except to prove
to the satisfaction of the Air Force that UFOs
should not be given further attention.³ Since 1969
when the Condon committee finished its work and published its report, there has been no official clear-
inghouse of information on UFOs within the U.S.
government. UFOs are now officially studied only by
various private organizations.

In this article (which has been followed by many
other articles and two books that he has since written), Mr. Hynek presented four categories to include
the several explanations for UFOs. They are as follows:

1) UFOs are sheer nonsense and can be explained
in every instance as the result of hoaxes or hallucinations.

2) UFOs are advanced military weapons belonging
to either the Soviet Union or the United States
which for security reasons the U.S. government does
not wish the general public to learn about.

3) UFOs do exist in fact and come from outer
space.

4) UFOs are natural phenomena that exist but for

which we have no scientific explanation—which is to
say that we do not know or understand their origins.[4]
It seems clear that the general public puts considerable credence in the second and third explanations. On the other hand the scientific community
for the most part dismisses UFOs as so much moon-
shine, but the believers among the scientists would
incline to the fourth explanation, which includes a
religious or mystical origin. Since Mr. Hynek wrote
this article, things have gotten vastly more complicated; and various matters concerning UFOs are far
from being settled.

Hynek now, fifteen years later, is not minimizing
the problems that face believers. When he addressed
three hundred members of the largest organization of
UFO buffs in the country, Mutual UFO Network, at its
annual meeting in Cambridge, Massachusetts, in the
fall of 1981, he said: "Ufology today is where chemistry was when it was alchemy," adding: "We have to
develop professional standards. Otherwise the buffoonery will continue."[5]

The buffoonery has taken many different forms, the
most obvious of which is the outright hoax perpe-
trated by jokesters. There are many more hucksters
than jokesters, however; and a good many people with
dubious credentials have made money writing and lecturing about UFOs. A reporter commenting on MUFON's
meeting at MIT's Kresge auditorium in Cambridge

wrote: "If a UFO were to land on the lawn . . . , most
members of this gathering would fall to their knees
or run for their measuring instruments, but some
would be jockeying the aliens for exclusive publication rights."[6] One of these zealots is a police pho-
tographer who claims to have photographed over 175
UFOs over Hillsborough, New Hampshire, and gathered
375 affidavits from as many witnesses. Still, according to Hynek and other reputable scientists,
roughly 20 percent of the reported sightings have
never been satisfactorily explained, even in the
Condon report.

There are many explanations for UFOs and their origins. One of the most popular is another version of
the conspiracy theory that appeals to many Americans
at one time or another. Many people believe that the
federal government, particularly the U.S. Air Force,
is suppressing evidence that would show once and for
all that UFOs exist and are here to stay. One of the
most outspoken of MUFON's members, Stanton Friedman,
says that a UFO crashed in Roswell, New Mexico, in
1947 and that the army covered up the evidence, including not only the crashed space ship but its hu-
manoid occupants. Mr. Friedman says that this and
other similar incidents constitute a "Cosmic Watergate."[7]

The conspiracy theory, however believable in some
respects, does not account for the origins of UFOs:
it merely tells us why no one in the U.S. government

has come forward and said that UFOs are not a fiction. There are more theories about the origins of
UFOs than there are hard facts to support the
theories. Each theory has its champions, which include distinguished scholars and thinkers. The most
popular theories involve religion, and various com-
mentators, particularly Ted Peters, a Lutheran minister with a Ph.D. in religion, believe that the
extraterrestrial beings manning UFOs are in some way
divinely created and motivated by the benevolent
God.[8] Edward Boudreaux, a professor of chemistry who
believes the literal truth of the Bible, says that
UFOs are the product of Satan, who is leading us to
idolatry and away from God.[9] Other theories include
speculations based on anthropology (one version is
that extraterrestrial beings come to earth to study
its civilization the way Margaret Mead studies prim-
itive tribes in exotic lands; another related version is that UFOs came to the earth hundreds or
thousands of years ago and left evidence to this effect), psychology (UFOs are psychic projections),
and studies in time (UFOs are spaceships coming from
our future into the present).[10]

The scientific explanations based on the claims
that UFOs are mirages or illusions are also many and
varied. In 1973 *U.S. News & World Report* put these
scientific explanations under the heading *electronic
phenomenon theory.*[11] These chiefly involve ball
lightning (a rare but natural electrical discharge

that produces fireballs). Another natural phenomenon
is the sundog, an effect caused by the interaction
of sunlight and ice crystals in which a disklike
image is projected. There are many such specific explanations and rebuttals.[12]

Scientists such as Carl Sagan who seek to disprove
the existence of UFOs have made strong cases that
most laymen would find compelling. But most laymen
do not read books by Carl Sagan, before or after
they witness strange occurrences in the sky. In one
of Sagan's latest reports on the subject, he says:
"Despite all the novelties of our times, there is a
kind of drudgery to everyday life that cries out for
profound novelties; and the idea of extraterrestrial
visitation is a culturally acceptable novelty."[13] In
the decade that has passed since Sagan made this observation, UFOs have become still more acceptable to
the general population. Even though the public is
increasingly inclined to believe in the existence of
UFOs as actual objects from other worlds (including
other galaxies or solar systems and other dimensions
of time and space), it appears that we are still a
long way from proving their existence in a way that
satisfies scientific canon. In "The Nature of Scientific Evidence" Philip Morrison describes proper
scientific procedure and deduction as resting on
"independent and multiple chains of evidence, each
capable of satisfying a link-by-link test of meaning." He continues: "If we are to believe any hy-

pothesis, however plausible or implausible,
concerning new events—particularly those that do not
satisfy the easy quality of being reproducible at
will . . . we must find a case clearly filled with
multiple, independent chains of evidence." Professor
Morrison makes a related logical point in an effort
to clinch his case. To present sufficient reason to
prove a particular matter, he argues, "you do not
simply multiply hypotheses, you try to get by with
the least you can."[14] Every argument for the existence of UFOs depends upon a series of hypotheses,
none of which rests on incontrovertible evidence.
The discovery of such evidence seems a long way off.
According to Jeremy Bernstein many of the most tal-
ented physicists in the country are "too concerned
with the really significant questions about science
to have given this matter more than a passing
thought."[15]

One does not have to ascribe corrupt motives to any
particular group or person to see that the various
parties involved in the UFO controversy are all
driven by powerful urges and moved by considerations
that are often deeply personal to the point of being
irrational. What they have in common besides a fascination (scientific, religious, or otherwise) in
UFOs is the economic motive, whether or not they are
willing to acknowledge that motive. Chief among
those moved by economic considerations would seem to
be George Adamski, a short-order cook who parlayed

his alleged meeting and conversations with the space people from Venus into fame and fortune. Adamski's notoriety resulted from his writing and lecturing about his experiences in the 1950s. Of course one can argue that many of the skeptics have the same economic motive as the popularizers, but the skeptics (who are called debunkers by the true believers) doubtless have a good deal less at stake, especially since there is less market for their point of view.

As time goes on, UFOs are being used to invoke explanations for more and more mysteries about human experience and the universe. Sir Fred Hoyle, a London scientist, in January 1982 presented his theory that life on this world was started by organic materials sent here thousands of years ago by a dying civilization.[16] Presumably these materials were transmitted by what we would now call UFOs.

Such a viewpoint joins physical and metaphysical theory. The word metaphysical is used here to characterize the realm of experience that is ultimately nonrational, transcendental, and religious. Hoyle's theory will probably be carefully examined by the creationists, who are arguing that the world was created along the lines that are described in the book of Genesis. Ministers such as Ted Peters may soon be arguing that God's chariots are UFOs, giving us a new version of Erich von Däniken's immensely popular theories of the early 1970s.

It is interesting to see how UFOs started in the late 1940s and early 1950s as being the instruments of totalitarian governments (especially the German Third Reich and the Soviet Union)[17] and have "progressed" in the popular mind to being the instruments of a benign God. The vision has changed from being malevolent and secular to being benign and utopian. It would appear that many people feel forced to invent new myths in order to understand the mysteries of this world and the worlds beyond. As Donald Menzel has written, "Man has traditionally tended to construct a myth to explain anything he cannot understand."[18] One thing seems to be sure: UFOs will be a fact of cultural life in the United States for a long time to come, but so far they have told us more about our own culture than they have revealed about other worlds. Joseph Wood Krutch put the matter well as long ago as 1969 when he wrote: "The saucers have already taken their place with the mystery of Atlantis, the secret of the pyramids, and the question of who wrote the works of Shakespeare." (He added the Loch Ness monster and the abominable snowman to this list of mysteries.) Mr. Krutch went on to say: "Deprived of such harmless fantasies, many an enthusiast might fall victim to more dangerous obsessions."[19] It is easy to agree with Krutch that such thinking is essentially harmless and that, as obsessions go, this one seems unusually persistent as well as unusually benign.

UFOs for the time being at least seem to have a
stronger mythic force than a scientific factuality.
The interest of evangelical and other religious
groups seems to guarantee their acceptance among increasingly larger numbers of the American public.
UFOs, it seems safe to predict, will be with us for
the foreseeable future and probably a long while
after that—probably a lot longer than the Loch Ness
monster or the abominable snowman. The reason boils
down to this: there is something in UFOs for everybody, even the unbelievers.

NOTES

[1] These statistics appear in the most persuasive
studies of the subject. See, for example, J. Allen
Hynek, *The UFO Experience: A Scientific Inquiry*
(Chicago: Regnery, 1972), esp. the table on p. 27,
the notes for chaps. 5–10, and app. 1.

[2] J. Allen Hynek, "Flying Saucers—Are They Real?"
Reader's Digest, 90 (March 1967), 62–63.

[3] See, for example, Carl Sagan and Thornton Page,
eds., *UFO's—a Scientific Debate* (Ithaca: Cornell
Univ. Press, 1972), esp. James E. McDonald, "Science
in Default: Twenty-two Years of Inadequate UFO In-
vestigations," pp. 52–122.

[4] Hynek, "Flying Saucers—Are They Real?" pp. 64–65.

[5] Paul Restuccia, "Revelations in a Flying Saucer:
The Theology of UFOs," *Boston Monthly*, 3 (Dec.
1981), 15.

[6] Ibid.

[7] D. Keith Mano, "Cosmic Watergate," *National Review*, 32 (5 Sept. 1980), 1096. Don Berliner makes an
observation that answers the conspiracy theory: "It

seems clear indeed that the main interest of the
USAF all those years concerned—and, seemingly, still
does—not the nature of UFOs but the concealment of
its own inability to cope with the elusive problem."
See "What Were Those 585 Objects the USAF Failed to
Identify—and Why the Cover Up?" *Science Digest,* 82
(Aug. 1977), 28.

[8] Ted Peters, *UFOs—God's Chariots? Flying Saucers in
Politics, Science, and Religion* (Atlanta: John Knox
Press, 1977).

[9] Ibid., pp. 167-68.

[10] For a good summary of these theories see Anthony
Feldman, *Space* (New York: Facts on File, 1980), pp.
292-99.

[11] "Are 'Flying Saucers' Real? Latest on an Old Mystery," *U.S. News & World Report,* 75 (5 Nov. 1973),
75-76.

[12] Of these instances one of the most interesting is
described in Philip Morrison, "The Nature of Scientific Evidence: A Summary," in Sagan and Page, eds.,
UFO's, pp. 281-82. In this case a sighting recorded
on motion-picture film turned out to be the distorted image of "the tail of the very aircraft in
which the camera was riding, perceived through the
extraordinarily astigmatic lens of the thick edge of
one of those round plastic windows set into the
pressure cabins in some aircraft" (p. 282).

[13] "UFO's: The Extraterrestrial and Other Hypotheses," in ibid., p. 273.

[14] Ibid., pp. 280, 283.

[15] Personal interview with Jeremy Bernstein, 21 Jan.
1982.

[16] Jessica Savitch, NBC Nightly News, 16 Jan. 1982.

[17] See Randall Fitzgerald, *The Complete Book of Extraterrestrial Encounters* (New York: Collier Books,
1979), pp. 109-11 et passim.

[18] Menzel, "UFO's: The Modern Myth," in Sagan and
Page, eds., *UFO's,* p. 123. Cf. this statement by

Menzel from his book with Ernest H. Taves, *The UFO Enigma: The Definitive Explanation of the UFO Phenomenon:* "This book is a solid steppingstone out of the morass of unconscious yearning for supernatural intervention" (p. xiv). Although Menzel does not mention it, Carl G. Jung writes of myth and UFOs in *Flying Saucers: A Modern Myth of Things Seen in the Skies* (1959). In reviewing the book, Philip Wylie says: "Dr. Jung's book is more interesting for its asides—which brilliantly present his theories and, with them, explore the unconscious terrors of modern men—than for its contemplation of the saucer-myth." "Of Stars and Saucers," *Saturday Review of Literature,* 42 (8 Aug. 1959), 17.

[19] "If You Don't Mind My Saying So," *American Scholar,* 38 (Summer 1969), 370.

BIBLIOGRAPHY

"Are 'Flying Saucers' Real? Latest on an Old Mystery." *U.S. News & World Report,* 75 (5 Nov. 1973), 75-76.

Berliner, Don. "Two Close Encounters of the 'Real' Kind in Air Force Files." *Science Digest,* 83 (Apr. 1978), 21-24.

_____. "What Were Those 585 Objects the USAF Failed to Identify—and Why the Cover Up?" *Science Digest,* 82 (Aug. 1977), 24-28.

Butler, David, "Touch of Venus." *Newsweek,* 93 (15 Jan. 1979), 47.

Feldman, Anthony, *Space.* New York: Facts on File, 1980.

Fitzgerald, Randall. *The Complete Book of Extraterrestrial Encounters.* New York: Collier Books, 1979.

Fowler, Raymond. *Casebook of a UFO Investigator: A Personal Memoir.* Englewood Cliffs, N.J.: Prentice-Hall, 1981.

Herbert, Roy. "Bathetic Case of Ball Lightning." *New Scientist,* 90 (28 May 1981), 544.

Huyghe, Patrick. "U.F.O. Files: The Untold Story."
    New York Times Magazine. 14 October 1979, pp. 106–
    12.

Hynek, J. Allen. "Flying Saucers—Are They Real?"
    Reader's Digest, 90 (March 1967), 61–65.

_____. *The UFO Experience: A Scientific Inquiry.* Chi-
    cago: Regnery, 1972.

_____, and Ford, Barbara. "Science Takes Another Look
    at UFO's." *Science Digest,* 73 (June 1973), 9–13.

Krutch, Joseph Wood. "If You Don't Mind My Saying
    So." *American Scholar,* 38 (Summer 1969), 370–75.

Mano, D. Keith. "Cosmic Watergate." *National Review,*
    32 (5 Sept. 1980), 1094–96.

Menzel, Donald H., and Taves, Ernest H. *The UFO
    Enigma: The Definitive Explanation of the UFO Phe-
    nomenon.* Garden City, N.Y.: Doubleday, 1977.

Peters, Ted. *UFOs—God's Chariots? Flying Saucers in
    Politics, Science, and Religion.* Atlanta: John Knox
    Press, 1977.

Restuccia, Paul. "Revelations in a Flying Saucer:
    The Theology of UFOs." *Boston Monthly,* 3 (Dec.
    1981), 13, 15–16.

Rojak, Barbara. Personal interview with Jeremy Bern-
    stein. 21 Jan. 1982.

Sagan, Carl, and Page, Thornton, eds. *UFO's—a Scien-
    tific Debate.* Ithaca, N.Y.: Cornell Univ. Press,
    1972.

Salisbury, Frank B. "Recent Developments in the Sci-
    entific Study of UFO's." *Bio Science,* 25 (Aug.
    1975), 505–12.

"Spy Satellite or UFO?" *Science Digest,* 89 (July
    1981), 108.

Von Däniken, Erich. *Chariots of the Gods: Unsolved
    Mysteries of the Past.* Trans. Michael Heron. New
    York: Putnam, 1970.

Wylie, Philip. "Of Stars and Saucers" (review of
    *Flying Saucers: A Modern Myth of Things Seen in the
    Skies* by C. G. Jung). *Saturday Review of Litera-
    ture,* 42 (8 Aug. 1959), 17.

A Writer's Checklist

Good prose is like a windowpane.

—George Orwell

The art of writing good prose or poetry lies in the art of correcting. This has to be painfully acquired.

—Gerald Brenan

The axioms that follow are drawn principally from this book as a whole and are a distillation of it, but some of them have not been discussed or even touched upon elsewhere, and others are presented with a new focus or fresh emphasis.

We are not implying that these suggestions describe the only way to write, but we firmly believe that the strategy and tactics that they delineate reflect the general approach of the vast majority of writers, not only professionals. Every writer writes in his or her own way—Hemingway while standing, Schiller while enveloped in the odor of rotting apples, Emily Dickinson while splendidly isolated from the mundane world, E. B. White while listening to the waves lap against the pilings of his boathouse—but all good writers share certain basic procedures that we are describing here in a way that is specific enough to be useful but elastic enough not to be confining.

1. Don't start writing before you are ready to begin—before you have accomplished whatever preparation is necessary for the job at hand and have thought through your subject. But don't wait until your material (reading, notes, ideas) has gotten cold before you get your essay or narrative under way.

2. Remember always that writing is a lonely pursuit (Robert Penn Warren calls it "Being alone with the alone") and that no one can give you any real help while you are in the throes of writing. You can be given effective help only after you have written at least a first draft.

3. Be sure that your beginning is a true beginning and not a warm-up exercise. Try to introduce the subject in the first sentence. Do not delay the introduction beyond the first paragraph.

4. Write as much as possible in a single sitting. Writing only a paragraph or two at a time will probably give your essay a choppy effect because it will lack consistent patterns of style, tone, and development. Try to maintain the momentum of your writing.

5. Don't be afraid to start over if you find that in spite of your best efforts your writing is clumsy and your material resists your efforts to organize it into a coherent whole. The fault may lie in your original conception. Look once more at your beginning and at the principles on which you planned your essay. See if the design that you are following is workable as a whole and is sufficiently specific.

6. Make sure that your paragraphs are generally the same length. Some will naturally be longer than others, but if some consist of a few lines and others of a page, you may be having trouble with organization and proportion. For emphasis or development you may occasionally write exceptionally short or long paragraphs.

7. Avoid lengthy and unnecessary transitions and don't give traffic signals to the reader by announcing what you plan to do or have done. If your material is properly organized and developed, you will not ordinarily have to explain how one idea or incident logically follows another. Resist the temptation to sum up the ideas in one paragraph or section as a means of getting into the next paragraph. The best technique is to invent and continue to move forward. Do not circle your quarry or back away from it.

8. Whenever you make a generalization, be sure that you give at least one concrete instance to support it.

9. Don't include in your piece all the material that you have gathered. Choose the most important and representative parts or scenes. If, however, you are in doubt concerning whether to include a scene in a narrative or a point in an essay, put it in, because when you are revising it is easier to delete extraneous material than to add something essential.

10. Conclude when you have covered your subject, but don't slight your ending. Many inexperienced writers simply quit at the end, stopping without having clinched the point toward which they have been moving throughout.

11. Try to write far enough in advance of your deadline so as to give yourself a day or two for the manuscript to sit between its completion and its final revision. In that revision, work straight through your copy. Make the easiest changes first. Cut superfluous words and repetitious sentences. Rework awkward constructions. Skip over particularly difficult passages and return to them later. If the essay seems poorly constructed or badly executed throughout, make an outline of what you have written and determine what logical or dramatic flaws exist in your structure.

12. After your final revision make another check of your facts. This includes facts proper (e.g., the year that prohibi-

tion ended in the United States) and the accuracy of any quoted material. Proper names, titles, quotations, and dates should be checked with special care.

13. When your revision is as good as you can make it, go through your fair copy one final time before submitting it.

14. Write always by ear as well as by eye. If you are in doubt about the idiom of a construction, read it aloud. Remember that your reader will often be as aware of the sound of what you write as of its appearance on the page.

15. If you use colloquial expressions, dialect, and slang for a special effect, do so without apology: do not put the word or phrase in quotation marks. Make sure that your use of such language is both occasional and accurate.

16. The cliché should always be avoided. If you suspect that the expression you have in mind is a cliché, ninety-nine times out of one hundred (itself a cliché) you will be right. Clichés have become bankrupt through overuse and have lost their power to convey meaning.

17. Write always with the emphasis on strong nouns and strong verbs. Don't say *querulous old man* for *codger* or *irritable, ugly old woman* for *crone*. Say *blame*, not *lay the blame on; praise*, not *give praise to; plead*, not *make a plea*. Don't use two or more words when one will do. Avoid the use of the passive voice.

18. Avoid the overuse of modifiers. Don't pile up adjectives and adverbs in an effort to compensate for having chosen vague nouns and weak verbs (see number 17). Ordinarily one modifier is enough; frequently it is too much. When you find that you are regularly using two or three adjectives to describe every noun, you need to make the noun more specific and rein in the modifiers. The same principle applies to adverbs and verbs.

19. Don't regularly begin your sentences with a conjunc-

tion. The worst possible way to begin a sentence is with the conjunctive adverb *too* or its cousin *also*. To use a coordinate conjunction such as *and* or *but* or a subordinate conjunction such as *however* is not much better. If you cannot effect a transition without using such an obvious device, the whole logic and development of your writing are questionable. This axiom applies particularly to the opening sentence of a paragraph, which seldom, if ever, should begin so lamely as with a conjunction.

20. Be careful in using expletives and vulgar language generally. There is a considerable difference between using such a word because it is the only possible remark (usually in dialogue) and using it because you are showing off.

21. Puns should be regarded with caution. The pun has been in ill repute since the 1600s, and one should not swim against the current of usage in such matters unless the given pun is extraordinarily apt. In any event the pun should be used only rarely.

22. Verbal tics, whether your own or common property, should be held to a minimum. Some examples are *you know, by and large, on the other hand, the fact that, indeed.*

23. Use the natural idioms of the English language in preference to foreign phrases and tags, jargon, slang, and cant terms. The accent should be American, not British.

24. Use words exactly. Don't assume that a journalist—or anyone else—knows what a word means, especially when it is a popular word. If you have any doubt about the meaning of a word, look it up in a good current dictionary. If you see or hear a word used recklessly and often, find another to use in its stead.

25. Avoid indirection and elegant variation in language. If you are discussing a spade, don't call it a digging instrument. Use common language in preference to parlor language:

sweat, not *perspiration; die,* not *pass away.* Don't write as though you have swallowed either an unabridged dictionary or a thesaurus. Use simple language (the nickel word) in preference to complicated language (the twenty-five-cent word), short words of Anglo-Saxon origin in preference to long words of Latin origin.

26. Don't hedge. Writers who regularly salt their prose with such words as *somewhat, rather, perhaps, kind of* (and worse, *sort of*), and *possibly* give their readers the idea that they are afraid to make a judgment and that they don't know what their position is.

27. Avoid a succession of similar sentences and structures. Don't, for example, write a series of short choppy sentences or a series of complex sentences, each of which begins with a subordinate clause. (The overuse of inversions by *Time* reporters led Wolcott Gibbs to write "Backward ran the sentences until reeled the mind.")

28. Don't write according to formula. The usual scholarly article states the subject to be investigated, surveys the relevant scholarship, and works out the "problem." Any such procedure is likely to be crippling to the writer.

29. Our axioms should not be taken as absolute. As George Orwell said in a similar context, "Break any of these rules sooner than say anything outright barbarous."

A Glossary of Diction, Grammar, and Usage

Most of the grounds of the world's troubles are matters of grammar.

—Montaigne

'Tis very difficult to write like a madman, but 'tis a very easie matter to write like a fool.

—Nathaniel Lee

The glossary that follows covers a wide range of grammatical and stylistic matters. There are definitions of grammatical terms—e.g., verbs (including separate entries on verbals, infinitives, mood, and tense); there are entries devoted to commonly confused pairs of words such as *imply* and *infer;* there are pointed discussions of subjects such as dictionaries and stylebooks; there are brief inclusive entries on habits and tendencies such as adverbial shortcuts, overblown language, qualifiers, and vulgar language. The glossary provides a short synoptic grammar and a succinct comprehensive stylebook. Unlike the text that precedes it, the glossary is mainly negative in force, usually containing advice on what not to do rather than what to do.

Abbreviated expressions are a form of verbal shortcut that, with a few exceptions such as *e.g.* *(for example)* and *i.e.* *(that is)*, have little or no place in formal writing. There are well-known instances of such usage *(ad* for *advertisement, taxi* or *cab* for *taxicab, bra* for *brassiere, exam* for *examination, lifestyle* for *style of life)* that have passed into accepted usage, but the careful writer should be chary of curtailed words. *Vibrations,* for instance, becomes *vibes; hyper* is used for *hyperactive* or *hypersensitive* (which?); *God bless you* becomes *God bless* (whom?); *duplicate* (noun) is shortened to *dupe,* a misleading usage in many contexts. Avoid the use of initials for words or phrases (except for such well-known instances as *RSVP).* See **Adverbial shortcuts.**

Absolute words. *Certain, complete, crucial, dominant, equal, perfect,* and *unique* are among the words that properly should not be used in the comparative degree. Something is *unique* or it is not; something cannot be *more unique* than anything else, just as John's setter cannot be more pregnant than Jill's dachshund (although one pregnancy can be more advanced than the other). The current tendency to inflate the commonplace by using overstatement results in such incorrect usages as: Kareem Abdul-Jabbar and Keith Benson were the *most dominant* players on the floor tonight. *(Correct:* Kareem was the dominant player on the floor tonight.) *Crucial* means critical, not important (hence: The success of the heart operation was crucial to John's living for another five years). To add an adverb such as *absolutely, perfectly, purely,* or *wholly* to an absolute adjective is as bad as or worse than using an expression such as *most dominant. Wrong:* We are absolutely certain that Smith will win the race. *Wrong:* That is the most complete account of the expedition. *Right:* That is the most nearly complete account of the expedition. There are famous instances of the comparative degree's being used with absolutes (as in "more perfect union" in the Declaration of Independence), but unless you are a master of prose, avoid such constructions.

Abstract words. In a famous passage in *A Farewell to Arms* Hemingway inveighs against abstractions such as *honor* and *patriotism* and *heroism,* suggesting that they are often phony, especially in war. Abstractions are used by totalitarian governments to manipulate the masses; they are as readily used by advertisers in capitalist nations—and by people in many other walks of life. "The unemployment situation in the auto industry has deteriorated to a tragic position of near-record levels," a union representative says solemnly at a news conference. Translated into concrete language, this reads: "More auto workers are unemployed now than at any time since the 1930s." To be concrete and specific is usually to be direct and succinct. Consider the difference between saying "The weather will be of a showery nature" and "It will rain sporadically." Avoid the lure of the abstract.

Adapt, adopt. *Adapt* means to make fit, often by change; *adopt* means to take something as it is (To adopt a successful defensive strategy at El Alamein before assuming the offensive against Rommel, Montgomery realized he must adapt his tanks into fixed artillery to protect them from damage or loss).

Adjectives are words that modify nouns or pronouns. *Attributive* adjectives usually come before the word modified (the *shabby, frail* derelict), predicate adjectives *after* the word (The day was *overcast*). Adjectives are classified as *demonstrative* (this, that, these, those); as *descriptive (common:* young, red, fat; *proper:* English, July, Shakespearian); as *indefinite* (each, both, either, such, some); as *interrogative* (which, whose, what); as *limiting* (the articles *a, an, the);* as *numerical* (one, ten, twenty;

first, fifth; triple, fourfold); as *possessive* (my, Martha's); and as *relative* (whose, which, what: We know *which* students were late). For *concrete* and *abstract adjectives* and other related matters, see Chapter 8: "Words."

Adverbial shortcuts. Americans often think of themselves as being so driven by the fast pace of life in the United States that they must use shortcuts in language. These shortcuts often result in ambiguity, comical or otherwise. One of the most notorious and widely used is *hopefully* to mean *I hope* or *It is hoped. Wrong:* Hopefully they will be able to come to the party. *Right:* They hope they will be able to come to the party, or We hope that they will be able to come to the party. Other examples include *curiously* and *curiously enough, fortunately* and *unfortunately, happily* and *unhappily, interestingly* and *interestingly enough,* and *thankfully.*

Adverbs modify verbs, adjectives, or other adverbs. The adverb characteristically ends in the suffix *-ly* (*lightly, thinly, wisely*), but there are many exceptions (such as *here, now, so, very*). Consider these examples: an adverb modifying a verb (The sick child slept *fitfully*); an adverb modifying an adjective (The explosion threw debris *too* close for the engineer's safety); an adverb modifying another adverb (His gouty foot was *so* exquisitely painful that the man nearly cried out when he stumbled). See Chapter 8: "Words," **Adverbial shortcuts,** and **Conjunctive adverbs.**

Afflict, inflict. *Afflict* means to hurt, try, or torment someone; *inflict* means to give or cause pain or punishment (Job felt himself afflicted by fate as one trial after another was inflicted upon him and his family).

Allusion, illusion. An *allusion* is a hint or an implication; an *illusion,* a misapprehension (The teacher's allusion to the poetry of Hardy led the student to remember how often Hardy's characters are the victims of illusion).

Alternate, alternative. An *alternate* is a substitute; an *alternative*, properly one of two courses of action (The alternate for the regular driver saw he had no alternative but to take the longer route when he learned the bridge on the main road was blocked).

Antecedents are the words or phrases that a pronoun represents *(Joan and David* proclaimed *their* independence from fads and fashions). The antecedent of a pronoun should always be unmistakable. A vague antecedent has occurred whenever the reader is unsure what or whom the pronoun refers to. *Vague:* Smedley spoke to his father, and he said that the result was predictable. *Clear:* Smedley said to his father that the result was predictable. *Or:* Smedley spoke to his father, who said that the result was predictable.

Apostrophe. See **Contractions** and **Possessives**.

Appositive. A word or group of words that identifies or repeats the meaning of another word or group of words (My great aunt *Prudence* was devoted to Ruggles, *a springer spaniel).* An appositive can be a *phrase* introduced by expressions such as *namely* or *that is* (He filed his flight plan at the Miami airport—*namely, to go to Honduras by way of Guatemala)* or a *clause* introduced in the same way (The law means what it states— *that sheep and cattle may not graze in unfenced pastures).* Appositives are useful in achieving clarity and emphasis, but you should remember that they can quickly become mannerisms and can result in repetition and redundance. See **Restrictive and nonrestrictive modifiers.**

Bankrupt words. Dozens of words have been worn out by careless and excessive use. Most of these have had the juices squeezed out of them by promiscuous use in conversation and in the communications media. *Cute, interesting, meaningful, nice,* and *worthwhile* are representative, being bland at best and trite and lifeless in nearly any circumstance. That "interesting" book you're reading—is it *absorbing, amusing, appeal-*

ing, diverting, engaging, provocative? Or is it *insipid, flat, vapid, tasteless?* Employ fresh and pointed words to achieve exact expression. See **Clichés, Euphemisms,** and **Overblown language.**

Beginning words and phrases. The opening words of a sentence, like the opening words of an essay or a narrative, are essential to the sentence's development, momentum, and impact. The worst way to begin a sentence is to use such words as *also, however,* and *too* because the sentence will seem more nearly like an appendage to the preceding sentence than an independent entity. Such formulaic phrases as *on the one hand* (and *on the other hand*), *this having been said, the fact is,* and *however this may be* are usually tired and colorless means of getting a sentence under way. Don't make readers cut their way through a thicket of conjunctions, prepositional phrases, and participial phrases before they get to the heart of your sentences. See **Adverbial shortcuts** and **Transitional words.**

Blatant, flagrant. *Blatant* means noisy or clamorous; *flagrant,* conspicuously objectionable (The drunken lout's blatant behavior at the opera was a flagrant breach of good taste, and he was escorted out before the first act ended).

Briticisms (Britishisms). Americans—i.e., citizens of the United States—should follow American usage. To use British spellings rather than American is pretentious: hence *theater,* not *theatre; center,* not *centre; gray,* not *grey; program,* not *programme;* and so forth. The same principle applies to British slang and other forms of British usage, including vulgarisms.

Capitalization. Capitalize proper nouns and adjectives (Shakespeare, Shakespearean) but not such words that are a variety of the common classification (Panama, panama hat; Roman soldiers, roman numerals); geographical divisions, regions, and districts (Western Hemisphere, Arctic Circle, Eastern Europe, Urals); religious names and terms (Jehovah, the Bible, Ten Commandments, Original Sin, Catholic church); historical epochs (Dark Ages, Renaissance, Augustan Age); significant periods and events (War of the Roses, World War I, Battle of the Bulge); historic documents (Magna Carta, Declaration of Independence, Bill of Rights); political and government organizations and departments (Democratic party, U.S. Marine Corps, Third Army, Department of State); legislative bodies (Congress, the Senate, House of Commons, Politburo); academic degrees (B.S., LL.B., M.D.); holidays (Christmas Eve, New Year's Day); peoples, races, creeds, tribes (Aryan, Oriental, Islamic, Apache); personifications and abstractions (Courage, thy name is Woman); titles when they precede a name (General Jones, but the general); trademarks (Levi's, Scotch tape, Jack Daniel's). Remember to deify only God (King James, but the king; President Kennedy, but the president). When in doubt (with such obvious exceptions as the first word of a sentence) don't capitalize.

Clause. A group of words containing a subject and a predicate. An independent (or main) clause can always be detached from a larger and more complicated sentence to make a simple sentence *(The cabinetmaker not only made furniture but designed it* when he was a young man). A dependent (or subordinate) clause can take any of three forms: noun *(That Smith was drunk at the time of the accident* was stipulated by his attorney at the hearing), *adjective* (Smith, *who is notorious as a drunkard,* was charged by the prosecutor for driving under the influence of intoxicating beverages), and *adverb (After Smith spent three hours in his favorite tavern,* he drove toward home and had a serious accident *when he and his automobile struck up an acquaintance with a large immovable elm).* See **Sentences by grammatical structure.**

Clichés are expressions that have become worn out through overuse and abuse. Here is a representative list: *back(s) to the wall, explore every avenue, fall victim to, go on a rampage, grind to a halt, in nothing flat, leave no stone unturned, limp into (port), lion's* *share, move into high gear, shroud in secrecy, skate on thin ice, stand shoulder to shoulder, view with alarm, wreak havoc.* The cliché, as George Orwell shows in "Politics and the English Language," is a way of avoiding thought rather than enabling thought and its expression. If you suspect that an expression is a cliché, drop it. See **Metaphor.**

Cf. See **Latin tags.**

Colloquialisms. Colloquial language is natural and idiomatic speech. There are thousands of such expressions that you hear more often than you see them in print. Be sure that you know the exact meaning of such idioms as *leadpipe cinch, a hard row to hoe, spit and image, scarce as hen's teeth, elbow grease, putting on the dog, pull up stakes, shirtsleeves to shirtsleeves in three generations* when you use them. Use colloquialisms sparingly and accurately. You do not have to be a farmer to know it is absurd to say *It is a hard road to hoe* or to know why hen's teeth (and elbow grease) are scarce.

Colon. The colon has fallen into disuse except to show that a series will follow ("Martha," Juliet wrote to her sister, "there are three things I detest about you: your devotion, your beauty, and your intelligence") or a quotation will follow (The scoutmaster said: "Do not carry too much baggage, boys") or to mark the end of a salutation in a formal letter (Dear Sir: Please be advised that for many years we have not stocked chesterfield overcoats). The colon is also still used in bibliographical notation (Acts 7:3). The colon, not the semicolon, should be employed in a compound sentence to show cause and effect (The overdrafts accumulated quickly: Sam was astonished to learn that his bank account was suddenly $196 in arrears).

Comma. The principal uses of the comma are (1) to separate three or more parallel elements in series, in which other punctuation is not present (Mailboxes are red, white, and blue. Note the final comma); (2) to separate coordinate adjectives (the ancient, doddering, senile retired postman); (3) to separate the coordinate clauses of compound sentences that are joined by conjunctions and in which there is little or no other punctuation (Amanda took a bus to Chapel Hill, and she then drove from there to Lexington with Annie); (4) to set off parenthetic elements—nonrestrictive modifiers (Ruggles, a springer spaniel); (5) to set off dialogue ("Get out of Dodge," Marshall Dillon said to the interloper).

The comma may be properly used with quotation marks (the comma appears *within* the closing quotation marks) and with parentheses (the comma seldom can properly appear *before* a parenthesis).

The comma is the only universally used mark of interior punctuation, and it is the most misused of all punctuation. You can avoid error by remembering that the comma should often be used in pairs, especially to set off parenthetic words, phrases, and clauses. To leave out either comma in a pair is to commit one of the most egregious of all comma faults (The stranger, an old man in khakis[,] looked suspicious); the worst fault of all is to separate the subject from its predicate (The question is, whether a divided nation can endure); in the list of cardinal sins involving the comma this mistake is closely followed by the comma splice (or run-on sentence)— the substitution of a comma for a semicolon or a period *(Wrong:* Most of the new owners knew what television had done for professional football, they wanted a piece of the same action for basketball). The comma is often used unnecessarily to set off introductory words and phrases (James Thurber, in criticizing the comma in the sentence "After dinner, the men went into the living-room," facetiously said the comma was there to give them time to push back their chairs). The comma is also often misused in an adjectival series preceding a noun, a series in which the adjectives are not coordinate *(Right:* The runaway team in its *mad headlong* rush carried the wagon and driver over the precipice); in such cases the adjective modifies the idea expressed by the second (and perhaps subsequent) adjective(s) and noun: hence commas should not be used. See *run-on sentences* in Chapter 7: "Sentences" and **Restrictive and nonrestrictive modifiers.**

Compose, comprise. *Compose* means to fashion, constitute, arrange, or produce; *comprise,* to include, contain, or be constituted of (The conductor composed a piano concerto that was comprised of three movements).

Conjunctions are connective words that join sentences, clauses, phrases, and words. Conjunctions fall into three classes: *coordinate,* which connect elements of equal rank *(and, but, or); correlative,* which are coordinate conjunctions used in pairs *(both . . . and, either . . . or, neither . . . nor, not only . . . but also);* and *subordinate,* which are used to join adverb clauses to main clauses *(after, although, as, as soon as, because, before, even if, if, in order that, provided that, since, than, that, though, unless, when, whence, where, whereas, while).* Note that many subordinate conjunctions are adverbs and are called *conjunctive adverbs.* Avoid starting sentences with coordinate conjunctions: this applies particularly to the opening sentence of a paragraph, especially when that sentence begins a piece of writing (But no matter what Huizinga and all his followers declare, I cannot feel that the Big Game really is religious). See **Conjunctive adverbs.**

Conjunctive adverbs make connections in a more definite way than ordinary conjunctions, and therefore they must be used precisely. You should distinguish among the conjunctive adverbs *accordingly, therefore,* and *thus,* each of which has an exact shade of meaning: they are not synonyms. *Therefore* means consequently (We have, therefore, an airtight case, the attorney declared after seeing the last bit of evidence); *thus* means in this manner (We will proceed thus to develop our argument along the lines of this case, the defense counsel said). *Therefore* indicates a conclusion will be made; *however,* in contrast, means that a qualification will follow (The evidence seems to indicate the defendant's guilt; however, this is not the case, his attorney said to the judge before making his final argument). Among these adverbs are *again, also, anyhow, besides, consequently, finally, futhermore, hence, indeed,* and *likewise*. See **Conjunctions** and **Transitional words.**

Continual, continuous. *Continual* means occurring regularly over an indefinite time; *continuous,* occurring without cessation or interruption (The continual wracking pain finally reached such an acute level that the patient thought the throbbing hurt was continuous, although it was not).

Contractions. As writing has become less formal, the rule against contractions in written prose has become more relaxed. (Contractions have always been acceptable in dialogue, of course.) When you are deciding whether a contraction is more appropriate than its unabbreviated form, consider the context and the tone of the passage at hand. Too many contractions can result in a breezy and clipped effect. (Note that the forms *I'd, she'd,* and *we'd* can mean either *I had* or *I would, she had* or *she would,* and so forth; and this ambiguity can mislead readers, forcing them to backtrack.)

Credence, credibility. *Credence* means belief or trust; *credibility,* a quality of inspiring belief or trust (The witness's testimony inspired little credence in the jurors because he was a person of little credibility, having once been convicted for perjury).

Crucial. See **Absolute words.**

Cute. See **Bankrupt words.**

Dash. This punctuation mark's most important use is for rhetorical emphasis. It is stronger and bolder than the comma. Like the comma it should often be used in pairs if it doesn't appear at the beginning or the end of a sentence (or in special cases between clauses). Parentheses are used for an aside or an insertion; the dash, in contrast, to highlight the elements within. We hold these rights—life, liberty, and the pursuit of happiness—to be self-evident, Thomas Jefferson might have written.

Dates. Note the following forms and follow them consistently: January–February 1980; January 5, 1980; from January 15 to March 15 (not from January 15–March 15); January 5th. If the comma precedes the year, another comma must follow the year: hence 5 January 1980 is in some ways preferable to January 5, 1980. Write the abbreviation B.C. (before Christ) after the year but the abbreviation A.D. (in the year of our Lord) before the year: hence 15 B.C. but A.D. 500. Spell out a date that begins a sentence (or reframe the sentence). For a series write 1940s, 50s, 60s, not 1940's, 50's, 60's; for a decade write forties, not 'forties or '40's or 40's. Write *seventeenth century* (noun) and *seventeenth-century* (adjective) not *17th century* or *Seventeenth Century*. Here are some examples of inclusive dates: January 1940–September 1941; 1900–1909 (or 1900–9, not 1900–09); 1849–1876 (or 1849–76). See **Numerals.**

Dead metaphors. See **Metaphor.**

Dictionaries. No dictionary is comprehensive and infallible because the language changes so quickly that any dictionary needs regular revision. The greatest of dictionaries is the *Oxford English Dictionary,* whose original twelve volumes were reissued in two microform volumes in 1971. The *OED* is now being slowly supplemented and brought up to date. Other standard unabridged dictionaries are *Webster's Third International Dictionary* and the *Random House Dictionary.* Anyone looking for the full history of a given word in English should check these sources. Everyone should own a good desk dictionary: we recommend the current editions of *Webster's New World Dictionary* and *Webster's New Collegiate Dictionary.* You may need to consult your library's specialized dictionaries: for contemporary language and new words—the *Longman Dictionary of Contemporary English* and *The Second Barnhart Dictionary of New English;* for slang—*Dictionary of American Slang* and *Dictionary of Slang and Unconventional English* (7th ed.); for quotations—*Bartlett's Familiar Quotations* (15th ed.) and *The Oxford Dictionary of Quotations* (3rd ed.). See **Stylebooks.**

Discourse can be *direct* (quoted speech): "I saw fourteen turtledoves and three partridges in a pear tree," the little boy said to his mother; or *indirect* (reported speech usually appearing in a subordinate clause): The little boy said to his mother that he had seen fourteen turtledoves and three partridges in a pear tree. In writing or quoting dialogue you will find quickly that speech is often uneconomical, repetitious, and rambling: hence indirect discourse, used occasionally, provides not only economy but a change of pace for the writer and reader.

Disinterested, uninterested. *Disinterested* means objective, detached, unbiased; *uninterested,* indifferent, not interested (The judge may have been properly disinterested about the suit's outcome, but there was no doubt of his uninterest when he nodded off briefly during the summation by the plaintiff's lawyer).

Dominant. See **Absolute words.**

Ellipses. An ellipsis shows that a sentence trails off and is incomplete or that material has been omitted from a quoted passage. In American usage there are two kinds of ellipses: the ellipsis used by itself has two functions—to mark an unfinished sentence ("Dad," he choked, "I didn't mean ...") and to show the omission of quoted material *within* a sentence ("Let him twist slowly ... in the wind," Ehrlichman said to Dean). The ellipsis is also used with terminal punctuation (usually a period but sometimes a question mark or exclamation point) to show the omission of material between two or more quoted sentences: the ellision marks the omission of material at the end of the first quoted sentence or the beginning of a succeeding sentence ("I think we ought to let him hang. . . . Let him twist slowly, slowly in the wind"). Since all quotations are taken from larger contexts or wholes, there is usually little point in indicating such by using ellipses at the beginnings and ends of quotations.

Eminent, imminent. *Eminent* means conspicuous, lofty, prominent; *imminent,* immediately threatening (The yachting party, which contained several eminent figures from public life, was suddenly confronted by an imminent typhoon which threatened to cut it off from the mainland).

Et al. See **Latin tags.**

Etc. See **Latin tags.**

Euphemisms are the genteel counterpart of vulgarisms and should be equally avoided. Use *dead,* not *deceased* or *departed; die,* not *pass away.* Avoid colloquial variations such as *bought the farm, headed West,* and *gone home* unless you intend comedy. Current euphemisms include *appropriate* and *liberate* for *steal, act of God* for *catastrophe* or *disaster, aversion therapy* for *electroshock treatment, categorical inaccuracy* or *cover story* or *fabrication* for *lie, disadvantaged* or *underprivileged* for *poor, professional car* for *hearse, sanitation engineer* for *garbage man,* and *undocumented person* for *illegal alien.* Euphemisms are often deliberately misleading, as in the case of *camisole* for *straitjacket;* and at their worst (as in the Nazis' use of *resettlement in the East* to mean *extermination)* they shield corrupt motives and behavior.

Exceedingly, excessively. *Exceedingly* means to an extreme degree; *excessively,* going beyond an acceptable limit (The exceedingly genial stranger struck the remote townspeople as being excessively friendly).

Exclamation point. This mark of punctuation appears at the end of exclamations that are either words or phrases (Great

Scott!) or sentences (As the dam burst he shouted to the Boy Scouts: Run for your lives!). It may also appear after interjections within a sentence (The patrol leader barely restrained himself from shouting Damnit! when he stumbled over the barbed wire in no-man's land). The exclamation point should seldom be used for rhetorical emphasis: your meaning should be conveyed by your language first and foremost *(wrong:* Mrs. White has had three serious accidents in the past two weeks!).

E.g. See **Abbreviated expressions** and **Latin tags.**

Fact is, the. See **Beginning words and phrases** and **Intensifiers.**

Farther, further. *Farther* means at or to a greater distance or extent; *further,* to a greater degree (The plainsman pushed his horse to go farther, but he realized when the animal foundered that he had gone much further in pressing the animal than he should have).

Feasible, possible. *Feasible* means capable of accomplishment; *possible,* which is less definite, means within the limits of realization (The plan, which looked feasible on paper, did not as a practical matter turn out to be possible).

Finalize. See **-ize** and **New words.**

Flaunt, flout. *Flaunt* means to behave ostentatiously or impudently; *flout,* to act scornfully or contemptuously (After Gordon Liddy flouted the law of the land before and during the Watergate hearings, he flaunted his bravado so actively that he received the longest prison term of any conspirator).

Foreign expressions. Avoid foreign expressions, except for a few common terms, chiefly in French and Latin, for which there is no brief, precise, and idiomatic English equivalent. Some representative examples are *bon vivant* (a lover of the good life), *hors de combat* (disabled and unable to return to combat), *in loco parentis* (in the place of a parent), *ménage à trois* (three at housekeeping), *sine qua non* (the indispensable condition or thing upon which all depends). Note that some foreign expressions such as *ad hoc, pro tem* (for *pro tempore*), and *status quo* have become so thoroughly anglicized as to be English words. Technical terms such as *zeitgeist* (the spirit of the age), *Gemeinschaft* (community order), and *Gesellschaft* (economic order), and *nalevo* (getting goods "on the left" or "under the counter") are also acceptable. If you must use a foreign expression, be sure you know its exact meaning and idiom. See **Latin tags.**

Fortuitous. See **Words commonly misused.**

-ful. This suffix principally means *full of;* secondarily, *having the quality of.* These meanings often shade into a single ambiguous meaning that is inexact and unclear, as in the word *thoughtful* (does it mean *contemplative* or *considerate?*). *Wonderful* and *awful* were originally synonyms describing the state of being wonderstruck or awestruck. Each has been so distorted by misuse and overuse that you should avoid both in your writing. *Awful* now means bad; *wonderful,* good. *Impactful, stressful,* and *insightful,* words that are unnecessary and pretentious, illustrate the unfortunate potency of such coinages. *Acute, perceptive,* and *shrewd* are far better words than *insightful.* Use such adjectives cautiously or not at all. See **Bankrupt words** and **Overblown language.**

Gentleman. See **Sexist language.**

Hopefully. See **Adverbial shortcuts.**

Humankind. See **Sexist language.**

Hyphenation (and compound words). Hyphens show syllable breaks when you get to the end of a line and cannot finish writing or typing a word. Compound nouns tend to be spelled open or closed (solid), not hyphenated. Remember that more and more words are being run together to form single words *(boardinghouse, bedroom, mastermind, pocketbook).* The hyphen is chiefly used in temporary compounds, especially modifiers. When in doubt consult your desk dictionary. Remember that the necessity for a hyphen or hyphens often indicates a clumsy and wordy construction *(too-much-forgotten* is a roundabout way of saying *neglected).*

I.e. See **Abbreviated expressions** and **Latin tags.**

Imply, infer. *Imply* means to suggest; *infer,* to conclude or deduce or gather (The diplomat implied that Great Britain might go to war if the agreement were violated again; his German counterpart across the table wrongly inferred, however, that the British were spineless and would let Germany have its way).

Infinitives. The infinitive is the fundamental form of the verb (to come, to see, to conquer). By itself or as a phrase it has great latitude and can be used as a *noun* (The best policy is *to tell the truth)* or an *adverb (To hear him talk,* you would think him the greatest renaissance man since Leonardo da Vinci) or an *adjective* (Next fall this apartment will be *to let).* You should avoid the split infinitive *(incorrect:* Old crocodiles are too big to quickly adapt themselves to captivity; *correct:* Old crocodiles are too big to adapt themselves quickly to captivity) but not at the cost of ambiguity *(ambiguous:* To lose your patience often indicates a lack of self-discipline; *clear:* To often lose your patience indicates a lack of self-discipline). In general avoid split infinitives but not at the cost of writing circumlocutions.

Insightful. See **-ful** and **Overblown language.**

Intensifiers. Such words as *absolutely, actually, certainly, definitely, indeed,* and *literally* usually add little or nothing to your intended meaning and may lead your reader to wonder why you are overstating your case. To this list should be added *so, very, in point of fact,* and dozens of others.

Interesting. See **Bankrupt words.**

Italics. Use italics (shown by underlining in manuscript or typescript) for the names of books, periodicals, motion pictures and plays, works of art, ships, aircraft. Italics, not quotation marks, should be used when you refer to a letter, number, word, or expression as such (The mysterious new verb *globalize* is running rife in State Department circles these days). Use italics for foreign words and expressions *not* in current English usage (hence ibid., bon voyage, i.e., a priori, mea culpa, élan, and ménage à trois are not italicized). For occasional rhetorical emphasis italics are always more appropriate than quotation marks.

-ize. Many useful verbs have been created by adding this simple suffix to a noun or an adjective, but be wary of faddish new coinages. *Editorialize, hospitalize, organize, summarize, scrutinize,* and *temporize* are good additions to the language; *accessorize, containerize, dichotomize, prioritize, trialize,* and *trivialize* illustrate the impulse to create new and unnecessary verbs at its most extreme and awkward. For example *containerize* is a foolish, roundabout, and lengthy way of saying *package,* and *dichotomize* is a poor substitute for *split* or *divide* (in two). That *customize, finalize, verbalize,* and other such bastard coinages have been casually embraced by many people, especially bureaucrats, provides little or no reason for you or any other careful writer to use such words except in dialogue or for purposes of satire. If you are tempted to use such verbs or, worse still, coin them, repeat this sentence by E. B. White until the impulse passes: "I would as lief simonize my grandmother as personalize my writing." See **New words.**

Lady. See **Sexist language.**

Latin tags. These expressions, especially abbreviations such as *e.g., i.e., etc.* and *et al.,* can be useful; but you should employ them sparingly as well as correctly. *Etc.* stands for *et cetera* (and so forth) and should be applied to things in series, not to people; *et al.* stands for *et alii* (and others) and should be applied to people, not to things. *Cf.,* the abbreviation for Latin *confer,* means *compare* in English. When is doubt, you should always use the English equivalent. See **Foreign expressions.**

Legal expressions. Many legal terms are popularly misused. Note that *alibi* properly means a defense of having been elsewhere than at the scene of the crime of which one is suspected; that *corpus delecti* does not mean the body of a victim but evidence that a crime has been committed; that indictments are handed up, not down; that *liable* means exposed to legal action, not *likely* or *inclined;* that *party* is not a synonym for *person.*

Lie, lay. *Lie (lay, lain)* is an intransitive verb and always carries the sense of repose or rest (Sometimes I *lie* awake for hours, gripped by insomnia. Just yesterday I *lay* awake for hours. I have often *lain* in bed all night). *Lay (laid, laid)* is a transitive verb; it means to place or put something down, and it requires an object (Every night I *lay* my head on my pillow, hoping for sleep to come. Last night I *laid* my head on the pillow at 9 P.M. but stayed awake all night. Sometimes I have *laid* my head down on the desk and fallen asleep at work twice in one day).

Lifestyle. See **Abbreviated expressions** and **Vogue words.**

Massive. See **Overblown language** and **Words commonly misused.**

Meaningful. See **Bankrupt words** and **-ful.**

Metaphor is the chief form of figurative language and as such provides the backbone of poetry. It has less place in prose, partly because in prose dead or dying metaphor (e.g., *sifting the evidence)* is often used. Another common failing that you must avoid is the mixed metaphor. To describe a ticklish matter as *skating on thin ice* is to use a dead metaphor (and a cliché); to propose *fighting fire with fire* in the same context is again to use a dead metaphor and to mix metaphors in a comical fashion. In a classic mixed metaphor Gerald Ford once said: "If Abraham Lincoln were alive today, he would turn over in his grave." The simile ("My love is like a red, red rose"), like the metaphor, should be used infrequently. You should also note that many words, such as *backlog* and *target*, have a metaphoric nature or aura, and you must be careful to use such words (and metaphors) accurately and realistically. To say that a target (rather than a goal or a finish line) is in sight is to talk nonsense: no marksman fires on unseen targets. See **Clichés.**

Modifiers of all kinds should stand near the word or words modified. Most of us follow this principle when using adjectives and adverbs, but when we use phrases—especially participial phrases (and also gerund, infinitive, and prepositional phrases)—we may tend to become vague and slipshod. The *dangling modifier* can be represented by this dangling participle: *Having discussed abortion,* nuclear power was then addressed by the committee *(correct:* Having discussed abortion, the committee then turned its attention to nuclear power). Here is an example of a *misplaced modifier:* The ranger drove off the troublesome black bear *in an orange vest (correct:* The ranger in an orange vest drove off the troublesome black bear). See **Restrictive and nonrestrictive modifiers.**

Mood. The *indicative* mood, which indicates the manner of doing or being, comprises the *declarative* (The baby is crying), the *interrogative* (Is the baby crying?), and the *exclamatory* (That squalling baby is insufferable). The *subjunctive* mood involves a wish, a condition contrary to fact, or a demand (I wish that baby would stop howling). The *imperative* mood states a command (For God's sake and mine make that baby stop howling). Do not arbitrarily shift mood within a given piece of writing and never shift mood within a sentence (dialogue excepted).

New words appear at a bewildering rate. The words most often manufactured or coined are verbs. These are usually created by the technical process known as *back formation:* hence *donate* is derived from *donation* (not the other way around) and *sculpt* from *sculptor.* Some newer formations include *escalate, fission, housesit, safekeep,* and *thermoregulate* (all verbs). In deciding whether to use a new word, you should ask yourself whether it serves a genuine need—or if it is arresting and useful only by virtue of being new. New words are frequently ambiguous: *finalize,* invented in the 1960s, is such a word: often we don't know whether it means *complete* or *put an end to.* Here are some dubious verbs of recent vintage: *access, accessorize, advantage, author* (John Cheever authored *Oh, What a Paradise It Seems*), *delawyer, deplane, flack* (The actor flacked his movie for the studio), *fuel, chopper* (The president and his wife choppered from the White House to Camp David), *ghettoize, globalize, impact* (The congressional committee will investigate how crime impacts on property values in urban areas), *obsolete,* and *Watergate.* See **-ize.**

Numerals. Spell out numbers under three digits that appear singly (e.g., ninety-three), but give numbers that appear in series (related groups) in numerical form (The company had 4 platoons, with 3 squads each, and each squad had 10 riflemen and 2 machinegunners). Spell out figures that begin sentences (Twelve was the number of ducks killed by the hunters: 2 by Brown, 4 by Batson, and 6 by Godby). Percentages should be shown in figures (Unemployment has risen to over 10 percent in parts of the United States). Inclusive numbers can be written in full (178–181) or condensed (178–81) form. Zeroes cause complications: 1700–1782 or 1700–82; 108–109 or 108–9, not 108–09 (use the same form for numbers as for dates). Be consistent. See **Dates.**

Oral, verbal. *Oral* means having to do with the mouth, hence spoken; *verbal,* relating to words (The oral testimony of the defendant was presented in verbal form by the court reporter when he typed a transcript of the testimony).

Overblown language is the idiom of bureaucracy and of politics. Be careful not to indulge regularly in overstatement (Jimmy's getting a blood blister early in the Boston marathon was a *tragedy* that cost him the race. Mary's being late for the wedding was a *catastrophe* since she was a bridesmaid). Some words tend to be overblown by nature: *insightful* and *massive* as popularly used are examples. E. B. White puts it well: Avoid fancy words. See **Absolute words.**

Parallelism. Coordinate elements—words, phrases, clauses— should be parallel grammatically and substantively. *Wrong:* I suspect his integrity and whether he intends to do the right thing. *Right:* I suspect his integrity and his intentions. *Wrong:* The Apache scout ran for many miles, stopping only occasionally, never breaking stride except to rest, and maintained the same pace day and night. *Right:* The Apache scout ran for many miles because he stopped only occasionally, never broke stride except to rest, and maintained this pace day and night. Note that some elements cannot be made coordinate and put in the same sentence. *Wrong:* For the rest of his life Churchill was able to keep himself by his journalism, took a siesta in the afternoon, and smoked cigars. *Right:* For the rest of his life Churchill was able to keep himself by his journalism. He continued to take a siesta every afternoon. He smoked cigars to the end of his days. In your writing be sure that the parallel elements, whether a series of words, phrases, or clauses, are coordinate and that the punctuation shows the relation.

Period. The period has a unique use that is its principal reason for being—to end a sentence. Remember that most sentences do not end quickly enough and that the period is therefore not discharging its proper function as often as it should. Whenever you have a long complicated sentence that seems needlessly drawn out, ask yourself whether it should be broken into two or more shorter sentences. The period's other use is to mark an abbreviation, but periods are often dropped in abbreviations, particularly for government agencies (The lecturer explained to the audience that the FBI and CIA perform some functions that overlap).

Plurals. Be aware that certain plural forms (especially when the words are derived from Latin) cause considerable confusion. The plural of *datum* is *data;* don't use *data* for both singular and plural. The singular of *media* is *medium (wrong:* The media in the United States has a vast authority with the general public). Some words that appear to be plural are not (Politics, it is said, is the art of the possible).

Possessives. Do not confuse the plural forms of words with the possessive forms. The plural of an English word is *never* formed with an apostrophe. The possessive of a personal pronoun is *never* formed with an apostrophe: there is no such word as *your's* or *her's* or *its'*; and *it's* can never be anything but the contraction of *it is.* The plural possessive pronoun is *their; they're* is the contraction for *they are.* The general rule is to form the possessive singular by adding *'s* (exceptions: Jesus', Moses', Aristophanes'; for conscience' sake). The possessive plural is formed by *s'.* Remember that the preposition *of* can and should often be used to form the possessive (the family of Charles Dickens).

Precede, proceed. *Precede* means to come before; *proceed,* to issue, carry on, begin, or advance (The commander instructed his officers to proceed on schedule, with the reconnaissance force preceding the main body of the troops by one hour).

Prepositional phrases. The prepositional phrase generally functions as an adjective or adverb, acting as a modifier in the same ways as those parts of speech. Avoid a series of such phrases: if you find yourself writing three or more prepositional phrases in a row, recast your sentence, trying to insert a verb or at least a participle (*weak:* The little boy at the top window of the old house across the street watches me every day when I am working in the yard; *better:* The little boy who sits at the top window of the old house that is across the street watches me every day when I am working in the yard).

Prepositions. Avoid using verbs composed of prepositions and verbs (and occasionally other parts of speech). *Consider* or *weigh* is far preferable to *pay attention to; forge* is superior to *hammer out on an anvil* or even *hammer out; bear* or *tolerate* or *brook* is superior to *put up with.* In general you should not end sentences with a preposition, but this is a word of caution, not a rule. Churchill's rejoinder to such a "rule" is well known: "This is the sort of English up with which I will not put." Often the preposition attached to the verb (as in *order off after, admit to, face up to*) is superfluous and hence should be cut *out.*

Punctuation. Every careful writer has a philosophy of punctuation. Good punctuation, like nearly every aspect of writing, is more akin to an art than to a science. Punctuation can vary considerably in the hands of different writers and editors and still be correct in several versions, but this is not to say that comma splices, misplaced apostrophes, and other such lapses can ever be acceptable. Remember that the careful writer should use the full resources of punctuation: don't forget the colon and the dash. Don't overuse commas, and don't fall into the habit of using underlining (italics), quotation marks, and exclamation points for rhetorical emphasis. For more on punctuation see the entries **Comma, Semicolons,** etc.

Qualifiers. If you regularly qualify statements, your style will be so guarded that the reader will wonder why you are timid or what you have to hide (I am somewhat amused by the mayor's campaign promises). This habit can be called the somewhat-rather syndrome. *Somewhat, rather, slightly, pretty, sort of, to a degree, to some extent, by and large, more or less,* and similar expressions tend to undercut your intended meaning by overly qualifying it. This is particularly true when a vivid word such as *astonishing* or *terrifying* is used. To say *He was frightened* is far more effective than to say *He was rather terrified.*

Quotation marks. The principal uses of quotation marks are to quote excerpts from spoken or written sources; to show the titles of articles, poems, chapters, or other short or subordinate parts of periodicals and books; and to set off dialogue from other kinds of writing. In dialogue remember to begin a new paragraph each time the speaker changes; if a given speech runs beyond a single paragraph, each paragraph begins with quotation marks, but only the last one ends with quotation marks. Quotation marks should not be used for rhetorical emphasis or to apologize for slang, colloquialisms, and other informal language. Closing quotation marks usually appear *before* colons, semicolons, and dashes; *after* commas and periods; and *before* or *after* question marks and exclamation points, depending upon the sense of the sentence. See **Italics.**

Redundancies are expressions that are flabby by nature. Examples include *general public* for *public, good and sufficient reason* for *good reason* (or *sufficient reason*), *huge throng* for *throng, a period of months* for *months* (note the application to any length of time), *at this point in time* for *at this time* or *now, stalling for time* for *stalling, trained expert* for *expert, the reason is because* for *the reason is* or *because.* The redundancy often has a pleasant ring, but on inspection we find that the ring is hollow and the phrase merely pompous repetition. See **Overblown language.**

Restrictive and nonrestrictive modifiers. A restrictive modifier is not purely descriptive or parenthetic: if it is excised from the sentence the meaning is radically changed (Here is the soldier *who won the Congressional Medal of Honor*). A nonrestrictive modifier amplifies the sentence but is not necessary to its essential meaning (The American bald eagle, *which has been on the list of endangered species for some years,* is thought by many ornithologists to be the greatest of living birds). The demonstrative pronoun *which* should be used to introduce nonrestrictive clauses; either *that* or *which* is proper for restrictive clauses. Restrictive and nonrestrictive modifiers include appositives. The rule for punctuation applies to appositives in the same way: set off parenthetic elements with commas.

Run-on sentences. See Chapter 7: "Sentences" and **Commas.**

Semicolons have several essential uses: (1) to set off elements in a series when commas appear within one or more of those elements (The private zoo contained lions and tigers, toothless and lean; reptiles of all kinds; an ancient polar bear; and various other poor creatures, most of whom were in bad shape); (2) to separate independent clauses within a sentences, especially when those clauses are not joined by coordinate conjunctions (After the carnival the crowd dispersed slowly; most of the people walked to the distant parking lots and then drove home); (3) to prevent confusion from occurring when a comma would create ambiguity in the grammar or syntax of a sentence, particularly in compound-complex sentences (At the party Alice, who danced a jig and played a flute with gusto, had great fun; Tommy pinned the tail on Sammy rather than the donkey, and Sammy retaliated by hitting Tommy in the nose; David cried when he did not win a prize; and various other incidents, expected and unexpected, kept the chaperones busy); and (4) for occasional purposes of rhetorical emphasis where a comma would otherwise be usual and appropriate ("We are all in the gutter; but some of us are looking at the stars"—Oscar Wilde).

Sensual, sensuous. *Sensual* means fleshly or carnal; *sensuous,* having to do with the senses in an appealing way (Their afternoon at the abandoned farm, which began innocently as an exploration of the sensuous pleasures offered by a picnic in the lush countryside, turned sensual after the couple stumbled into each other in the empty barn).

Sentence fragments. See Chapter 7: "Sentences."

Sentences by grammatical structure. The grammatical forms of the sentence are the simple, compound, complex, and compound-complex. *Simple* (one independent clause): Fishing is usually a sedentary sport. *Compound* (two or more independent clauses): Fishing is usually a sedentary sport; the same applies to playing the horses. *Complex* (one independent clause, one or more dependent—here two): Fishing, although usually a sedentary sport, can entail strenuous activity if you are fly-fishing for bass in a deep swift-running stream or deep-sea fishing for marlin. *Compound-complex* (two or more independent clauses—here three; one or more dependent—here two): Fishing is usually a sedentary sport, but it can entail strenuous activity if you are fly-fishing in a deep swift-running stream or deep-sea fishing; playing the horses in contrast never involves strenuous activity unless you are running from your bookie or the mobsters he works for.

Vary your sentence structure both grammatically and rhetorically as much as you think reasonable and effective. In other words do not use a succession of similar structures, sentence by sentence, paragraph by paragraph, and page by page.

Sentences by rhetorical structure. The principal types of rhetorical structure are *loose, periodic,* and *balanced.* See Chapter 7: "Sentences."

Sexist language. Avoid language that is sexist; at the same time do not part company with common sense and natural expression. Hence *firefighter,* not *fireman,* but *policeman* and *po-*

licewoman; humankind, not *personkind.* Use *he or she,* not *s/he.* Employ *Ms.* like any other form of address—accurately and sparingly. *Lady,* now a loaded term, a cliché, a euphemism, or a combination of all, should be avoided; it, like its counterpart *gentleman,* should be used with the utmost precision and only when nothing else will do. When in doubt consult *The Handbook of Nonsexist Writing* by Casey Miller and Kate Swift.

S/he. See **Sexist language.**

Simile. See **Metaphor.**

Sit, set. *Sit (sat, sat)* is an intransitive verb and therefore does not take an object; it means to take or occupy a seat (I *sit* down and watch the national news each night before eating supper. Last night I *sat* down and watched several news programs before eating a late supper. Lately I *have sat* down and fallen asleep several times while watching the nightly news). *Set (set, set)* is a transitive verb and takes an object; it means to place upon (The policeman *sets* his pistol on the nightstand before going to bed. The policeman *set* his pistol on the nightstand last night as he always does. The policeman *has set* his pistol on the nightstand hundreds of times over the past several years).

Slang. Nothing is deader than outdated slang *(23 skidoo!, hep cat, zoot suit).* Some slang makes its way into standard usage *(hangup),* but the vast majority does not. If you insist on using slang, don't make matters worse by putting the expression in quotation marks. Some examples of current (or already dated) slang are *blows my mind, bottom line, bumming, jamming, rip off,* and *uptight.*

Sports lingo. This special branch of journalese combines overstatement with inexactness as the writer searches for new and colorful language. Hence *praise* or *honor* becomes *accolade.* Sportwriters do not know the difference between *faze* and *phase* and are unsure whether the slangy vogue word for *zero* is *zit* or *zip*. In general you should use sports lingo only in dialogue or when the expression has technical significance (e.g., *red dog, nickel defense, transition game*). Avoid words and phrases such as *accolade, a legend in his (or her) own time, cheap shot, game plan, situation* (as in *punting situation*), *engineer* (verb), and *wizardry* made trite by overuse in the sports pages. In general you should be wary of using the jargon of any profession or walk of life.

Stylebooks. The best of all stylebooks, *Fowler's Modern English Usage* (revised by Ernest Gowers in 1965), is the most idiosyncratic; it should be supplemented by Roy H. Copperud's *American Usage and Style: The Consensus* and the *Chicago Manual of Style* (13th ed.). Strunk and White's *Elements of Style* (3rd ed.) and William Zinsser's *On Writing Well* (rev. ed.) are the best succinct yet comprehensive books on writing prose. See **Dictionaries.**

Tense. Once chosen, the tense of a given piece of writing should be maintained and should not be arbitrarily changed. If you decide to write in the present tense, try to maintain that tense throughout, using the present perfect tense to show past action. There are obvious exceptions: if a person has died, you cannot present him as talking in the present tense (unless he is a well-known writer, in which case to write Shakespeare *says* is both expected and proper). The *historical present* is a tense used by historians and fiction writers to impart the sense of present time to events that occurred in the past (In the fog and falling snow shrouding the Ardennes Forest the German troops move into position to counter attack the advancing American armored divisions).

Thoughtful. See **-ful.**

Transitional words. If you continually find yourself signaling your transitions with such words as *furthermore, however, nevertheless, then, thus,* and *therefore,* you are probably forcing the development and logic of your writing and failing to achieve a smooth flow of thought and expression. Well-written prose is a seamless web; the seams in poor prose often begin to bulge and unravel at the junctures marked by transitional words. The point involves proportion as well as sense: use transitional words sparingly and exactly, checking the logic of your expression if you begin to rely on them frequently.

Transpire. See **Words commonly misused.**

Unique. See **Absolute words.**

Verbals are words derived from verbs—infinitives or gerunds or participles—that combine the meaning and force of verbs with the functions of the noun, adjective, or adverb. Verbals can be used alone or in phrases. *Gerund* (verbal noun): *Running* is strenuous exercise for beginners. *Running a marathon* is strenuous for amateurs and professionals alike. *Participle* (verbal adjective): *Running,* the dog turned the corner and headed toward home. *Running easily but hard,* the young greyhound crossed the finish line well ahead of the pack. *Infinitive: To run,* rather than *to walk,* would put him there well ahead of the appointed time. *To run up and down the steps of the football stadium* in order *to get in shape for crew* was not the coxswain's idea of fun or sport. See **Infinitives** and **Modifiers.**

Verbs. The transitive verb expresses an action that affects an object (I *broke* the window). Some verbs that can take a direct object may also be intransitive (*Transitive:* He farms forty acres. *Intransitive:* For a living he *farms*). Intransitive verbs, such as *appear, come, lie,* and, most important, *be,* do not take objects. They express intransitive actions, states, or conditions (He *lay* prone on the carpet), or they are linking verbs that connect a predicate adjective or noun with the subject (Sam *looked* unhappy). When a verb is conjugated fully, the forms in its paradigm will appear as follows: *voice*—active and passive (the intransitive verb is voiceless); *mood*—indicative (declarative, exclamatory, interrogative), subjunctive, imperative; *tense*—present (I *go*), present perfect (I *have gone*), past (I *went*), past perfect (I *had gone*), future (I *will go*), future perfect (I *will have gone*); *person*—first (I), second (you), third (he, she, it); *number*—singular and plural. The paradigm might also include the tenses formed with auxiliary verbs such as *do, can, may, might, should,* and *ought* and the progressive forms (present: I *am going*; past: I *was going;* future: *I will be going*). See Chapter 8: "Words" and **Infinitives, Mood, Tense,** and **Verbals.**

Vogue words. Words, like clothing, are subject to the currents of fashion. Some now fashionable words are *escalate, interface, lifestyle,* and *parameter.* Fashionable words often are derived from the world of technology, and frequently their meaning is fuzzy. Avoid them except in dialogue. See **New words.**

Vulgar language. Avoid obscenity and profanity. Always ask yourself whether the vulgar word is the only possible expression in the given circumstance—or whether you are just showing off. Usually vulgarisms should be restricted to dialogue and then used sparingly. To use British vulgarisms or those of another language (such as French or Yiddish) makes the expressions no less offensive.

-wise. *Clockwise, lengthwise, likewise,* and a few other words coined with this suffix are acceptable English; but most words coined with it are not, including *fuelwise, pricewise,* and *cosmoswise. Wrong:* Weatherwise the day was perfect. *Right:* The day was sunny and mild. See **Adverbial shortcuts.**

Words commonly misused. Words misused more often than not are *chronic, dastardly, exotic, fortuitous, massive, moot,* and *transpire.* Many careful writers use *fortuitous* to mean lucky in a good sense; it means *by chance,* and the luck can be good or bad (That the cars which were out of control collided on the interstate was fortuitous). *Transpire* does not mean *happen* or *occur* but *leak out*—hence *become known* (It transpired that one

U.S. senator and several congressmen were directly involved in the Abscam scandal). Never assume that another person, especially someone writing for the popular press, knows the exact meaning of any given words that he or she uses. You should avoid many of these words because the meaning has been distorted or wrung from them.

Index